A CONCISE
HISTORY OF
NAZI GERMANY

A CONCISE HISTORY OF NAZI GERMANY

1919–1945

Joseph W. Bendersky

Fourth Edition

Rowman & Littlefield Publishers, Inc.
Lanham • Boulder • New York • Toronto • Plymouth, UK

Published by Rowman & Littlefield Publishers, Inc.
A wholly owned subsidiary of The Rowman & Littlefield Publishing Group, Inc.
4501 Forbes Boulevard, Suite 200, Lanham, Maryland 20706
www.rowman.com

10 Thornbury Road, Plymouth PL6 7PP, United Kingdom

British Library Cataloguing in Publication Information Available

Library of Congress Cataloging-in-Publication Data

Bendersky, Joseph W., 1946–
   A concise history of Nazi Germany / Joseph W. Bendersky. — Fourth edition.
     pages cm
   Includes bibliographical references and index.
   ISBN 978-1-4422-2268-7 (cloth : alk. paper) — ISBN 978-1-4422-2269-4
(pbk. : alk. paper) — ISBN 978-1-4422-2270-0 (electronic) 1. Germany—
Politics and government—1918–1933. 2. Germany—Politics and
government—1933–1945. 3. National socialism. 4. Hitler, Adolf, 1889–1945.
I. Title.
   DD240.B348 2014
   943.086—dc23
                                                                    2013011707

Printed in the United States of America

For Carmen

CONTENTS

PART ONE

The Origins and Development of Nazism, 1919–1928

PART TWO

The Seizure and Consolidation of Power, 1929–1934

ILLUSTRATIONS

Figures

Maps

Photo Gallery I—between pages 96 and 97

1. Nazi Storm Troopers on parade.
2. Nazi mass rally at the Berlin Sportpalast.
3. NSDAP Standard: "Germany Awaken."
4. Hitler as charismatic orator.
5. Reich propaganda minister Josef Goebbels.
6. Storm Troopers advancing with Nazi colors.
7. (Left to right) Deputy *Führer* Rudolf Hess, Hitler, and *Gauleiter* Julius Streicher.
8. Nazi parade through Nuremberg.
9. The annual Nuremberg party rally.
10. Nazi propaganda poster: "Yes, *Führer*, we will follow you!"
11. Nazi women greet Hitler.
12. The Hitler Youth.
13. Members of the German Girls' League performing domestic chores.
14. A standard-bearer of the German Girls' League.
15. Hitler's motorcade through Nuremberg.
16. Hitler meets with German workers.

Photo Gallery 2—between pages 146 and 147

pose in writing this book was to provide students and laymen with a systematic study that was both concise and comprehensible. Based upon the major historical studies and latest research, this book explains the crucial events and factors involved in the rise and fall of Nazi Germany. Although not designed for experts in the field of German history, it covers many important aspects of nazism often neglected in more specialized studies or biographies that deal with only certain dimensions of the Nazi movement or its illustrious personalities.

The popularity of this book has remained strong among students and general readers. However, the enormous amount of important new research and publications on this subject since *A History of Nazi Germany* first appeared has required several revisions. The second edition reorganized and expanded the text to include the fruits of the burgeoning field of Holocaust studies. It also integrated the new data and interpretations contributed by social history. Social historians, often assisted by quantitative methods, provided competing interpretations of the various social groups from which the Nazis recruited members and voters. They likewise broadened our knowledge of German women during the Nazi rise to power as well as of the multidimensional relationship women had to the nature and policies of the Third Reich. The third edition continued to reflect the trends in social history, while reemphasizing the crucial role played by racial ideology in determining the policies and practices of the Third Reich. This edition showed more of the complexity of social life within the Nazi state. It clarified the situation of average citizens negotiating their way with both the threatening power behind certain Nazi policies and the strong enticements to acquiesce or collaborate of others. German Christians struggled to preserve a central place for religion in social life against Nazi paganism and euthanasia programs. Simultaneously, individuals and groups in public, government, and business sectors became complicit in the persecution of the Jews out of economic or institutional self-interest. Although some young Germans were fanatical members of the Hitler Youth, many were as rebellious as any adolescent generation. It was a society, however, whose laws, policies, and expectations were increasingly determined by a Nazi racial ideology based upon a biological and Darwinian perception of life, society, and history. A fundamental Nazi domestic goal was to purify the Aryan race and German society by eliminating those Germans deemed unfit physically, mentally, or behaviorally. The Nazi objective for European civilization as a whole was the ethnic cleansing of the so-called inferior races across the continent through war, enslavement, and genocide. This racial purification would open the way for the domination of the Aryan master race in the Thousand-Year Reich envisioned by Hitler and Nazi ideologues.

The current, revised fourth edition continues to incorporate the incessant flow of impressive research published by the outstanding scholars working in the field of German history. The most recent literature has made it necessary to clarify and highlight the ideological and political distinction between nazism and conservatism found in earlier editions. Although these two forces shared certain common characteristics (nationalism, antiliberalism, anti-Marxism, anti-Semitism, etc.), they were starkly differentiated by their essence and their visions of a future for Germany and the world. Rather than being an extension of the extreme right, nazism was a unique synthesis of various previously opposing historical forces and ideologies, especially nationalism and socialism. At heart, the Nazis were not only fanatical racialists but truly social revolutionaries. As the advocates of sweeping revolutionary transformation of society, the Nazis were as much the enemies of conservatives and reactionaries as they were of democracy and the left. Only by perceiving this significant difference can one truly understand the essence of this new movement, or its appeal to such a wide-ranging constituency of followers and voters.

This edition addresses the illuminating new scholarship on war crimes trials and the controversies over German memory and the Third Reich. And among other revisions, it expands coverage of often-overlooked persecuted groups such as homosexuals and Jehovah's Witnesses. In addition, given the technological advances in media that have made films readily available as educational instruments, a section has been included on highly recommended documentary and feature films from the period or about the Third Reich. If used properly, in conjunction with relevant readings, such films can bring the period to life while enhancing our understanding of the multidimensional aspects of the Nazi phenomenon. These films are invaluable tools in grasping the nature and horrific consequences of the National Socialist movement, as well as in comprehending the varied responses to nazism from the 1930s through World War II and into debates over its legacy for contemporary Germany and its historical memory.

This new research has been integrated while retaining the strengths of the earlier editions, particularly their brevity and reliability. One of this work's most attractive features, however, has been its organization and writing style, which combine narrative storytelling with analysis. Students, general audiences, and historians have found it captivating reading as well as an easily understandable explanation of the origins, nature, and consequences of nazism. In essence, this book remains an intriguing account of the Third Reich for those seeking a brief, though thematically comprehensive, study of a subject that retains its historical significance and widespread contemporary fascination.

THE ENDURING IMPORTANCE OF NAZISM: AN INTRODUCTION

Within three years of their first electoral success, the Nazis acquired political power in Germany when Adolf Hitler became chancellor on January 30, 1933. That evening Hitler stood in the window of the Reich Chancellery waving to thousands of Storm Troopers who staged parades through the streets of Berlin. By June 1940, Hitler toured Paris as conqueror of the French nation the *Wehrmacht* had defeated in a matter of weeks. The Nazis proclaimed that their Third Reich would be the greatest civilization in history and last for a thousand years. But the meteoric rise of Hitler and National Socialism was followed by an almost equally rapid defeat. The Third Reich lasted a mere twelve years. By 1945, Hitler was forced to retreat to his underground bunker, where, surrounded by the ruins of his empire, he took his own life.

Within the entire scope of modern history, the Nazi era occupies a minuscule span of time. Yet during that brief period, the Nazis instituted one of the most oppressive dictatorships known, launched a world war, dominated most of the European continent, and perpetrated crimes against humanity of staggering enormity. Indeed, the Third Reich drastically altered the political structure of Europe and the course of world history.

For these reasons, nazism still occupies a distinctive place in the collective consciousness of the Western world almost a century after the founding of this political movement. This remains the case long after the end of the Cold War eliminated the postwar territorial, political, and ideological divisions of Europe caused by Hitler's war. Few other historical developments of such limited duration have plagued our consciences and attracted such widespread interest throughout the Western world so long after the event. In stark contrast, interest in Soviet Communism has dropped precipitously, despite the significance of that oppressive regime, which lasted seventy years. And for the Germans the Nazi dictatorship still looms like a dark shadow—an "Unmasterable Past"—over the political culture of that nation, even though for the past fifty years the German republic has proven to be one of the most democratic and progressive societies in human history. The study of the Third Reich has also recently taken on a global dimension, as Chinese and Latin American academics display a serious interest in the subject. And increasingly political scientists and commentators invoke nazism as a historical framework for understanding and assessing militant Islamic movements.

From research scholars and university classrooms to popular culture, books, and film, nazism stands as a subject that both fascinates and horrifies. The term *Nazi* has become almost synonymous with evil itself. For millions of people, the disturbing emotional response to anything associated with the Third Reich has certainly not lessened with the passage of time. The mere mention of nazism still immediately conjures up in the minds of many persons ghastly images of destruction, barbarism, and the murder of innocents on a massive scale. When historians, philosophers, writers, and even laymen seek an extreme case to substantiate some ethical or moral argument, they more often than not cite an example from the Third Reich. In a Western world characterized by uncertainty and moral relativism, nazism appears to be one of the few subjects about which a universal moral consensus exists.

Widespread interest, revulsion, and moral condemnation do not, however, in themselves indicate historical understanding. Over the decades, I have encountered general audiences and numerous students who have read widely about various aspects of the Third Reich. But often I have been surprised at how little they have grasped the nature of nazism or the reasons for its successes and failures. Despite their general knowledge, they could not explain the ability of the Nazis to seize power so quickly and implement their barbaric policies in such a culturally advanced society as Germany. Yet these and other key questions are exactly what historians have argued over for almost a century. How could a nation once guided by the brilliant statecraft of Otto von Bismarck follow the reckless foreign policy of Adolf Hitler? How could the humanistic educational ideals of Wilhelm von Humboldt, respected and emulated around the world, be replaced so easily by the anti-intellectualism and hateful propaganda of Josef Goebbels? Why was nazism attractive to so many, and why did Germans (and others) fail to resist the racial policies of the Third Reich that led to the extermination of millions of human beings? Was the Nazi rise inevitable, the natural culmination of German history or manifestation of a peculiar German national character? Or was it caused by a particular set of historical and social circumstances?

Answering such questions and comprehending the essence of this movement requires an understanding that can only be derived from a systematic examination of the origins and history of the Third Reich. My original pur-

PART ONE

The Origins and Development of Nazism, 1919–1928

The National Socialists are increasing their strength rapidly. Hitler, their leader, is of Austrian origin and a pure and simple adventurer . . . a real character . . . exploiting all latent discontent to increase his party's strength. . . . Whether he is big enough to take the lead in a German national movement is another question; probably not.
—Captain Truman Smith, Assistant U.S. Military Attaché, Berlin, 1922

1919–1928

CHAPTER 1

Weimar Democracy in Crisis

On November 10, 1918, an obscure German soldier named Adolf Hitler lay grieving on his bunk in a military hospital. He had just learned that the emperor of Germany, Kaiser Wilhelm II, had abdicated and that a republic had been proclaimed in Berlin. What shocked Hitler even more was the news that the war had been lost. The armistice signed the following day was, in fact, tantamount to a German surrender. In Hitler's mind the armistice and the new republic had not resulted from German defeats on the battlefield. They were the work of Jews and Socialists who, out of lack of courage, disloyalty, or self-interest, had undermined the government and the war effort. Hitler considered the creation of the republic and the subsequent acceptance of the Treaty of Versailles political catastrophes for Germany. Thereafter, he blamed most of Germany's economic and political ills on the republic and the treaty. Yet it was these developments, which Hitler so lamented, that allowed him to emerge from obscurity to become one of the most powerful and infamous dictators in history. Although the roots of the Nazi ideology can be traced back to certain cultural and intellectual currents in the nineteenth century, the rise of Hitler and the Nazis as political forces can be attributed directly to the Versailles Treaty and the crises that plagued the new republic from the very beginning.

Within two months of the declaration of the republic, Communists incited revolutions in Berlin and several other major cities. Their goal was to establish a Soviet state in Germany similar to the one founded by Lenin in Russia. By April 1919, a Communist republic had also been declared in Munich. These revolts were brutally suppressed by the army and volunteer units, called the Free Corps, but throughout the winter and spring of 1919, Germany remained in a state of civil war. It was under these circumstances that elections took place for a National Assembly that would draft a new constitution. The capital, Berlin, was in such turmoil that the constitutional assembly had to convene in the city of Weimar. As a result, the new democracy became unofficially known as the Weimar Republic.

Despite difficulties, there were initially some encouraging signs that democracy might take root in Germany. In the elections to the constitutional

MAP 1.1
Germany under the Versailles Treaty, 1919–1936

Demilitarized Zone   Territorial Losses—1919

assembly, in which 80 percent of the electorate cast ballots, the supporters of the republic received three-quarters of the vote. A democratic constitution was adopted by an overwhelming majority of the assembly. The Weimar constitution guaranteed all citizens basic civil rights (equality before the law, freedom of speech, press, and religion, and so on) and abolished the privileges of the aristocracy. The Reichstag (parliament) was elected by universal suffrage and was to serve as one of the major institutions of self-government as opposed to the authoritarianism of the former monarchy. The chancellor and his cabinet were directly responsible to the parliament and could remain in office only with the confidence of a majority of the deputies in the Reichstag.

The framers of the Weimar constitution were as concerned about political stability as they were with parliamentary government. Therefore, the constitution also provided for a strong president, who was independent of the Reichstag and directly elected by the people for a seven-year term. The president had broad powers that were intended to provide for strong leadership and a stable government. He controlled the armed forces, directed foreign policy, appointed and removed the chancellor, and could dissolve parliament and call new elections. Equally important, under Article 48 of the constitution he assumed special authority in a state of emergency. In such circumstances, he could temporarily suspend parts of the constitution, institute emergency measures, and intervene with the armed forces to reestablish order and security. Although this clause was later referred to as the "dictatorship article," its purpose was to preserve the existing state and constitution; it was not intended to serve as the basis for a dictatorship. A president could not alter the constitution, and the Reichstag had the right to rescind any emergency decree. Moreover, it was only through decisive executive action under this article that the republic was able to survive as long as it did. On paper, at least, the Germans had finally laid the foundations for a modern and stable democracy.

In practice, the new government had great difficulty in stabilizing the country and getting the democratic system to function properly. At the heart of the problem was the lack of a political and social consensus among the Germans. Before the war, the nation had been ruled from above by an authoritarian regime, and as a result, political parties did not learn democratic governmental responsibility and tactics of political compromise. The majority of Germans also lacked political education. These problems were especially acute in Weimar, for no political party acquired a majority in the Reichstag, and it was extremely difficult to form coalition governments from among the various antagonistic parties. Furthermore, many Germans never supported the republic, and many of those who accepted it did not have a real commitment to democracy. The political right associated the republic with defeat, shame, betrayal, and weakness; rightists never accepted the legitimacy of the new government and favored either the restoration of the monarchy or an authoritarian state. The old aristocracy also resented the loss of its special privileges and would not adjust to a democratic government and society. Many middle-class Germans originally voted for the republic not out of sympathy for democracy but because they saw the republic as a bulwark against a Communist revolution. Even this pragmatic support began to erode in less than a year as the middle and lower-middle classes held the republic responsible for their economic decline. On the other hand, the Communists regarded Weimar as a middle-class capitalist state that had to be overthrown by revolution; they never ceased in their efforts to destabilize the republic. For one reason or another, most segments of German society were disappointed by Weimar.

Weimar was not completely without republican sympathizers. Although most Socialists and workers were disappointed by the limited nature of social and economic reform in Weimar, they enthusiastically supported the new republic. Similarly, Catholics in general and a minority of the middle classes were loyal to the new constitutional order. But these republican sympathizers remained in a minority, and in their efforts to make democracy work, they had to rely upon other segments of society that were unenthusiastic about, if not hostile to, the republic. Weimar was not a republic without republicans, as often claimed; it was a republic without a republican majority.

Another serious problem for Weimar was the political party system itself, which reinforced already existing divisions within German society. German parties were not open associations that developed platforms during elections to attract a broad group of voters. They were tightly organized and exclusive institutions that represented the interests of distinct and antagonistic segments of society, and their programs had little appeal to those outside their particular social, economic, or ideological group. Many parties developed their own bureaucracies, social clubs, newspapers, and auxiliary organizations; in some cases, parties had their own paramilitary groups with thousands of members. Not just the political life but the social life of members as well was centered around the party. The result was that party members tended to become even more segregated from other segments of society. In elections, voters did not vote for a particular candidate but for "party lists" of candidates decided on by each party. The electorate, which had no influence over the selection of these candidates, was forced to accept or reject the entire list. Thus, parties had tremendous control; until the 1930s, most voters remained loyal to their respective parties. This control also extended into parliament, where party discipline was enforced and deputies voted according to the wishes of their party leadership. The flexibility of these parties was limited further by the fact that many of them viewed each other not merely as the parliamentary opposition but as the "enemy," with whom only limited compromises could be made. Since different party interests conflicted so often, it was difficult to pass significant legislation; frequently the parliament would be paralyzed by the intransigence of several parties. Critics of the republic referred to Weimar as a *Parteienstaat* (party-state).

Before 1930, the Nazis were an insignificant political force and a minor factor in the crises caused by the party system. For most of Weimar, the greatest right-wing opposition to the republic came from the German National People's party (DNVP). This party was extremely nationalistic, antirepublican, and reactionary. Originally, it favored a restoration of the monarchy, but later it sought a substitute in the form of an authoritarian state. It received its support from devoted nationalists, the aristocracy, the upper-middle class, part of the middle classes, and big business. While it had an anti-Semitic faction, this party viewed the Socialists and Communists as the greatest danger and the source of most of Germany's problems. Although the DNVP sought the eventual demise of the republic, it participated in several cabinets to keep the Socialists out of power. Very often the DNVP found itself in alliance with the German People's party (DVP), which was also nationalistic and conservative, but more moderate in its ideological orientation and politics. The DVP was the party of most of the German middle classes; consequently it opposed further social and economic reform. Unlike the DNVP, the German People's party tolerated the republic and was willing to form coalition governments with the Socialists in order to ensure domestic stability. Yet it preferred a reduction in Socialist power and the rise of a stronger German state at home, one that could then again play a major role in international politics.

Although most middle-class Germans voted for either the DNVP or DVP, a small minority of them belonged in the republican camp. Politically, they were represented by the German Democratic party (DDP), which held a middle ground between the reactionary right and the radical left. The DDP was part of the Weimar Coalition, an alliance of those parties that had dominated the National Assembly in 1919 and remained devoted to the republic and its constitution. The major partners in the Weimar Coalition, however, were the Catholic Center party and the Social Democratic party. The Center party was actually the center of the entire political system, because it was the only party that cut across class lines. It attracted Catholics from all classes, occupations, and regions of Germany. Though it had authoritarian traditions and tendencies, the Center recognized that Catholics had benefited greatly from the new democratic constitution; therefore, it was one of the staunchest supporters of the republic. As a broadly based party, it could form coalitions and make compromises with various parties; before 1932 no government was ever formed without its participation. The largest party in Weimar was the Social Democratic party (SPD), which was Marxist in its ideology and rhetoric, though reformist and democratic in practice. While it still favored gradual socialization, it was no longer a revolutionary party, and it proved to be the party most loyal to the Weimar system. But as a working-class party that frequently used Marxist rhetoric, the SPD continued to alarm the middle classes, and its defense of the rights of labor prevented lasting cooperation with parties that represented middle-class and business interests.

Members of the Weimar Coalition had to contend not only with the power and popularity of the antirepublican right but with the radical left as well. The German Communist party (KPD) still adhered to an orthodox version of Marxism and exploited every crisis in order to incite revolution against what it considered the "oppressive" and "bourgeois" Weimar regime. A small party that increased in size during times of crisis, the KPD attracted devout Marxists, workers disillusioned with the moderate course of the SPD, and radical leftist youths who desired quick and drastic solutions to social and economic problems. The political process was further complicated by the emergence at different times of various small parties; sometimes as many as twenty-five took part in an election. Since these parties usually represented narrow special interests (for example, small farmers), they greatly hampered the formation of coalition governments. The failure of Weimar was probably due as much to the nature of this multiparty system as it was to the antirepublican opposition of the radical right and left.

An added burden for Weimar was that important public institutions were staffed with antirepublicans who could not be removed for political reasons, because their rights of tenure were protected by law. Organized and staffed under the monarchy, the bureaucracy remained essentially unchanged after 1919 and was dominated by officials who either detested or, at best, tolerated the new government. They had little loyalty to the government they were sworn to serve; often they favored rightist causes and opposed republican policies. Similarly, university professors, who trained the nation's elites, were usually either apolitical or tended to be conservative nationalists and harsh critics of Weimar. Though a very limited number of professors had a democratic orientation, most relentlessly attacked the Versailles Treaty and the weaknesses of the republic in their lectures and publications, reinforcing the sense of disappointment and the antagonism toward Weimar already felt by their students and the public in general. The army, supposedly the defender of the state and constitution, also displayed little enthusiasm for the republic, preferring an authoritarian state. Weimar governments were never sure if they could count on the army to protect the republic. Certainly there was good reason for such doubt: when the terms of the Versailles Treaty became known, there was serious discussion within the army high command about replacing the republic with a military dictatorship.

The provisions of the Versailles Treaty came as a shock to every German. Had the republicans in control of the government had any choice, even they would have rejected it immediately. The Germans had expected a treaty freely negotiated along the lines of President Wilson's Fourteen Points, but they were never involved in the actual drafting of the treaty. They were confronted with the options of signing the treaty or facing occupation by the victors. Thereafter, the Germans accurately referred to the Versailles Treaty as a *Diktat* (or dictated peace) designed to weaken and punish their country. The treaty, which was reluctantly signed in June 1919, was based on the assumption that Germany had intentionally started World War I, and it was intended to prevent Germany from ever reemerging as a military or political power.

Territorially, Germany lost large, economically valuable areas, including Alsace-Lorraine, Upper Silesia, and its colonial empire; East Prussia was cut off from the rest of the country by the Polish Corridor. Germany was to be almost entirely disarmed: the military draft, air force, most of the navy, war colleges, the general staff, and armaments industries had to be eliminated, and its army was limited to 100,000 men. Most humiliating was Article 231 of the treaty (the War Guilt Clause), which held Germany totally responsible for the war and thus for all its damages. Germany was forced to pay extensive reparations to the victors, which became a permanent economic, psychological, and political burden that hindered efforts at stabilizing the new democracy. Because so many Germans held the Weimar government accountable for accepting the treaty, the *Diktat* issue would easily be exploited by the right in its attempts at undermining the republic.

The Versailles Treaty, frustrations with the ineffectiveness of the Weimar government, and pressure by the victors to compel rapid German demobilization set off a series of events in 1920 that almost destroyed the republic within a year of its birth. In March, the so-called Kapp *Putsch* forced President Friedrich Ebert and the legal Weimar government to flee from Berlin. The leaders of this rightist coup, former General Walther von Lüttwitz and a politician named Wolfgang Kapp, were backed by Captain Hermann Ehrhardt, whose Free Corps brigade took over the city. Their goals were to resist the implementation of Versailles and to overthrow the republic. During this first overt challenge to the power and authority of the Weimar political order, the army remained neutral. The republic was saved only by an effective general strike called by the SPD and labor unions, which brought about a quick collapse of the Kapp government. However, the danger to the republic had not ended. The German Communists exploited this crisis to start a revolution in the Ruhr, the industrial heart of Germany, and by the end of March a Red army of more than fifty thousand had seized control of several major cities. While the army had been reluctant to act against the right to defend the republic, it never hesitated against the left in order to save Germany from communism. A brutal suppression of the Communist revolution followed.

The reaction against the treaty, the turmoil of recent months, and middle-class fear of communism produced further loss of faith in the republic. The June 1920 Reichstag elections signaled a drastic political shift to the right.

The parties that constituted the prorepublican Weimar Coalition lost their majority, never to regain it, and the strength of the rightist DNVP and

DVP greatly increased. For the rest of Weimar, coalition governments could be formed only with the participation of rightist parties, which were less than sympathetic, often hostile, to democracy.

The return to normalcy and order desired by most Germans did not follow. The gains made by the right did not satisfy the extremists for whom the republic itself symbolized defeat and betrayal. Rightists labeled those associated with the formation of Weimar and the treaty "November Criminals," because the armistice of November 11, 1918, was considered the beginning of the betrayal of Germany. Certain right-wing extremists took it upon themselves to punish the November Criminals. In August 1921, Matthias Erzberger, a republican leader of the Center party, was assassinated. He had been involved with arranging the armistice. Another prominent republican who favored fulfillment of the treaty, the intellectual and industrialist Walther Rathenau, was assassinated the following June. Rathenau's murder also pointed out the connection between anti-Semitism and antirepublicanism in the minds of the extreme right. Many on the right charged that the republic was created and controlled by Jews to the detriment of "true" Germans. In their propaganda such rightists frequently referred to Weimar as the "Jew Republic."

The year 1923 brought even greater disasters. On the grounds that Germany had failed to meet its reparation obligations, French and Belgian troops occupied the Ruhr in January. The German policy of passive resistance to this action revealed the weakness of the republic and produced an almost complete collapse of the economy. Shortly thereafter, Germany experienced the most catastrophic inflation in its history. By November 1923, the German mark was worth only one-trillionth of its 1914 value. Middle-class savings and investments became worthless; those on fixed incomes and many of the self-employed were cast into poverty almost overnight. Government deficits reached close to 99 percent. These problems generated massive unemployment, food riots in certain areas, as well as widespread social and psychological distress. All of this provided opportunities for the extreme right and left. Communist strength in several states increased dramatically, and leftist political violence was just the prelude to a planned Communist revolution. At the same time Bavaria had become a hotbed of right-wing radicalism, which culminated in Hitler's famous Beer Hall *Putsch* of November 8 (see chapter 4). The political crisis was so intense and the danger so great that President Ebert declared a state of emergency under Article 48 of the constitution and authorized the army to restore order. This decisive executive action was sufficient to counteract these overt threats, but political and economic conditions remained critical. The long-range impact of the inflation and disorders of 1923 would affect the entire history of Weimar.

The political repercussions of the Great Inflation were most noticeable among the middle classes. Before World War I, middle-class Germans had enjoyed increasing prosperity, but by 1923 many of them suffered economic ruin. Already doubtful about democracy, they became even more alienated from the republic as a result of their recent economic misfortune, and this greatly accelerated the middle-class move to the right, a movement already begun in 1920. Searching for an explanation of their plight, they became easy prey for the propaganda of the reactionary right. The source of the inflation, the right claimed, was the republic itself; a weak Weimar government had turned Germans into slaves of the Allies. Only a strong German state could restore the nation's prosperity, as well as its national sovereignty and integrity.

Today, most historians agree that the inflation was caused by war debts inherited from the monarchy and reparation payments, two factors beyond the control of the republican government. In the 1920s, however, the inaccurate explanations of the reactionary right proved quite convincing to the middle classes. Germans from all classes, of course, had lost confidence in the government during the crisis of 1923, but middle-class hostility toward the republic endured beyond this period. When the next economic crisis struck in the 1930s, a greatly disproportionate number of middle- and lower-middle-class citizens would either join or vote for the Nazi party, which promised them an economic and national rejuvenation. In return for these things, they were quite willing to sacrifice a democracy in which they had so little faith and on which they blamed their economic and social decline.

From the early years of the republic, the crisis of Weimar democracy was also aggravated by Germany's intellectuals. Weimar granted intellectuals greater freedom and creative opportunities than they had ever known, yet they reacted to the republic with hostility and disdain. Instead of creating enthusiasm for Weimar, intellectuals raised additional doubts and increased popular disillusionment and despair. Some thought their criticism of Weimar's failures and weaknesses would lead to necessary change, but others believed that the republic's problems were inherent in the system itself, and they looked forward to its demise. None of them found the existing situation tolerable, and together they had a devastating psychological impact on Weimar's political climate.

Among the countless left-wing intellectuals of this era, those associated with the journal *Weltbühne*, such as Carl von Ossietzky and Kurt Tucholsky, held a place of distinction. To these intellectuals, Weimar had failed because it had instituted neither socialism nor true democracy. They were not anti-republican per se, but wanted a republic that would fulfill their Socialist and democratic ideals. To reach their goal of a social-democratic republic, they advocated revolutionary measures to destroy rightist influence in society and politics, which would involve democratization of the army, bureaucracy, and judiciary, as well as the socialization of the economy. Moreover, they were unrestrained in their criticism of cherished German traditions, values, and symbols. Often their writings and artworks were not merely unpatriotic but blatantly anti-German. The satirist Kurt Tucholsky, like the artist George Grosz, depicted Germans as dumb, crude, even barbaric. The targets of their scathing attacks were not just the right, German cultural traditions, and the republic, but also the SPD, because it had abandoned the cause of revolutionary socialism. However, instead of bringing Germany closer to their ideal social-democratic state, these intellectuals helped undermine the progress Germany had already made toward a democratic form of government. By constantly pointing out Weimar's failure to realize economic and social justice, they intensified the dissatisfaction of the left and the working classes. Likewise, their vicious assaults on German society and culture shocked the middle classes, who viewed these intellectuals as cultural nihilists. Many middle-class Germans were thereby confirmed in their belief that democracy was leading toward the destruction of all social and moral standards. Their reservations about Weimar multiplied accordingly.

The association of cultural decadence with Weimar democracy was a favorite theme of right-wing intellectuals. They elevated Weimar's problems to the level of a general cultural crisis. According to their pessimistic assessment, modern trends in such areas as lifestyle, art, literature, and morality—all supposedly characteristic of the new democracy—were destroying traditional German values and culture. Some right-wing intellectuals attributed these trends to Communist or foreign influence. Others, such as Oswald Spengler in his popular book *The Decline of the West*, saw them as a manifestation of a larger historical process of the rise and fall of civilizations, which if not reversed would mean the end of German culture. The racists and anti-Semites on the right, of course, drew a connection between Germany's cultural decline and the alleged rise of Jewish influence.

Although the right-wing intellectuals were a diverse group with varying, often contradictory, explanations for real and alleged problems, they generally agreed that democracy was a major cause of Germany's ills. In their ideological campaign to discredit democracy, they argued that parliamentary government was a sham and democracy an illusion, because people did not rule but were manipulated by political parties and special-interest groups that controlled elections and parliament. In the process, the welfare of the nation as a whole was sacrificed for the benefit of these powerful special interests. As a solution, many rightist intellectuals advocated a "conservative revolution" that would eliminate Weimar and establish what Moeller van den Bruck called a "Third Reich" and others labelled the "New State," a political system in which traditional conservative ideals and German values could be realized. But there was no agreement on the exact nature of this new conservative order or on how such a conservative revolution might be brought about. In a general way, these intellectuals envisioned an authoritarian state ruled by an elite.

Although right-wing intellectuals were as hostile to nazism as they were to the republic, they were an unwitting asset to the Hitler movement. They contributed to the German mood of despair, and much of their terminology and many of their works were taken over and distorted by the Nazis as useful propaganda. Concepts such as the "Third Reich" and a "state above parties" soon became Nazi slogans. Perhaps more significant, the intellectuals' persistent assaults on parliamentary government found a receptive audience among Germany's middle classes, for there were major problems with the practice of parliamentary government and political parties in Weimar. The result of party strife was almost perpetual governmental instability and ineffectiveness. In its short fourteen-year history, Weimar would have twenty-one different cabinets and fifteen chancellors, six within its first five years.

Nevertheless, after Weimar weathered the crisis of 1923, antirepublican activities and sentiments subsided dramatically. Between the end of the Great Inflation and the onset of the Great Depression, Weimar experienced its most stable and prosperous interlude. The figure most responsible for this recovery was Gustav Stresemann, leader of the DVP, who served briefly as chancellor in 1923 and thereafter as foreign minister until 1929. Still a monarchist and antirepublican as late as the early 1920s, Stresemann became one of the strongest advocates of the new republic; without his leadership Weimar might not have survived as long as it did. By 1922 he was convinced that the political collapse of Weimar would end in civil war or in a seizure of power by the extreme right or left, and he was determined to prevent these events. As a nationalist, Stresemann wanted Germany to regain its lost position among the great powers of Europe. He realized that this could not be accomplished unless Germany first put its own house in order. Stresemann believed that these objectives could best be achieved by stabilizing the republic rather than by remaining in opposition to it.

Considering that Germany had been at the brink of political and economic collapse, Stresemann's accomplishments were tremendous. Currency and fiscal reform ended the inflation; the Dawes Plan of 1924 set a more reasonable schedule and amount for German reparation payments; and a program of international loans assisted Germany's economic recovery. In foreign policy, Stresemann favored fulfillment of the treaty obligations, because he felt that Germany's recovery at home and of its lost status in international politics could be achieved only through cooperation with the Allies. Stresemann ended the policy of passive resistance and negotiated the withdrawal of the French and Belgians from the Ruhr. By confirming Germany's new frontiers with France and Belgium and by accepting the demilitarization of the Rhineland in the Locarno Treaties of 1925, Stresemann initiated a new era of international cooperation. He brought Germany into the League of Nations in 1926 and arranged a plan for British and French evacuation of the Rhineland. Not only had Stresemann become the dominant political figure in Germany, but he received international recognition as well. In 1926 he was awarded the Nobel Peace Prize.

These successes were accompanied by domestic political stabilization. Under Stresemann's leadership the conservative DVP pursued a moderate political course aimed at making democracy work in Germany, and the Center-Right Coalition government (1924–1928) was one of the most durable of the Weimar era. The election of Field Marshal Paul von Hindenburg as president in 1925 was also significant. Although his election was initially viewed as a victory for the reactionary forces, Hindenburg took his oath to the constitution quite seriously. He knew little of democracy and politics in general, but he did his best to uphold the constitution and to stabilize the Weimar Republic. Instead of using the presidency to support the reactionary policies of the rightist groups that had helped elect him, Hindenburg kept his office above partisan politics and ideological disputes. He saw himself as a neutral force, acting in accordance with the constitution and representing the welfare of the nation as a whole. Equally important, the Hindenburg presidency provided many Germans with a sense of political and psychological security. To republicans, his constitutional stance was reassuring; to the middle classes, he was a symbol of authority and a bulwark against further disorder.

By 1928 Weimar had reached its most politically stable and economically prosperous point. The Reichstag elections of that year showed a significant trend away from the right. The SPD gained votes, while the DNVP lost almost a third of its previous support. An even more positive sign for the republic was that Stresemann had managed to get the conservative DVP to participate in a new government with the Social Democrats to the exclusion of the reactionary right. More encouraging still, the largest party and the strongest supporter of the republic, the SPD, was once again in power. Its man, Hermann Mueller, became the new chancellor. The future of the republic looked brighter than ever before.

But events would soon show that, despite these positive developments, Weimar had not overcome its fundamental problems. Very little had changed in the relationships between the various segments of German society. The nation was still deeply divided by class, ideology, and economic interests; the republic had acquired only the toleration, not the enthusiastic support, of the bulk of the German people. In retrospect, it is clear that the years of tranquility and stability were dependent upon the leadership of Stresemann and prosperity. When these crucial factors were removed, Germany would again lapse into political and economic turmoil. Weimar parties would revert to their habitual squabbling, confidence in the republic would quickly disappear, and political radicalization would return.

To a large extent, the early 1930s in Germany would be reminiscent of the first years of the republic. Only this time, a well-organized and dynamic Nazi party would be waiting to exploit the situation.

CHAPTER 2

The Rise of Hitler and Nazism

Despite all of Weimar's problems, the Nazi triumph was not inevitable. Certainly before the 1930s, the possibility of a Nazi seizure of power appeared highly improbable even if Weimar were to collapse. Shunned by the more reputable segments of society and dwarfed by the more established political parties, the Nazi party was a political failure throughout the 1920s. During these years, there was little to suggest its future success. In fact, from its beginning, the Nazi party seemed doomed to obscurity. The original group that formed the basis for the Nazi party in Germany was so pitiful that Hitler himself called it "this absurd little organization."

The Nazi movement developed out of one of countless radical revolutionary groups that appeared in Germany during the period of postwar dislocation. Munich, in particular, where there existed approximately fifty different political organizations, was a hotbed of radicalism. In January of 1919, this city became the birthplace of the German Workers' party (DAP). The organizers and early leaders of this new party were Anton Drexler, a locksmith, and a sports journalist, Karl Harrer. The DAP attracted at most about forty members; it lacked an organizational structure and had no program to guide it toward more direct political activity. Hitler was correct when he later described this group as more of a club than a political party. Members gathered in Munich beer halls to hold discussions and to complain about Germany's ills. The group was racist, anti-Semitic, nationalistic, anticapitalist, and anti-Communist, and it lacked a coherent and developed ideology. Although each member had his own pet ideas, all generally agreed that the sources of Germany's problems could be found in a Jewish conspiracy, the Bolshevist menace, and capitalist exploitation. They wanted to root out these evils and restore Germany to its previous national and military status.

The orientation of the DAP was definitely toward the masses, because it considered the middle classes and old aristocracy politically and morally bankrupt. It was Drexler's intention to win the working classes back to the cause of German nationalism. To accomplish this, Drexler advocated a type of German socialism that would eliminate capitalist exploitation of workers and provide for the economic and social welfare of all Germans. Workers supposedly would abandon international Marxism in favor of this national form of socialism. Their allegiance to the fatherland would again be assured. But the general idea of reconciling nationalism and socialism was not developed into a program for political action.

The DAP was for the most part a collection of social misfits, malcontents, political amateurs, and pseudotheorists. The uneducated Drexler, though he could ramble on about the causes of Germany's misery, was as ineffective at public speaking as he was incompetent at organizing. Similarly, Harrer, whose leadership potential was also nil, proudly assumed the title of national chairman of a nonexistent national organization. The self-proclaimed economic expert, Gottfried Feder, an engineer by training, lectured endlessly about his bizarre theory of "interest slavery." Even those with some talent or potential were distinguished by their social deviance and ideological extremism. Dietrich Eckart, for example, was a poet and journalist, but his vehement oral and written assaults on Jews knew no limits. Eckart was also concerned with preserving the purity of the "Nordic race," and he prophesied that a national savior would soon appear in Germany.

One of the few early members with any real ability in organizing or in political affairs was Captain Ernst Röhm. A devoted soldier who had proven himself under fire, Röhm had as his original objective the reemergence of a strong army within a rejuvenated nation. It was the DAP's goal of rallying the working classes behind the nationalist cause and the army that brought him into the party. But he, too, had his personality problems, and by 1923 his wild-spirited behavior and uncontrollable temper led to his forced resignation from the officer corps. It was difficult to imagine that any party that had such a group as a foundation would amount to anything politically, let alone dramatically change the course of human history.

The beginning of the transformation of this small, disorganized lot into a major historical movement can be traced to a party meeting held on the evening of September 12, 1919. That night, a political instruction officer was sent by the army to investigate the DAP. Although the army spy was completely unimpressed by what he saw and heard, a few party members took a distinct interest in this stranger after he engaged a critic in debate. The party felt that such a speaker could be useful and decided to recruit him. At first the soldier reacted with amusement to their invitation to join the DAP, because he had so little respect for the group and intended to establish his own party. After some agonizing, however, he decided to join. He did so not only because he agreed with many of their ideas, but also because he saw that the group was so new and disorganized that he could transform it into the type of party he envisioned and could determine its future political course. Later, he said that this was the most important decision of his life. It was a decision that the rest of humanity would soon regret, for that soldier was Adolf Hitler.

Although he always felt superior to other members, Hitler was a perfect candidate for this group because of his personality, background, and life experience. Like most DAP members, he was a misfit, alienated from a middle-class society he had come to detest and was determined to destroy. His family origins were quite humble, if not disreputable, and he was not even a citizen of the country with which he identified and of which he would become the political master.

Hitler was born on April 20, 1889, in the small town of Braunau in Austria. His father, Alois, was the illegitimate son of a peasant girl named Maria Schicklgruber. Later, Alois changed his family name to Hitler, since it was assumed that his father had been a wanderer named Johann Hiedler. Despite numerous stories spread later, there is no evidence to suggest that Adolf Hitler had a Jewish grandfather, and historians generally discount this possibility. Through years of hard work, Alois was able to overcome the social stigma of his birth and his peasant origins. Eventually, he achieved the respectable position of a customs official for the Austrian state. His public position contrasted sharply with his private life. He had three marriages, one illegitimate child, and two children born shortly after he married their mothers. Alois's third wife, Klara Pölzl, was his second cousin and twenty-three years younger than Alois. When Klara gave birth to Adolf, Alois was already over fifty years old. In 1895 the family moved to Linz, where Alois soon retired.

In Linz, the Hitlers had a comfortable lower-middle-class existence. There young Adolf certainly had opportunities that could have led to a good career and most likely to middle-class economic and social status. After Alois died, his pension was sufficient to provide for the needs of the family and for Adolf's education. Alois tried to instill in his son the values of industry and education necessary for success in the middle-class world. Klara was a devoted and loving mother. The reasons for the young Hitler's failures, therefore, are to be found not in the social circumstances of his early years, as he tried to make others believe, but in his own personality. Apparently pampered by his mother, Adolf became egotistical, lazy, obstinate, and moody. His behavior was characterized by indecisiveness, anxiety, and an inability to concentrate on a particular task or issue for any length of time. He was a dreamer who was always at the center of his own dreams. He fancied himself a leader, yet he had no followers and few friends. He believed that he deserved recognition and success, even greatness, and was sure that these were awaiting him in the future; but he lacked discipline and avoided the hard work necessary for success. The young Adolf felt superior to others, but aside from his own exaggerated estimation of himself and his talents, he could point to nothing, no achievement or recognized ability, that could justify this self-image. He blamed his failures on others, or on society, and he developed a strong resentment of the middle-class world he was convinced had unjustly rejected him.

His first major rejection occurred quite early. Between 1900 and 1904 he attended the *Realschule* in Linz, which prepared pupils for technical or commercial careers. Hitler later created the myth that his poor performance and ultimate failure in school arose from an enduring dispute with his father over Adolf's desire to become an artist. The fact is that Adolf's laziness and lack of discipline were the roots of the problem. He failed several subjects, performed only adequately in others, and had to repeat a grade twice. After his father died in 1903, Adolf's performance did not improve; a year later he had to transfer to another school, which he was forced to leave in 1906 before graduating. His second failure followed shortly thereafter. In 1907, convinced of his artistic talents, he applied for admission to the Academy of Fine Arts in Vienna. The academy's negative decision and a second unsuccessful attempt to gain entry to this institution in 1908 came as bitter shocks to Hitler. All of his egotistical hopes and dreams of future greatness as an artist seemed in jeopardy. Nonetheless, since his feeling of superiority rested on his belief in his own artistic talent, he was determined to become an artist without formal schooling. For the rest of his life he regarded himself as an artist and came to pride himself on his special talent for architecture as well. But these experiences had left him embittered; throughout his life he displayed a deep dislike and distrust for intellectuals, experts, and traditional educational systems. Behind his criticism, however, there remained a sense of inadequacy and rejection. Hitler always felt hampered by his lack of formal education; he was uncomfortable in the presence of intellectuals and specialists.

Hitler stayed in Vienna until 1913, living a meaningless and aimless life. He was by no means destitute and could have used his resources and time to learn a trade or acquire steady employment. But again, his personality prevented him from making any decision on his future; he lived from day to day. He used up a pension, a small inheritance, and some money from his aunt. In all these years he had no regular employment and finally ended up in shelters for the homeless among the lower classes of the society he detested. A good deal of his time was spent drawing and painting and dreaming. He visited art galleries and museums, attended the opera (Wagner was his favorite), and became an avid reader of newspapers. As time passed, his income came solely from an occasional job and from his paintings and commercial drawings, including one advertisement showing Santa Claus. Hitler's dress and behavior remained eccentric. He was given to fits of anger and violent arguments; he continually annoyed others with his monologues and political harangues. Lasting personal relationships were impossible for him, and he showed no interest in women. Indeed, this fellow who neither smoked nor drank struck others as a rather strange individual, one to be avoided.

Although Hitler considered these years the worst of his life, they were crucial in terms of his political and ideological development. During this period, he formulated his basic philosophy of politics and history; equally important, he acquired insights into the behavior and baser instincts of the masses that he would later skillfully exploit as a politician and demagogue. The components of his grand philosophy were not original; instead, they were selectively gathered from a variety of sources. He did not approach subjects in a systematic manner, but moved from field to field in his reading, depending upon his mood and passing interests. His knowledge came mostly from newspapers and pamphlets and books published by the popular, often anti-Semitic press in Vienna. His grandiose ideological statements could not withstand critical analysis, and he rarely tried to provide sufficient evidence to back up his arguments. The foundation of his political outlook was his own unshakable belief that he was correct. Yet Hitler's beliefs have been shared by many before and after him.

Among the most important influences on Hitler's ideological development were the writings of Lanz von Liebenfels and Houston Stewart Chamberlain, two promoters of the theory of the "Aryan master race." Both argued that evolution had produced races with different intellectual characteristics and potential, among which the "Aryan" or "Nordic" race was the most advanced on the evolutionary scale. This Aryan race was the only race capable of advanced cultural and technological achievements, and all of the great civilizations in history were its creations. Lanz and Chamberlain held that racial purity was essential to the survival of the Aryan race and therefore of higher civilization itself. They thought other forces in the modern world were at work trying to poison and undermine the Nordic race; a struggle for survival was underway. The primary threat came from the allegedly inferior, though supposedly parasitic and crafty, Jewish race, but other forces such as the Slavs and Marxism also presented a danger. Lanz's call for a political attack against the menaces of Judaism and Marxism was echoed by Georg von Schönerer, a fanatical anti-Semite and German nationalist, who urged the creation of a unified empire of Austria and Germany to replace the decaying Habsburg monarchy that he claimed was being overwhelmed by Jews and Slavic minorities.

The Vienna of this period also witnessed the spread of a type of political anti-Semitism that was socially and economically based. The Christian Socialist party, with the mayor of Vienna, Karl Lueger, as its leader, repeatedly emerged triumphant in elections by playing upon the economic and social insecurity of the workers and lower middle class. Lueger's politics consisted of a shrewd manipulation of anti-Semitism combined with government programs to meet the social and economic needs of what he called the "little man." His anti-Semitism was not racial but economic. Lueger charged that Jews were behind big finance and capitalism, that consequently Jews were the source of the most pressing problems of the lower classes, and that the average man had to be protected from this exploitation. The ideas of Lueger, like those of Lanz and Schönerer, were reinforced by the writings and speeches of countless other writers and political activists. Pseudoscientific theories about race and Jews, pamphlets promoting chauvinistic German nationalism, and treatises warning about the Marxist, as well as the capitalist, menace abounded. Anti-Semitic societies and publications, along with the campaigns of political demagogues, made racism, anti-Semitism, and extreme nationalism integral parts of the cultural and political atmosphere of prewar Vienna.

Hitler's philosophy was a reflection of many of these ideas and trends. Like Lanz and Chamberlain, he came to believe that nature had established certain "racial laws" that must be observed and that world history was the story of the struggle between races for survival. As Hitler stated, "Those who want to live, let them fight, and those who do not want to fight in this world of eternal struggle do not deserve to live." The "genius-race" consisted of those of Aryan stock who were endowed by nature with superior talents, intelligence, and potential that allowed them alone to be the creators of science, art, and culture. Other races could borrow ideas and technology from the Aryans but never create them. In Hitler's mind, the progress of humanity depended solely upon the Aryans. This superior race could maintain its dominance and fulfill its great cultural mission only if it retained its purity and its instinct for self-preservation. The Jewish race was the mightiest opponent of the Aryans, according to Hitler, precisely because Jews had maintained their racial purity and had a strongly developed instinct for self-preservation. Hitler maintained that in the racial struggle throughout history, the Jews, who have no potential to create culture and civilization, seized upon the achievements of other races to survive. In effect, the Jews were seen as cultural and economic parasites, who would use any means, adopt any ideas, and associate themselves with any historical movement that would temporarily suit their needs. Liberalism and the Enlightenment, democracy and parliamentary government, capitalism and industrialization, Marxism and trade unions were all viewed by Hitler as forces either created or exploited by the Jews as a part of their plan for the "enslavement and with it the destruction of all non-Jewish peoples."

The susceptibility of Hitler to Aryan race theories was not surprising. Such ideas allowed this impoverished social outcast, who remained convinced of his own superiority and self-importance, to identify himself as part of a superior race with a unique historical mission. He grasped racial concepts in the same way that many of the newly urbanized European masses, uprooted by industrialization from the traditional cultural and social patterns of the countryside, embraced the cult of nationalism. For those suffering from alienation in the mass society of the cities, nationalism provided a needed group identity and a feeling of belonging. It furnished them not only with a sense of pride but also with a feeling of superiority. No matter how lowly their status in society, they were, as part of a distinct racial or national group, better than others and destined to share in the historical greatness of the larger group. Moreover, in Hitler's case, the alleged Jewish conspiracy also provided a clearly definable enemy against whom he could vent all the frustrations emanating from his failures and anxieties. Hitler's anti-Semitism was not merely political or ideological; it was irrational and emotional, as his hatred for Jews knew no bounds. From his harangues directed at vagrants in flophouses to his writings and speeches as leader of Germany, he continually reproached Jews in the most vicious and threatening language, calling them liars, filth, maggots, and a pestilence. For the rest of his life Hitler was psychologically obsessed with the so-called Jewish question.

It was also during this early period that Hitler's racial ideas became intermixed with the Pan-German nationalism of Georg von Schönerer. Hitler believed that the core of the Aryan race was the Germans and that biologically and culturally all Germans constituted a distinct natural grouping. In the modern world, Germans were separated by geography and artificial state boundaries. The preservation of the race required that those of German blood be reunited in a single state; otherwise, a divided German race would remain weak and face bastardization as Germans assimilated with the peoples of the various states in which they resided. Living in the multinational Austrian Empire of the Habsburgs, Hitler was quite concerned that Austrian Germans would perish as a result of intermixing with various ethnic groups. In Vienna, he felt personally threatened by the cultural and political influence of Czechs, Hungarians, Jews, and other minorities. For this reason, he found Schönerer's Pan-German nationalism and his call for the unification of Austrian Germans with the German Empire created by Prussia particularly attractive.

Although he was an Austrian citizen, Hitler became a German nationalist who shared Schönerer's hatred for a declining Habsburg monarchy that prided itself on ruling such an ethnically diverse empire. Hitler felt no loyalty toward the Austrian Empire, and thereafter he identified himself with the more powerful state of Germany, for there he saw the strength and vitality he knew were necessary in the struggle for survival. Nation and race were synonymous for Hitler, and the determining factor was the biological makeup of a people, not state boundaries or citizenship. Austria and Germany must be brought together into a natural racial unit.

In Vienna, Hitler learned more than the ideologies of racism and German nationalism. The streets and political arenas of the capital provided him with an understanding of political behavior and tactics. His greatest lesson was that the best chance of acquiring power is through a well-organized and ruthlessly led movement that was directed at the masses. His years of association with the lower classes gave him insight into their needs, fears, weaknesses, and political reactions. He came to know their basic instincts and learned from others how to manipulate these. In this regard, one of his greatest teachers was Karl Lueger, a man for whom Hitler had immense admiration. Hitler saw that Lueger's success was due to his broad-based mass movement that appealed to members of various classes, whereas other parties usually represented the interests of one particular class or group. Equally significant, Lueger's support came from those segments of society that felt alienated and economically insecure. As a shrewd demagogue, Lueger played upon their real needs and their emotions. He enhanced their fears with rhetoric and offered concrete social and economic programs to alleviate their burdens. He launched vicious attacks against their alleged enemies or causes of their problems. Usually this meant the Jews or other ethnic minorities. And he used emotional slogans to appeal to nationalistic and patriotic sentiments.

Hitler also was impressed by the growth of the Social Democratic party. Of course, he despised this Marxist group as much as he did the trade unions, because he thought it was merely a means used by Jews to control workers. Nevertheless, he respected the organizational and propaganda techniques of the Social Democrats that allowed them to develop a powerful party with devoted and disciplined followers. They addressed the real economic plight of the workers on the one hand, while on the other, they used the Marxist rhetoric of class hatred to capitalize on the emotions of workers. The weakness of the Social Democrats, Hitler correctly observed, was that their Marxist ideology limited their constituency to the working classes, and their internationalist orientation and attacks against the state prevented them from exploiting the nationalism and patriotism of the masses. His political schooling in Vienna led Hitler to conclude that a successful mass party must be both nationalistic and socialistic, and that skillful leadership, organization, and propaganda were essential.

When he left Vienna for Munich in 1913, Hitler still intended to pursue a career as an artist. Although his interest in political affairs was stronger than ever before, he had not yet decided to enter politics. It is doubtful that the political ideas and attitudes he had acquired had been formulated into a coherent ideology. Hitler moved to Germany to avoid being drafted. Military induction would have interfered with his artistic pursuits, ended the freedom of his bohemian lifestyle, and placed him in the service of the Habsburg state for which he expressed such loathing. His life in Munich was as aimless as his existence in Vienna had been, though his determination to become a professional artist seemed to decline as his fascination with politics increased.

The outbreak of World War I in 1914 proved to be a turning point in Hitler's life. He was swept up in the initial nationalistic enthusiasm that accompanied the declaration of war, and he volunteered for service in a Bavarian regiment. The young Pan-German nationalist, who saw life in terms of struggle, now had the opportunity to participate in a conflict of major historical importance. In the army, he found many of the things his life had lacked—a purpose, a sense of order, and a place to belong. The army was a substitute for the home and the family he did not have. For the first time, he learned toughness and discipline, two assets that would later benefit him as a political leader. Will power and ruthlessness would be distinguishing characteristics of the future Nazi *Führer*. All indications are that Hitler was a brave soldier. He fought in one of the most brutal battles at the beginning of the war, won an Iron Cross, second class, was subsequently wounded twice, and eventually was awarded an Iron Cross, first class. In October of 1918, he was blinded during a gas attack and evacuated to a hospital in Germany. To Hitler, the war was both an idealistic crusade for Germany and a way of life. Until the very end he remained quite confident of a German victory, and defeat was a devastating psychological blow.

It was the events of 1918 that finally prompted Hitler to enter politics. He believed that the loss of the war, the revolution that overthrew the Kaiser, and the establishment of the Weimar Republic were the work of Jewish and Communist traitors. At first, he apparently viewed his political activity in terms of avenging this betrayal and of assisting those forces struggling to return Germany to its former position as a great power. Hitler's first political experience was as a political instruction officer for the army. His duties consisted mainly of educating soldiers in the evils of democracy, communism, and pacifism and in reporting on various radical political organizations in the Munich area. This service not only brought him into contact with the DAP but also awakened in him a recognition of his skill and effectiveness as a political speaker. As he became more confident in his own political ability, Hitler gradually came to believe that it was his destiny to be the historic savior of Germany. Hitler suffered from what some historians have called a "messiah complex." It was Hitler's unwavering belief in his special mission and his ability to convince others of this that account in large measure for his success in attracting a following and in holding the movement together.

Hitler entered the DAP with the intention of transforming this fringe group into a mass movement under his sole command. He started out as member number 7 of the party's central committee in charge of propaganda and recruitment. Although the leadership of the party was still in the hands of Drexler and Harrer, Hitler shrewdly used his position to change the nature of the party and to enhance his own power. In accomplishing this, Hitler had certain advantages that his associates lacked. With no regular job or profession, he was the only member who could devote himself full-time to the party. Such party activity also suited his personality, because he could work irregular hours and avoid being tied down by specific duties or obligations. He worked hard at developing the party organization and recruiting new members. Neither Drexler nor Harrer could compete with Hitler's organizational skill and talents as a speaker. Hitler carefully established the foundations of the future party bureaucracy and improved propaganda techniques. To enhance the enthusiasm and loyalty of existing members and to enlist new recruits, he introduced the practice of holding mass meetings that projected the image of party unity, vitality, strength, and determination.

It was soon clear that Hitler possessed a certain charisma, an irrational quality that captivated the emotions and eventually the devoted loyalty of others. As a result, most of those who joined the party were attracted by Hitler himself, and they gave their allegiance to him. At the first successful mass meeting, held at the Hofbräuhaus in Munich on February 24, 1920, the spotlight was on Hitler rather than on Drexler or Harrer. Hitler himself had the honor of introducing the new party program and proclaiming a change in the party's name. Henceforth, the DAP was to be known as the National Socialist German Workers' party (NSDAP), from which the term *Nazi* was derived.

Hitler used his position as propaganda director to manipulate the flow of information within the party and to the public so as to promote himself and his ideas while undermining his opponents in the party. One year after he had joined the party, Hitler had expanded party membership to over three thousand. His influence within the organization and his indispensability to the movement increased accordingly.

In 1921, threatened by the influx of new members loyal to Hitler and by Hitler's obvious ambition to seize control of the party, Drexler, Harrer, and others among the old guard attempted to purge Hitler from the organization. But Hitler's position was so strong that he not only thwarted these efforts but emerged from this confrontation as first chairman of the party, with essentially dictatorial power over its central organization in Munich. Drexler and Harrer soon faded into obscurity, and Hitler proceeded to centralize additional power in his own hands at the expense of the independence of local Nazi groups in other parts of Germany. As time passed, the future political and ideological direction of the party would be determined by Hitler to such an extent that nazism became more and more a reflection of the ideas and personality of the *Führer*. Supporters and detractors alike often referred to the Nazi party as the "Hitler movement."

Almost a decade passed before the historical implications of Hitler's triumph over his early party rivals became evident. In retrospect, it is clear that this leadership struggle was a watershed in the development of the party and an important stage in Hitler's rise to political power in Germany. But at the time, few outside the party took note of this change of leadership. For the most part, Hitler and the Nazi party were unknown beyond Munich, where they were identified as simply one minor radical group among many. It would take years of intensive effort before even a significant minority of Germans would take the Nazis seriously. Hitler and his followers, however, never doubted that ultimately the German people would grant them recognition and power.

The Nazi movement was not merely an extreme version of the traditional right or radical conservatism. Nazism, like fascism generally, was a unique historical development that embodied a variety of aspects from the right and left. Nazism created a distinctive synthesis of the formerly opposing ideological forces of nationalism and socialism. It was not a reactionary movement, attempting to return Germany to some previous political and social order. Quite the contrary, this novel historical force of nazism was very much a forward-looking and -thrusting movement. It shared the fervent nationalism of the right. From the beginning, however, it distinguished itself from conservatives and reactionaries by its social revolutionary ideas and commitment. As social revolutionaries, the Nazis would pose a serious challenge to the traditional elites, ideas, and institutions of the German right. This unique synthesis also created uncertainties among potential followers and ardent opponents about nazism's true nature. For this reason, many would misinterpret and perilously underestimate nazism. The left misperceived and attacked the Nazis as part of conservative Germany. In their efforts to combat nazism, the left further alienated the middle classes that identified with that conservative Germany under leftist assault. The traditional right meanwhile misunderstood nazism's populist appeal to their own middle-class constituencies, eventually losing these voters to the NSDAP. The traditional right would ultimately underestimate the allure that Nazi social revolutionary promises had to the middle classes in a period of prolonged desperation, resentment, and hopelessness.

CHAPTER 3

The Historical Roots
of Nazi Ideology

From the beginning, Hitler envisioned the Nazi party as more than just a political organization. It was an ideological movement; its distinct philosophy, rituals, and symbols constituted almost a secular religion. Since his Vienna days, Hitler was aware that men were motivated by symbols and ideas. He attributed the success of the Social Democrats to their ideological doctrines that provided workers with the inspiration for action and sacrifice. Socialist ideals unified workers behind a common cause and justified their struggle against the existing system with moral and historical imperatives. The strongest and most enduring historical movements were those that were the most dogmatic, because their intransigence affirmed the absolute validity of their beliefs. Hitler claimed that the stability and power of the Catholic Church were due to its uncompromising stance on doctrine. He also believed that ideological movements such as Marxism could not be defeated through force or by attacking their ideas, but must be challenged by a new philosophy with claim to absolute truth that would inspire its followers to fanaticism and at the same time provide the masses with a substitute for the ideology being destroyed. Hitler did not view the Nazi ideology as merely a tool for manipulating and controlling the masses; no one was more confirmed in his ideological convictions than Hitler himself. To him, the Nazi ideology embodied self-evident truths.

Nazi ideology contained no original elements. The underlying assumptions and basic ideas of the Nazi creed had existed in German and European civilization since the nineteenth century. The Nazis combined many of these preexisting currents into a unique, though often vague, ideological synthesis. This new formulation of established ideas, prejudices, and traditions allowed the Nazis to play upon traditional identities, symbols, and beliefs, while at the same time making the party appear fresh and revolutionary. It was a movement that would preserve, in some cases rejuvenate, cherished values and traditions from the past, yet it would also develop a new dynamic social and political order. The Nazi ideology was full of inconsistencies and contradictions. However, these proved to be a major source of strength rather than a weakness, because they gave the party flexibility and allowed it to encompass a wide spectrum of ideas as well as diverse interests and classes. As many historians have pointed out, nazism promised to be all things to all men.

The Nazi ideology provided millions of disillusioned and desperate Germans with an explanation for their plight, a focal point for their discontent, and a hope for the future. It must be noted, however, that most Germans did not accept this ideology, and many found it totally absurd. Even in the most hopeless days of the depression, Hitler could attract the support of only a third of the German people. The combined strength of the Communist, Socialist, and Catholic parties showed that a solid majority of Germans adhered to ideologies hostile to national socialism. A good many of those who joined the party or merely voted for it did not necessarily accept major parts of the ideology as valid. Most were attracted by one aspect of the ideology or another, or by certain programs and promises offered by the Nazis. Many disregarded the more extreme elements of the ideology as mere propaganda. Various factions had different perceptions of national socialism, and each was sure that its version was the correct one. As will be seen, even among party leaders and theorists there existed significant ideological differences.

But there were also millions of true believers in nazism who regarded its ideology as a coherent philosophy and who were either unconcerned with or unaware of its contradictions. To them, nazism was an absolute faith, an accurate reflection of historical and political realities. One of the more remarkable things about the highly ideological Nazi movement was that it failed to generate a theoretical work offering a coherent and fully developed explanation of the various tenets of national socialism. Hitler stated that he wrote *Mein Kampf* so that the basic elements of the Nazi doctrine would be set down for all time and be disseminated uniformly and coherently, but this disorganized and poorly written volume fell far short of this mark and failed to provide a comprehensive theoretical exposition of Nazi ideology. Moreover, Nazi ideology continued to evolve after the publication of *Mein Kampf* in 1925 and through the Third Reich. When we speak of Nazi ideology, we are referring to a set of general tenets and beliefs, some specific and others rather vague, drawn from a variety of sources in addition to Hitler's book. Among the more important of these are the Party Program of 1920, Nazi propaganda, the policies of the Third Reich, and the speeches and conversations of Hitler and other party leaders, as well as the writings of Nazi theorists.

At the heart of the ideology stood the concept of the *Volk*, a term that can be translated as people, nation, or race. This concept first became important as a part of the German romantic movement of the early nineteenth century from which a variety of *völkisch* movements eventually evolved. At that time, a *Volk* was generally perceived as a cultural rather than a biological entity. Romantic *völkisch* writers, like Friedrich Ludwig Jahn, argued that each *Volk* constituted a natural cultural group that had unique characteristics produced by its specific cultural-historical development and its peculiar environment. Some writers claimed that each *Volk* embodied its own distinct "life force" that helped to account for the different values, outlooks, and characters of various nations. These common values and cultural experiences united members of a particular *Volk* into an organized unit or *Gemeinschaft* (community).

Not individuality but identification with the group and the welfare of the *Volk* as a whole were paramount. Like many romantics, *völkisch* writers tended to paint a glorified, essentially mythological and inaccurate picture of medieval times, when the ideal *Gemeinschaft* supposedly existed. In their medieval utopia, the community was rooted in the land and bound together by custom and tradition. Heroic leaders, peasants, and craftsmen lived together in harmony with nature and each other as part of an organic whole. Each knew his proper place in society and had a purpose and meaning to his life; there was no exploitation, class conflict, or selfish individualism; time-honored customs and traditions provided a sense of psychological security. Modern social and economic changes, urbanization and industrialization in particular, had undermined the foundations of this organic rural life and threatened the unity and continued existence of the *Volk*.

Since many of these thinkers equated Jews with modern intellectual and political trends, as well as with urbanization, commerce, and industry, the *völkisch* movement was inherently anti-Semitic. Jews also were considered a different *Volk*, an alien cultural force within the natural German *Gemeinschaft*; they were outsiders whose roots did not originate in Germanic soil and who, as a landless group, were not an integral part of the rural agrarian community. Consequently, they did not share the same values and experiences of the German *Volk*. The notion that the Jews were a disruptive and threatening element was reinforced by the traditional anti-Semitism that had existed in Europe since the Middle Ages. In much of the popular literature Jews were depicted as middlemen and moneylenders who lived as economic parasites off the hard work of the peasants and craftsmen. From the early nineteenth century, *völkisch* writers were preoccupied with the Jewish question and whether it could be solved by removal of the Jews or by cultural assimilation.

By the second half of the nineteenth century, *völkisch* writers found a growing following among those who had become disillusioned with the modernization of German society brought about by rapid industrialization. Social and economic change drastically altered the living patterns of millions within a very short period, and many Germans had great difficulty adjusting psychologically, socially, and economically. Uprooted from their rural life, they faced the alienation, tension, and uncertainty of an urban industrial existence and were confronted with new value systems and lifestyles for which they were unprepared. A certain nostalgia developed for the lost innocence, simplicity, and stability of an earlier age.

Many of the disillusioned blamed their economic and social problems on modernization. Their anxieties were reflected in the works of Paul de Lagarde, one of the most widely read *völkisch* writers of the day. He viewed the displacement of traditional German society through modernization as the result of the influx of non-German ideas and forces. The preservation of the *Volk*, he argued, required the cultural purification of Germany and a return to a premodern *völkisch* community. He identified many of the modern forces he feared and detested (such as democratic ideas, parliamentary government, economic progress, and so on) with Jews, and his writings were permeated with vicious attacks against Jews.

At about the same time, the nature of *völkisch* thought underwent a crucial transformation. Earlier *völkisch* thinkers, including Lagarde, had viewed the *Volk* as a cultural entity, whereas, more recently, the *Volk* became defined in racial terms, and its very nature was determined by biological or genetic makeup. Thereafter, race, not culture, was the decisive factor. A major proponent of this *völkisch* racism was Julius Langbehn, a popular writer who shared many of Lagarde's utopian dreams about a rejuvenation of the lost German *Gemeinschaft*. Langbehn was fanatical in his beliefs that Jews were a separate and dangerous race and that the Jewish question could never be solved by assimilation, because this would lead to the bastardization of the German *Volk*. *Völkisch* theorists, in general, no longer spoke only of the cultural and environmental factors that produced a certain *Volk*; the new emphasis was on *Blut und Boden* (blood and soil). Similar themes also were prevalent in numerous popular novels of this period, and in this way, *völkisch* ideas reached a wide audience.

This new *völkisch* orientation was an outgrowth of the rise of scientific racism in the late nineteenth century. As Darwinian ideas became more acceptable, it was widely assumed that evolution had created various races of men in the same way that it had produced different species of animals, and that the different genetic makeup of each race determined not only its physical characteristics but also its intellectual and behavioral ones. The national character and cultural traits of a people were to a large extent the result of its biology; thus different cultural achievements and levels of development could be explained by the evolutionary process. It was assumed, for example, that

Germans, Frenchmen, Jews, Slavs, and so on constituted genetically distinct races and that major genetic differences divided them into superior and inferior groups, depending upon their potential. These viewpoints were by no means restricted to fanatics or anti-Semites; they were widely held by reputable thinkers across Europe and America well into the twentieth century.

Numerous anthropological and biological studies, in fact, seemed to prove the case for scientific racism. Although the writings of France's leading racial theorist, Count Georges de Lapouge, were essentially pseudoscientific, scientific racism in England was promoted by the works of Robert Knox and James Hunt, two of that country's most distinguished anthropologists. The credibility of racial theories was enhanced further by the studies of heredity conducted by the respected British scientist Francis Galton, father of the modern eugenics movement.

It also became fashionable to equate the struggle for survival in the natural world with conflict in human history. This application of Darwinian concepts to the study of human behavior and society became known as Social Darwinism. Human history was interpreted as a brutal fight for existence between different groups, and in this Social Darwinistic struggle, the fittest would survive and the weaker perish. Eventually, Darwinian ideas, like those of other reputable scholars, were distorted and popularized in the form of pseudoscientific theories and publications that appeared to establish a scientific and factual basis for the concept of racial struggle.

The first systematic work that viewed race as the essential factor in the process of human history was written by a Frenchman and predates the spread of Darwinism. In his *Essay on the Inequality of Races*, published in the 1850s, Arthur de Gobineau theorized that only the superior white race could create civilization. Consequently, the survival of civilization was dependent upon the maintenance of the purity of the white race, and race mixing would mean the decline, ultimately the end, of civilization. His arguments were further developed and refined by Houston Stewart Chamberlain, an Englishman by birth, who later became a citizen of the German state he so greatly admired. In *The Foundations of the Nineteenth Century* (1900), a book that went through several editions, Chamberlain argued that the Nordic, or Aryan, race had created everything of significance in human culture, civilization, and history. The Aryan race, which he called "cultural creators," was involved in a struggle with the parasitic Jewish race ("cultural destroyers"), and in this struggle for survival and civilization itself, the Aryans needed a strong leader to assure their triumph. The scholarly and scientific pretensions of Chamberlain's work established the validity of his ideas in the minds of many readers; in essence, the book buttressed the existing prejudices of racists and anti-Semites with allegedly scientific arguments. Chamberlain exercised considerable influence on Hitler's thinking.

The evolution of the *völkisch* movement coincided with the emergence of modern nationalism, one of the most powerful ideologies of the nineteenth and twentieth centuries. While the *völkisch* movement had a limited following, the nationalistic ideology was embraced by most Germans and actively promoted by the country's political and educational elites. By the turn of the century, German nationalism had reached the stage of extreme chauvinism, as patriotism was transformed into a feeling of German superiority. Many nationalistic writers and politicians claimed that German culture was indeed superior to that of other nations and that Germany had a historic mission to spread its culture and expand its influence in the world. Such notions were interconnected with Germany's militaristic tradition, its glorification of the army and power, and its goal of enhancing its political status on the international scene. On the eve of World War I, Germany was at its peak of economic and military power. Its amazing technological and industrial advancement, like its intellectual creativity, were recognized around the world, and Germans looked forward to even greater power, prestige, and wealth in the future. During the early phase of the war, the Germans were confident of a victory that would greatly expand their empire in Europe and also establish German hegemony over most of the Continent. Many German intellectuals justified the war as a struggle of superior German culture against the decadent cultures of the Western powers.

The idea of German cultural superiority and uniqueness fit in perfectly with the *völkisch* ideology. In the years preceding the war, there was a partial convergence of the nationalist and *völkisch* movements. Several leaders of the Pan-German League, a small but influential radical nationalist organization, adopted *völkisch* racist and anti-Semitic views, and *völkisch* groups began to support the expansionist and aggressive political goals of the Pan-Germans. The result was that a segment of the German nationalist movement had become infected with biological racism.

Together, *völkisch* racism, Social Darwinism, and German nationalism formed the core of the Nazi ideology. Hitler referred to the "aristocratic idea of nature" when describing the inequality of races and the superiority and higher values of the Aryans on which all civilization rested. Through struggle and proper "breeding," the strong would increase their strength, subdue the weak, and raise themselves to a dominant position. A primary ideological objective was the unification of all those of Nordic stock into a purified and homogeneous *Volksgemeinschaft* (racial community). The Party Program of 1920 stated explicitly that only those of "German blood" were members of the *Volk* and could be citizens of the state. No one of Jewish descent, even though he or she might be culturally assimilated or baptized in the Christian faith, could be a German citizen. The nationalistic planks of this program also demanded the cultural purification of German society. Roman law, allegedly an anti-German foreign code, must be replaced by German common law. A German national press must be created to promote the "national welfare"; all foreign and anti-German publications must be suppressed; and a legal struggle must be waged against all trends in art and literature that might undermine the German way of life.

While most of these aspects of the ideology would be primarily attractive to racists, other planks had broader appeal. The call for reuniting all Germans, based upon the "right of self-determination" and equality among nations, addressed the legitimate grievances and the indignation of those Germans who felt humiliated and frustrated by the Treaty of Versailles. The inability to adjust to the sudden collapse of German power and to the disappearance of national prestige was especially acute among those who had developed a strong psychological and emotional attachment to the ideology of nationalism before and during the war. The forceful Nazi stand against the treaty and the promise of a restoration of Germany to its former greatness appealed in particular to those who, while outraged and vengeful, felt helpless.

Most of these more moderate nationalists, like many foreign statesmen, failed to give serious consideration to the extremism of the Nazi version of German nationalism and its foreign policy implications. Nazis believed that the preservation of the Aryan race required the establishment of a German empire, or Third Reich, that would extend far beyond Germany's pre-1914 borders. If the race were to survive, it would need space and resources for its expanding population—an empire large enough to compete with the United States, Great Britain, and Russia. The concept of *Lebensraum* (living space), which would serve as the ideological foundation of Nazi foreign policy, was a mixture of *völkisch* ideas, contemporary geopolitical thought, and the expansionist philosophy of the Pan-German nationalists. The fulfillment of this ideological goal would require not only the destruction of the Treaty of Versailles but also war, because Hitler believed that the necessary *Lebensraum* could be found in Eastern Europe and Russia and could be acquired only through force.

Realization of nationalistic aspirations was not the only lure that Nazi ideology held out to the masses. At a time of social and economic distress, the Nazis were quite cognizant of the "social question," the importance of which Hitler had learned from Lueger and addressed at length in *Mein Kampf*. According to Nazi theory, the state had the social responsibility to provide for the basic welfare of its citizens and to protect them from social injustice and economic exploitation. The original intention of the party had been to win the workers away from the left by combining Nationalist and Socialist ideologies. Unlike Marxism, the National Socialist ideology did not present a threat to the private property of the middle classes. In fact, amid the socialistic components of the Party Program, there was a statement demanding the establishment and maintenance of a strong middle class. Nazis claimed to represent the interests of the "little man"—whether worker, farmer, or middle class—against more powerful economic forces. The enemies were not the small property holder and businessman, but big capitalism, large corporations, and international finance. It was the duty of the state to promote the industry and livelihood of its citizens and to ensure that the economy functioned for the common good of the nation rather than the selfish interests of wealthy capitalists. "Income unearned by work" was to be abolished, and profits made through wartime speculation were to be confiscated. Large trusts were to be nationalized; big department stores divided up and their space leased to small shopkeepers; when necessary, land would be confiscated without compensation. Land speculation and interest on land loans would be eliminated. Usurers and profiteers "must be punished with death," the program stated. There would also be profit sharing in large corporations and extensive provisions for health, education, and old age.

Clearly, Nazi economic programs appealed more to the lower middle class than to the workers. In Weimar, the small businessman faced growing competition from big department stores and large corporations. Similarly, low incomes of clerks and white-collar employees denied them the social and economic status they felt they deserved. Economic circumstances made it exceptionally difficult for small farmers to survive; often they blamed their losses on the government or the banks to which they were indebted. Each of these groups felt either threatened or deprived economically by big capital. Their resentment was enhanced by the fear that economic failure would cast them among the lower classes they despised. More and more of them came to believe that national socialism would protect them from the danger from above and below.

Despite the socialist components of their ideology, the Nazis were less successful in acquiring working-class support, in part because their version of socialism did not offer the sweeping economic and social revolution advocated by the Marxists. National socialism would eliminate neither private property nor class distinctions. It would provide economic security and social welfare programs for the workers; employment, a just wage, and protection from capitalistic exploitation would be guaranteed. But economic equality and a classless society were never Nazi goals. What workers would receive, aside from economic justice, would be enhanced social status. The new image of the worker would be one of honor and pride in his station in life. Workers would no longer constitute an alienated and despised group. They would again take their rightful place in society; their importance and dignity would be recognized by the rest of the nation. In the ideal Nazi *Volksgemeinschaft*, classes would exist (based upon talent, property, profession, etc.), but there would be no class conflict. Different economic and social classes would live together harmoniously and work for the common good. A national consciousness would replace the class consciousness that had historically divided Germans and turned them against one another.

Although socialism and anticapitalism were significant parts of the Nazi ideology, compromises were made on these aspects before and after the Nazis seized power. Ultimately, many of the socialistic ideals and programs remained unrealized. Part of the reason for this was that within the party there was violent disagreement over the essence of national socialism. Hitler himself was more concerned with the racial, nationalistic, and foreign policy goals of the ideology than he was with socialism. While he glorified the workers in his speeches, he retained the contempt for the lower classes he had acquired in Vienna; he later downplayed socialism in his efforts to gain votes from the middle classes and funds from wealthy capitalists. However, the left wing of the Nazi party, led by Gregor and Otto Strasser, considered nazism essentially a socialistic and anticapitalist movement. Their goal was the destruction of capitalism and the establishment of a socialist state, and they vigorously protested Hitler's compromises. In most cases, Hitler's views prevailed, but the conflict between these party factions over such issues would last until the suppression of the left wing in 1934. In theory, at least, socialism and anticapitalism remained integral parts of the Nazi ideology, and they continued to play a very important role in Nazi propaganda and election campaigns.

The refusal to pursue the egalitarian goal of eliminating class distinctions was due to the Nazi belief in the natural inequality of men. Just as there were differences among races, there also existed different capacities among members of each race. Under national socialism, the state would advance those with special talents or intelligence to positions of leadership and influence, from which they would rule over the masses. The Nazis condemned Western democratic forms of government because the practice of majority rule left political control in the hands of the masses and prevented elites from assuming their proper leadership roles as nature had intended. Elitism and the *Führerprinzip* (leadership principle) were two crucial elements in the Nazi ideology and the party organization.

The National Socialist elite would consist of what Hitler called the "best minds" and most creative personalities within the *Volk*. This elite would be organized according to a hierarchy of talent ascending upward to a single *Führer*, or leader. The *Führer* would rise to this position as a result of a general recognition of his exceptional talents, and his authority would be absolute. Although the *Führer* would stand above the party and the *Volk*, he would embody the will of the people, whose interests he would represent. Since the *Führer* would be the personification of the *Volk*, there would be an identification between ruler and ruled. Nazi theorists referred to this form of government as a type of "Germanic democracy."

In contrast to the Western notion of democracy, however, the German leader did not rule by majority consent nor were there any checks on his power. The *Führer* was accountable only to himself and bore sole responsibility for his actions. All political authority emanated from him, descending through the various levels of the hierarchy to the people. According to the *Führerprinzip*, each member of the hierarchy owed absolute obedience to those above and exercised authority over those below. Thus, the Nazi organization resembled the command structure of military institutions.

The strongest proponent of the *Führerprinzip* was Hitler himself. *Mein Kampf* was permeated with statements espousing the importance of individual personalities as the source of all cultural creativity and political greatness. Every great revolution and historical development, Hitler wrote, was inseparably associated with the name of the person who accomplished the deed. Hitler was sure that he was the manifestation of the essence of national socialism and that his personality was the key to the future greatness of Germany. He was relentless in his efforts to promote what Marxists would call the "cult of personality," and nazism became inextricably linked with his name. Adolf Hitler considered himself a political messiah, and many of those who followed him had an almost religious devotion to and faith in the *Führer* they came to regard as their savior. Hitler's cultivation of this image was designed to ensure that he alone would be the dominant force within the party and eventually in Germany. In this respect, the *Führerprinzip* proved essential in Hitler's triumph over his competition in the NSDAP.

As indicated by the *Führerprinzip*, nazism was to a large degree a reaction against liberal ideology. The Nazis challenged the liberal principles of equality, individualism, and parliamentary government. Hitler charged that the notion of equality was a sin against nature, an idea that undermined the concept of leadership. He believed that liberal emphasis on individualism threatened the organic unity and common welfare of the *Volk*. He envisioned the result as chaotic, ineffective, and irresponsible rule by inferior segments of society who would use the parliamentary system to foster their own selfish interests at the expense of the nation as a whole. In addition, the liberal values of compromise, tolerance, and discussion were anathema to the Nazi belief that the basic fact of political life was struggle. Hitler took special pride in pointing out that national socialism was "intolerant" of opposing forces and "fanatical" in the pursuit of its objectives. What was needed was not discussion leading to political compromise, but leadership and decisive action. In the Nazi mind, liberalism was an insidious doctrine invented by Jews as a means of debilitating the Aryan race by denying it strong leadership and by dividing it into self-centered interest groups.

Nazis identified their other ideological rival, Marxism, as a Jewish construction. They never tired of repeating that Marx was Jewish or of claiming that the Communist movement, trade unions, the Social Democratic party, and the leftist press were Jewish-controlled. The internationalist orientation of Marxism destroyed loyalty to the nation, and the concept of class struggle caused internal disunity, turning German against German and alienating the working class from the rest of society. Marxism was viewed as just another part of the "international Jewish conspiracy" to conquer the world. Allegedly, the Jews instigated the Bolshevist revolution in Russia and supported those Communists who stabbed Germany in the back during the war.

The antimodernist cultural perspectives of the Nazis also were linked to anti-Semitism. The Weimar Republic had opened the way for tremendous freedom of expression and artistic experimentation. But most of the more traditionally inclined Germans reacted with anxiety and hostility to the resulting changes in lifestyles and to the new modes of cultural expression known as modernism. Many rightist intellectuals, as well as Nazi publicists, launched scathing attacks on these modern trends, charging that German culture was decaying and that society was on the verge of a spiritual and moral collapse. Modern art, literature, theater, and popular culture were foreign in origin and were eroding the traditional values and moral standards of Germany. Patriotism, heroism, and military duty and honor were being derided by antiwar novelists and the leftist press, while the moral fiber of society was being destroyed by cabarets and sexual permissiveness.

The critics of modernism pointed to the popularity of jazz as a sign of the bastardization of culture caused by Negro influences. Likewise, traditional standards of beauty and art were being subverted by expressionist, cubist, and futurist themes and styles, which the traditionalists viewed as decadent, irrational, and incomprehensible. As expected, the Nazis took the most extreme stance against modernism, labeling it "cultural Bolshevism." It was the cultural counterpart to the Jewish-inspired Bolshevist political assault on Germany and was aimed at the spiritual degeneration of the *Volk*. Hitler referred to "cultural Bolshevism" as a disease that would weaken the Germans and leave them prey to the Jews. A moral struggle was underway, and the outcome could determine the survival of the race. Thus a primary ideological objective of the Nazis was a cultural and moral purification of Germany that would eliminate Jewish, Bolshevist, and other alien influences, rejuvenate true German culture, and produce a vibrant *Volk*.

The purified and rejuvenated nation the Nazis had in mind was substantially different from the society Germans had known before 1914. Nazism was neither conservative nor reactionary; it was a dynamic and radical revolutionary movement. Its ultimate goal was the creation of a new society and, indeed, a new type of man—the National Socialist. Although the Nazis shared some common objectives with conservatives and reactionaries, Nazis and the traditional right were political and ideological enemies. Both groups desired the destruction of Weimar and the left, as well as a cultural revival and the restoration of German power and greatness. At times, they formed temporary political alliances and tried to exploit each other, but the conservatives and reactionaries looked to the past, whereas the Nazis had a vision of radical changes in the future. National socialism demanded the total transformation of German society and culture along the lines of the Nazi *völkisch* ideology and the *Führerprinzip*. The traditional right was a definite obstacle to the realization of this ideology, a force with which the Nazis had to compete and one which would eventually have to be eliminated. A key stanza in the Nazi anthem, the "Horst Wessel Song," referred to those comrades killed in the struggle against the "Reaction."

The Nazis, Hitler included, proudly declared themselves revolutionaries. They plagiarized the concept of the national revolution from reputable conservative writers and altered it to suit their own ideological convictions and political needs. To the conservatives, the national revolution meant the replacement of Weimar with an authoritarian state that would regain Germany's lost position in the world and revitalize traditional German values, a state in which private life and basic institutions such as the family, churches, state bureaucracy, and the army would remain inviolable. The Nazis sought the establishment of a *Volksgemeinschaft* and with it totalitarian control, the transformation of every aspect of life, and the destruction of all vestiges of traditional institutions and private existence.

The acquisition of political power and the destruction of Weimar democracy were to be only one phase in the Nazi national revolution. The revolution would be completed only when every institution and all facets of life had been nazified, when every German had become a zealous disciple of national socialism. The seizure of power would take years; the final transformation of all Germans into true National Socialists might require decades or even generations. No matter how long it took, the Nazis were committed to the struggle and would persevere until the national revolution became a reality. Their fanatical devotion to this cause was evident in the final statement of the Party Program: "The leaders of the Party swear to go straight forward—if necessary to sacrifice their lives—in securing fulfillment of the foregoing points." The reward for their faith and sacrifices would be, they were certain, the creation of the greatest culture and civilization in human history—the National Socialist Third Reich, which would last for a thousand years.

CHAPTER 4

Party Structure, Propaganda, and Followers during the "Early Years of Struggle"

During the gradual evolution of Nazi ideology in the decade of the twenties, the Nazi party developed the organizational structure and propaganda techniques that would later prove so effective. This was accomplished only after numerous mistakes and almost fatal failures. In Nazi parlance, these were the "years of struggle," a time in which the party existed as a fringe group fighting to survive under highly unfavorable circumstances. During this period, the party tried several different political strategies but was unable to discover one that gave it mass appeal and a realistic chance to defeat the Weimar state.

In the early twenties, the NSDAP pursued the revolutionary path to power through the forceful overthrow of the republic. Because of its limited size and strength, the party had to ally itself with right-wing groups and with antirepublicans in the army and Bavarian government. These organizations and individuals tolerated the Nazis because they shared similar antidemocratic and anti-Versailles political objectives. Conservatives and reactionaries thought they could use the Nazis to whip up support for the antirepublican cause and to suppress the left in the event of future Communist uprisings. The important link between the army and the Nazis was Ernst Röhm, who, as an officer, was able to facilitate a flow of funds and arms to the party. The army provided part of the funds for the purchase, in 1920, of the party newspaper, the *Völkischer Beobachter*, and demobilized soldiers constituted a large segment of NSDAP membership. Though not substantial, some finances also came from certain wealthy families and businessmen. Under the protection of the army and the Bavarian authorities, Hitler was able to expand his party and agitate against Weimar. The number of Nazi local groups outside Munich multiplied, with membership reaching fifty-five thousand by 1923, as Hitler prepared for the moment when the party and its conservative allies would launch an overt assault on the democratic system.

Many of those who joined the party at this point did so in anticipation of such revolutionary action. Among the new converts were several figures who would become prominent leaders in the Third Reich. It was the military, as well as the militant, character of the Nazi party that brought Hermann Göring into the movement. Although an extreme nationalist and anti-Communist, Göring was less concerned with ideology than with fulfilling his need for action, power, and the comradeship he had come to relish during the war. In return, he added a certain flair and a degree of respectability to the Nazis. A jovial personality with hedonistic tastes, Göring was of upper-class background and had married an attractive and wealthy Swedish aristocrat. He had also been awarded the highest decoration for bravery and was the last commander of the famous Richthofen fighter squadron. Göring's personality and background made him the exception within the Nazi elite.

More typical was Rudolf Hess, an ex-officer and student at the University of Munich, who had a psychological need to submit himself to an authority figure. A sullen man of limited intelligence, Hess held important party positions mainly because of his pathological devotion to Hitler, whom he believed was Germany's salvation. The *Führerprinzip* and the Hitler cult found one of their greatest prophets in Hess. In ideological conviction, Hess was matched by Alfred Rosenberg, who became the editor of the *Völkischer Beobachter* in 1923. An ethnic German from the Baltic region, Rosenberg had studied architecture in Moscow before immigrating to Germany. His knowledge of Eastern Europe and Russia allowed him to play the role of party foreign policy specialist, while his intellectual pretensions gained him a reputation as the philosopher of nazism. In his writings, particularly *The Myth of the Twentieth Century* (1930), Rosenberg portrayed nazism as a substitute for religion. Although he would eventually be overshadowed by more powerful leaders, Rosenberg served a useful purpose as an ideologue, whose anti-Semitic and anti-Bolshevist propaganda provided a justification for the most extreme Nazi racial policies, culminating in genocide.

Fanatical anti-Semitism was also a distinguishing characteristic of Heinrich Himmler and Julius Streicher, two members who had serious psychological problems. Himmler had been born into a lower-middle-class family in Munich and educated in agriculture. This neurotic man started out as a chicken farmer and ended up as the leader of the SS. Physically weak and unimposing, he was nonetheless brutal and without compassion in expanding his power and in fulfilling the most radical goals of the Nazi ideology. He loved animals but had no inhibitions about murdering millions of people to make room for the master race he wanted to breed. Himmler tried to elevate his anti-Semitic crusade to the level of an ideal, whereas Julius Streicher's assaults on the Jews were nothing less than pornographic. His paper, *Der Stürmer*, was perhaps the most bizarre and crude anti-Semitic publication that has ever appeared. This schoolteacher from Nuremberg had a psychological and sexual compulsion to print stories, with vicious illustrations, about Jewish ritual murders of Christian children, the rape of Aryan women by lustful Jews, and the conspiracy of Jewish elders to conquer the world. Streicher had been a leader in the German Socialist party, another *völkisch* group and strong rival of the NSDAP. In 1922 Hitler brought this competitor into the Nazi fold.

Although the leadership consisted mostly of lower-middle-class persons, the Nazi rank and file at this stage came from all parts of society. The influx of white-collar workers and small businessmen meant that the lower-middle class predominated, but there was also strong representation from workers who had not been integrated into organized labor or the Socialist movement. Nonetheless, compared to their actual percentage in the German population as a whole, workers were greatly underrepresented and would remain so throughout the history of the party. Members of the social elites (upper-level managers, higher civil servants, entrepreneurs, students, and academics) tended to be overrepresented in the party. Originating in the industrial areas of Munich, the early NSDAP was essentially an urban and south German movement that gradually spread out into the small towns and countryside by the mid-1920s. This growth pattern ensured the lower-middle class ultimate predominance within the party due to the influx of nonindustrial groups, especially farmers and peasants. These percentages, however, must be viewed in the context of the limited size of the NSDAP during these early years. For exceedingly few Germans joined this group, and before 1922 it had only three thousand members. Although it made great gains in the next two years, reaching about fifty thousand members by 1923, it was far from an imposing threat and easily overshadowed by opposing political organizations.

The shopkeeper and worker, the civil servant and student stood side by side, giving credence to the Nazi claim that their party was above class distinctions. These diverse individuals were united by their authoritarian tendencies, nationalistic zeal, and resentment of society. Undoubtedly, the NSDAP was the party of resentment and hope; it exploited people's fears and hatreds and offered quick, drastic solutions to their problems. Its semimilitary structure and leadership principle satisfied their need for authority, just as its militant tactics provided them with an opportunity to strike out against the objects of their hatred.

A male-dominated and male-oriented movement, nazism almost completely ignored women and women's issues during the early 1920s. The relatively few women who associated themselves with the Nazi cause in this phase of its development did so on their own initiative without encouragement, guidance, or control from the party. Although generally older than their male counterparts, Nazi women tended to share many similar characteristics with them. Of middle- and lower-middle-class origin, Nazi women were also predominantly Protestant, extremely nationalistic, anti-Marxist, and cultural traditionalists; some were also religious and anti-Semitic. Fearful of the rising tide of the socialist masses and distressed by the decline of the German middle classes after World War I, these women resented the modern economic and political trends of the Weimar Republic, which they held responsible for the social displacement of their class and the threats to their country. Moreover, these women were disillusioned with the female emancipation and legal equality provided by Weimar. To some traditionalists, the rise of the "modern woman" degraded and endangered the natural role of women as mothers and wives. For others, the promises of emancipation and equality turned to disappointment and disillusionment. Instead of improving their economic condition, such changes really meant low-paying work or poverty, while stripping away traditional protections as well as the respect and status afforded by traditional roles for women in society. Reacting against the supposed causes of their plight as women and Germans, Nazi women sought a movement that would save their country and class through reestablishing a strong state and return the protection and stability for women that had been provided by stable families and traditional society.

The formation of the *Sturmabteilung* (Storm Troop or SA) was a definite indication that the NSDAP was a party of radical action rather than of political debate and rational persuasion. Ostensibly organized in 1921 to protect Nazi meetings from leftist attacks, the SA soon became one of the largest and most powerful forces within the party. Its most vital function was offensive rather than defensive, as it became the spearhead in Nazi recruiting and election campaigns. The SA was an effective paramilitary organization, used to terrorize the opposition and intended as the force that would launch the final blow against the republic. Storm Troopers organized parades and meetings, distributed propaganda, fought street battles with opponents, and disrupted the political activities of leftist groups. Members were disciplined, trained to obey, and prepared for violent revolution in the near future. Under the leadership of Röhm, the SA enlisted fifteen thousand fighters by 1923. The military nature of the organization was further evident by their brown uniforms, which became standard in 1924.

Most of the early SA recruits were demobilized soldiers of lower-middle-class origin who could not adjust to the routine of civilian life or accept the loss of the social status they had formerly known as officers during the war. Comradeship, the status afforded by rank and uniforms, and the chance for excitement and action were especially attractive to these men. Nationalism and patriotism also were significant factors. A large percentage of those who joined the Nazi party regarded their service in the SA as a continuation of their wartime struggle for the fatherland. They were eventually joined by younger men who had not fought in the trenches. The limits placed on the German army by the Treaty of Versailles created a pool of youths whose hopes of military careers and experience remained frustrated in Weimar. The SA became an alternative for these youths. To others, the attractive features were the radicalism of the party and the search for adventure. But many were nothing more than young toughs and alienated antisocial elements. The activities of the SA offered them an outlet for their aggression.

The SA was tolerated by the authorities because officers in the regular army believed that this paramilitary force could serve as a trained reserve for the army. Hitler, however, regarded the SA primarily as a political tool in his drive to overthrow the state. His first opportunity to mobilize his troops for overt action came with the nationwide crisis of 1923. The French occupation of the Ruhr, the economic collapse and catastrophic inflation, and Communist uprisings had left the Weimar government temporarily paralyzed. The Nazis joined a conspiracy of several rightist organizations and Bavarian officials who thought the time had arrived to put an end to this disastrous democratic experiment of Weimar. Even the reactionary former general and popular war hero Erich von Ludendorff was a party to this conspiracy. Hitler assumed that, with Bavaria behind them, this coalition of forces would be joined by parts of the army for a march on Berlin. When the Bavarian officials decided against a revolution at the last moment, Hitler tried to force their hand by seizing control of the government in Munich. At a mass meeting in a beer hall on the night of November 8, 1923, Hitler fired his pistol into the ceiling and declared the beginning of the "national revolution."

Although Hitler then managed to trick Ludendorff into following him in this ill-conceived and theatrical attempt at a *Putsch* (coup), the Bavarian government resisted, and Hitler found himself engaged in a showdown with the police forces the following day. In a quick exchange of gunfire, fourteen Nazis and several policemen were killed. Many others, including Göring, were wounded. Hitler wrenched his shoulder in the action. But the real damage was to Hitler's reputation as a revolutionary leader, because he fled under fire and left his troops behind. He was arrested for treason two days later.

The so-called Beer Hall *Putsch* was a fiasco for Hitler personally and for the party, one that pointed out the weakness of the revolutionary strategy the

Nazis had utilized up to this point. Yet these results did not signal the end of the movement. There were few better examples of Hitler's political skill than his ability to turn a clear defeat into a political triumph. The publicity surrounding Hitler's trial provided him, for the first time, with a national audience, and he shrewdly exploited this forum to attack viciously the Weimar system and to accuse its leaders of turning Germans into slaves of the allies. The real treason, he alleged, had been committed by the "November Criminals," who caused the defeat of 1918, accepted the indignities of Versailles, and continued to betray their country. He had acted out of patriotic duty to Germany and was proud to assume responsibility for his deed; he had not engaged in treason, but acted according to a higher law and obligation to his people.

This defense found a sympathetic audience in radical nationalist circles throughout Germany and also among the basically antirepublican judges hearing the case. The history of Weimar justice showed that such nationalistic judges usually considered rightist defendants misguided patriots, treating them with exceptional leniency, while giving harsher sentences to leftists, whom they viewed as a danger to organized society itself. In this particular case, Hitler was given the minimum sentence of five years in prison, whereas Ludendorff was acquitted. Other Nazis were subsequently convicted, but many more had escaped the country and avoided trial.

This light sentence was only part of Hitler's political victory. Equally important was his ability to transform the *Putsch* into a sacred party myth in which he had a distinguished place as the central hero. In Nazi propaganda, the actual details of the battle were supplanted with a mythical version of the *Führer* leading his men in the revolutionary struggle. The dead became martyrs not only for the movement but also for the German national cause. Rarely did Hitler miss an opportunity to promote this myth or to recall the ultimate sacrifice of these men. Later, he would open the first volume of *Mein Kampf* with a dedication to those who fell "with loyal faith in the resurrection of their people." In the minds of those who were susceptible to this myth, Hitler had proven himself a revolutionary leader and hero under fire.

Hitler spent a year in Landsberg prison before being paroled on December 20, 1924. With the exception of confinement, Hitler's prison days were far from punishment. He lived in a large room, wore normal clothing, walked freely in the garden, and had almost unlimited visitors. Among Nazi prisoners he acted as party leader; he spent most of his time preparing for his political comeback. During this time he dictated the first volume of *Mein Kampf* with the assistance of Rudolf Hess, who had voluntarily joined his beloved *Führer* in prison. These months also granted Hitler sufficient time for reflection on the reasons for his recent debacle. He became convinced that the revolutionary strategy had to be abandoned, because the forces at the disposal of the modern state were too powerful to be assaulted directly. Henceforth, he would adopt the strategy of the "legal" conquest of power, using the constitutional freedoms and democratic rights granted by the Weimar Republic. Hiding behind the cloak of legality, his party would play the game of democratic politics until they were in control of the state. Their final goal would be the destruction of the very system that guaranteed them these legal rights, but their methods would remain for the most part legal and pseudolegal. After their "legal revolution" brought them to power, the true National Socialist revolution could be instituted with the machinery of the state rather than against it. In the meantime, so long as the Nazis did not engage in excessive violations of the legal system, it would be difficult for the existing state to suppress their movement.

After his release from prison, Hitler found the NSDAP in disarray and confronted with almost insurmountable problems. He had allowed party rivalries and infighting to flourish during his absence in order to prevent anyone from presenting a challenge to his leadership, and it was no easy task to reunite the divided movement. Röhm had reorganized the SA under his sole control with the intention of carrying on the revolutionary struggle, while Gregor and Otto Strasser, representing the Nazi left wing, had emerged as the dominant force over the party in northern Germany. The Strasser brothers were deeply committed to the Socialist and anticapitalist goals of the Party Program, which in effect would involve a social and economic revolution. These developments were a threat to Hitler's personal leadership and to his new strategy of legality. At first he was more successful in solving the SA question than he was in dealing with the Strasser brothers. Röhm resigned from the NSDAP early in 1925, and the SA was brought under party control and prohibited from engaging in illegal activities. The Strasser faction maintained its independence in the north. Under its influence the entire party followed an anticapitalist and proworker course in its rhetoric, propaganda, and political campaigns. It was not until 1926 that Hitler managed to bring the northern wing under the centralized control of the party headquarters in Munich, and the Socialist orientation of the party was not abandoned until 1927. In the end, the *Führerprinzip* and the legal strategy prevailed.

The rebuilding of the party was hampered by the fact that the aborted *Putsch* led to a ban on the NSDAP across Germany. In 1925, after promising to stay on a legal course, Hitler managed to have the ban on the party in Bavaria lifted, and the National Socialists continued to operate under various names in different parts of the country. The party remained at a distinct disadvantage, and even after most bans were removed, Hitler was kept under legal restraints. He was prohibited from speaking in public in Bavaria until 1927 and in Prussia until 1928, which made it more difficult for the party to recruit and campaign.

The first time the Nazis put their legal strategy into effect in a national electoral campaign was during the Reichstag elections of 1924. Although they tempered their earlier revolutionary rhetoric and asserted the sanctity of private property, the Nazis continued to attack big capitalism and modern corporations that were supposedly destroying the middle class. Their campaign propaganda tried to identify big capitalism and international finance with Jews while the Nazis championed the cause of the small business man, shopkeepers, and small farmers against these larger and supposedly anti-German economic forces. The Nazis also presented themselves as the defenders of the middle classes against the Marxist danger that they also associated with Jews. However, the Nazis still had limited appeal. And despite the economic and psychological damage done by the political crises and Great Inflation of 1923, the disaffected middle classes remained almost completely beyond the Nazi reach. Thus, in the 1924 elections, the Nazis received only 5 percent of the vote and fourteen seats in parliament. When they ran the national hero General Ludendorff as their candidate in the presidential election the following year, they attracted only 200,000 votes out of approximately 27 million. By 1926 the NSDAP had fewer than fifty thousand members compared to almost a million for the Social Democratic party.

The most difficult problems for the Nazis were created by the political climate that existed between 1924 and 1929. The political turmoil and economic crises of early Weimar, which had given the Nazis plenty of issues to exploit, had disappeared as Germany began to experience relative prosperity and stability in the era of Stresemann. Hostility toward Weimar had diminished significantly, and most Germans were wary of radical political groups that might disrupt this period of quiet and order. The Nazis seemed very out of touch with the times. Their familiar charge that the "November Criminals" controlled the state carried little weight since the rightist candidate, Hindenburg, had been elected president in 1925 and the reactionary German Nationalists began participating in the government. Economic recovery had lessened the appeal of Nazi economic anti-Semitism, and the absence of an immediate Communist threat meant that the Nazi anti-Marxist crusade was not as effective as previously. Nazi Socialist and anticapitalist propaganda, promoted most vigorously in northern Germany, proved equally counterproductive.

The Nazis failed to make inroads into the working classes, but in their attempts to do so by fostering a version of German socialism, they alienated big business and the middle classes. These groups perceived the Nazis as social revolutionaries and a threat to private property. Business leaders and the rightist parties that represented their interests were not about to support a party that called for the nationalization of corporations. Whereas the Nazis had benefited in the early twenties, especially in 1923, from financial contributions from industry and from their political alliance with traditional rightist groups, such financial and political support was no longer forthcoming. During this phase, capitalists and Nazis were political enemies.

Lack of money greatly inhibited party activity and occasionally led to crises within the organization. Hitler's efforts at acquiring money from industrialists and businessmen by arguing that Nazi anticapitalism was merely rhetoric were completely unsuccessful. Without major financial backers the party had to rely on dues from members as its primary source of revenue. This was augmented by fees from various publications, meetings, and events, as well as by some funds from contribution drives. These meager financial resources meant that the party had difficulty expanding its operations and even meeting printing costs for its propaganda. Often the party had to use part-time help; it would be several years before its bureaucrats could be paid a regular salary.

Undeterred by these problems, Hitler continued to plan for the future, when renewed popular discontent would swell the ranks of the party. He began to lay the foundations for a well-organized and highly centralized political machine that would allow the Nazis to campaign effectively throughout the country. For organizational purposes, all of Germany was divided into regional party districts, each known as a *Gau* and controlled by a *Gauleiter*, or regional leader. Within each *Gau* were various subdivisions reaching down to the local level. Each level of the organization was controlled by the one above, with each *Gauleiter* appointed by and responsible to Hitler personally. Under this scheme the number of party offices was greatly expanded, and the entire apparatus was staffed by Nazi bureaucrats. Regional and local groups were permitted flexibility in exploiting local issues, but autonomy was denied them. Policies and practices set forth by the Munich headquarters or Hitler were to be strictly followed without question. Obedience was more than a requirement; it was a National Socialist ideal. The totalitarian nature of this organization was further evident in the establishment of party courts to enforce discipline among its members. Factionalism and the potential for internal disintegration remained a problem, but the party bureaucracy gave Hitler a powerful instrument with which to counteract these tendencies.

Another facet of this bureaucratization involved the creation of numerous departments with responsibility for specific areas of politics and society.

Some of the specialized offices were labor, agriculture, economics, culture, propaganda, and foreign affairs. A Foreign Organization (AO) was even established to control party members living abroad. Various auxiliary organizations were founded: for the young there were the Hitler Youth and the Nazi student organization; lawyers, doctors, and teachers each had their own party organization; and women fulfilled their duty to national socialism by serving in the Nazi Women's Group. Recruitment, integration and control of members, effective political campaigning, and the development of expertise in specialized areas were only a few of the purposes of this bureaucracy. A long-range aim was the development of a shadow government in preparation for the day when the Nazis would seize the reins of power. Because the NSDAP was so tightly organized and because so many of its agencies duplicated the functions of essential government offices, the party was referred to as a "state within a state."

Women's organizations, however, were only brought within Nazi bureaucratic control rather late. Some Nazis, probably including Hitler, rejected any role for women outside the home and felt they must be protected from the vulgarity of politics. But certain Nazi leaders believed that women could perform public functions consistent with their feminine nature. Women took advantage of this opening to develop various groups devoted to health, education, and welfare. They ran soup kitchens for the unemployed and first-aid stations for wounded Nazi street fighters, and they provided a variety of other support functions to assist the activities of the males carrying on the political struggle. Ignored by the party for most of the 1920s, these scattered, often local or regional Nazi women's organizations enjoyed a tremendous amount of independence in their activities and thought. In 1931 these diverse associations lost their separate identities and independence when the NSDAP finally organized them into a single Nazi Women's Group, which henceforth would fall under the direction of the male-dominated upper echelons of the party.

Accompanying the development of this political machine was the refinement of Nazi propaganda techniques. Hitler considered the correct use of propaganda an art, and during the "years of struggle" the Nazis learned to become masters of the craft of psychological manipulation. The essence of the Nazi theory of propaganda was explained in *Mein Kampf.* Its first principle was that propaganda must always be addressed to the masses; its second precept was that effective propaganda must be aimed at emotions and not the intellect. The underlying assumptions were that the masses had limited intelligence and that their behavior was determined more by feeling than rational thought. Hitler also believed that the masses sought forceful leadership. Balanced and complicated arguments, which considered all sides and ramifications of an issue, would be totally ineffectual. Therefore, it was imperative that a piece of propaganda relate a direct, simple, one-sided message. It must go beyond presenting the party's position; instead, it must appear that this position is the only correct one. Propaganda should not stimulate thought, but rather elicit an immediate and deep emotional reaction such as enthusiasm, fear, or hatred. After reinforcement of the message through constant repetition, more and more people would come to regard it as an established truth. Hitler drew a comparison with the marketing techniques of the business world, referring to propaganda as "political advertising."

The grand master of Nazi propaganda, Josef Goebbels, was also among the most cynical members of the party. Like so many Nazis, Goebbels had become embittered by personal failure and rejection by society. Of lower-middle-class Roman Catholic origins, he earned a Ph.D. in German literature from Heidelberg University but was unsuccessful in his attempts to establish himself as a journalist and author of romantic novels. Goebbels's sense of social alienation also was related to his physical problems. He was short and thin and was handicapped by a clubfoot. Later, his opponents in the party would disparagingly refer to him as "Mickey Mouse" because he had large ears. Nonetheless, Goebbels was intelligent and a skilled writer and dynamic orator; some have claimed that, as a speaker, he surpassed Hitler. When Goebbels joined the NSDAP in the mid-1920s, he was a forceful spokesman for the Socialist policies of the Strasser brothers and an adversary of Hitler. But by 1926 he was converted to the Hitler cult and was rewarded with the position of *Gauleiter* in Berlin, where his talent as a propagandist blossomed. Cynical in his attitude toward the masses, Goebbels had no qualms about using lies or slander; he cleverly changed his position on issues at will. Often his pamphlets, newspaper articles, and demonstrations were expressly intended to incite violence in order to gain public attention for the Nazis. He was so effective in Berlin that in 1928 Hitler promoted him to director of the Reich propaganda office. His success in this new position would be so astounding that the name Goebbels has become almost synonymous with the word *propaganda*.

In the hands of Nazi propagandists like Goebbels, complex problems were reduced to emotionally charged and catchy slogans. "Honor, freedom, bread," a phrase from one Nazi leaflet, typified the simplistic approach to issues of foreign policy and economics. Political choices were presented in black-and-white terms, with no room for compromise or a middle position. If one stood with Germany and against Versailles, then one must side with Hitler. Otherwise, one was a traitor. This approach was especially noticeable in Nazi anti-Semitic propaganda. Goebbels wrote in one pamphlet, "He who thinks German must despise the Jews. The one thing makes the other necessary." Similarly, no distinction was made between the Social Democrats and Communists. The Nazis represented both the SPD and KPD as part of a barbaric Bolshevist movement sweeping westward out of Russia and threatening Western civilization and culture.

In deciding upon specific propaganda themes, the Nazis became quite astute at identifying the real problems, proclivities, and fears of particular audiences. They showed amazing flexibility in adjusting their propaganda to various groups. When recruiting or campaigning in working-class districts, they published statements such as, "The maintenance of a rotten industrial system has nothing to do with nationalism. I can love Germany and hate capitalism." One poster showed a huge Nazi demolishing the stock exchange, on which was written "International High Finance." The Nazis also exploited the basic needs of the lower classes. Beneath the words "Work and Bread" on one poster, there was a Nazi handing tools into the desperate arms of the unemployed. Another poster depicted a depressing scene of a crowd of poor and unemployed with the caption "Our Last Hope: Hitler." At the same time, the Nazis used anti-Marxist themes in other areas to capture middle-class support. Playing upon middle-class fears of communism's threat to religion and private property, one Nazi poster had a gigantic, fiendish-looking skeleton in a Communist uniform set against a glaring red background. The poster was so well designed that it conveyed a feeling of immediate danger, and the caption below stated that only Hitler could save Germany from Bolshevism. Taxes, the economic plight and future of the middle classes, nationalism, and the defense of religion were issues cleverly exploited by the Nazi propaganda machine. In those places where cultural anti-Semitism was prevalent, the Nazis found attacks on the Jews a convenient way of alleviating middle-class doubts about the Socialist wing of the party. Hitler maintained that the National Socialist anticapitalist campaign was directed primarily against the exploitive economic power of Jewish financiers and speculators—it was not aimed against the German businessman. The Nazis tried to draw a connection between Jews and the economic problems facing the middle classes. For example, they stressed that the large department stores, predominantly Jewish owned, were putting the small shopkeeper out of business. But where anti-Semitism was not an issue, the Nazis ignored this essential component of their ideology and concentrated instead on nationalism and anticommunism. Such duplicity was a distinguishing characteristic of Nazi propaganda.

Trying to broaden their overall electoral support in late Weimar, the Nazis began to appeal systematically and intensely to women for the first time.

Consistent with their own views on the inherent nature and appropriate social roles for women, Nazi propaganda repeatedly emphasized the traditional German vision of *Kinder, Küche, und Kirche* (children, kitchen, and church). Nazi literature and posters focusing on issues of family, education, and the evils of a decadent modern society were primarily targeted at women. Realizing the importance of religion for both Protestant and Catholic women, the Nazis identified themselves with the defense of religion against atheistic Marxism as well as the secular, hedonistic culture of Weimar that threatened family values and corrupted the young. Most Nazi propaganda on religion was, in fact, directed almost exclusively toward women. These themes became the core message of *Frauenwarte*, the magazine that the Nazi Women's Group started publishing for women in 1932.

Hitler knew that publications and visual propaganda alone would be insufficient to bring about the national revolution. Far more important were the "spoken word" and the activism of party members. Only the power of speech, he wrote, could motivate the masses to action. The French and Russian revolutions did not result from the treatises of Enlightenment writers and the theories of Karl Marx. They were the work of agitators and demagogues who excited the passions of the people. Therefore, direct, constant, and emotional contact with the masses was crucial. The early growth of the party owed much to Hitler's oratory, but during the years he was prohibited from speaking this essential task had to be performed by others. Although Gregor Strasser and Goebbels were natural speakers, the average party member needed training in rhetoric. For this reason the Nazis established schools that produced several thousand effective speakers who could be moved around the country to assist local groups in promoting national socialism.

In terms of style and content, Nazi speakers used techniques similar to those employed in visual propaganda. The appeal was always to the emotions, and they spoke in generalities. The final goal was the manipulation of the minds of listeners. The settings of meetings were carefully prepared and controlled. Speakers knew the general makeup and political orientation of a particular audience and geared their statements specifically to the concerns and prejudices of each group. Speakers received reinforcement from the symbols and rituals that were an integral part of such gatherings. Patriotic music, German flags, party banners, uniformed members, and special lighting effects created an unreal and romantic atmosphere. Questioning and opposing viewpoints were forbidden; applause was usually regulated by party members. Most meetings were held in the evening, because Hitler believed that the resistance of listeners would be greatly diminished by this time of day.

Aside from meetings designed to recruit members and supporters, the Nazis expanded the size and frequency of mass meetings for existing members. The purpose was to continue the "enlightenment" and to strengthen the commitment of those already converted, especially newcomers. At these meetings the consciousness of the individual gradually became blended into the mass consciousness of the National Socialist community of believers. A member no longer felt alone but saw himself as part of a great and powerful movement. His beliefs were confirmed, and he left the meeting with renewed enthusiasm and confidence.

The effectiveness of the Nazi organization in instilling enthusiasm, dedication, and an *esprit de corps* among its members cannot be overestimated. The NSDAP had a much higher proportion of militant and hardworking activists than any other party, including the Communist party. The dynamism of the party, like the romantic and exciting rituals of the mass meetings, was particularly attractive to the young. Compared to other parties, in fact, the Nazi movement had a youthful aura. Not only was it a relatively new and unique party, but approximately 40 percent of its members were under thirty, and its leaders were usually more than ten years younger than those holding similar positions in non-Nazi political organizations. This in turn gave the Nazis an added vigor and dynamism. It allowed them to keep up a constant pace of political activity. They staged more parades, rallies, and meetings than their opponents, and Nazi events were always elaborate and intense. Such activity was augmented by Nazi-sponsored films showings and a wide variety of sports and social events. The outcome was a slow but steady growth in the number of devoted followers. By 1928 membership had risen to over 100,000, most of whom could be considered either political militants or ideological dogmatists, and the party could mobilize twenty thousand SA troops for demonstrations at mass rallies.

A major political breakthrough eluded the Nazis, however, and more failures were in store for the movement before the "years of struggle" would come to an end. The Nazis had achieved breadth though not depth in developing their electoral constituency. Despite extensive organizational efforts and a definite Socialist orientation in their propaganda between 1926 and 1928, the National Socialists failed to crack the Communist and Social Democratic monopoly on the workers. The Nazis made some inroads among those employed in craft industries and small firms but not among the bulk of industrial workers or those integrated into the leftist political and social culture of the time. The results of the Nazi working-class strategy merely created a wider gap between the NSDAP and the middle classes. Only elements of the lower-middle class were attracted to the Nazi anticapitalist message. Throughout the

1920s, small farmers, shopkeepers, and artisans remained the core of the Nazi electorate. In the case of both the workers and the lower-middle class, the Nazis drew voters from the nonindustrial segments of society or from those whose economic existence had been declining for decades due to the rise of a modern industrial economy. Nonetheless, these constituencies were still not large enough to make the Nazis a serious threat at the ballot box.

Moreover, the party was struggling against a republic that seemed to have stabilized itself. Four years of economic improvement and domestic order had altered substantially the earlier climate of resentment and insecurity in which the Nazis thrived. The Reichstag elections of May 1928 showed that even the efficient Nazi political machine was useless against the formidable forces of prosperity and stability. In this election, those parties that supported the republic made significant gains, while the rightist parties suffered heavy losses. The Nazis were also handed their most devastating political setback since the Beer Hall *Putsch*, receiving only 800,000 votes out of the more than 30 million cast. Their worst defeats were in the urban areas, where they had campaigned most heavily and into which they had channeled the bulk of their resources. In the major cities and industrial areas, their share of the vote ranged from less than 1 percent to under 3 percent. The Nazis had employed the wrong strategy at the wrong time.

With only twelve seats in the new Reichstag, the Nazis had been reduced to the status of a splinter party that seemed to be on its way to political obscurity. Few political observers felt the need to take this group seriously. Yet, within a year, conditions would change dramatically, and the Nazis would make an astonishing comeback.

PART TWO

The Seizure and Consolidation of Power, 1929–1934

The ruling party can make use of the advantage that accompanies the mere possession of the legal means of power. . . . The majority is now suddenly no longer a party; it is the state itself. . . . When things have really gone that far, it ultimately depends upon who holds the reins of power at the moment when the entire system of legality is thrown aside and when power is constituted on a new basis.

—Carl Schmitt, *Legalität und Legitimität*, 1932

CHAPTER 5

Parliamentary Paralysis and the Nazi Breakthrough of 1930

The Nazis recovered from their defeat of 1928 before the onset of the Great Depression and the political crisis that accompanied it. Shortly after the elections, the NSDAP started to reorganize and reorient its political strategy. Voting patterns had shown that Nazi strength existed in rural areas and among the middle classes in small towns. This was another indication that the Nazi party could flourish only under conditions of economic crisis and insecurity, for in the midst of general economic and political stability, there existed an agrarian crisis. High costs, low yields and prices, taxes, and indebtedness created extreme hardships for the small farmer and led to increasing numbers of failures and foreclosures, and economic repercussions were felt in surrounding small towns. Farmers blamed their plight on banks, middlemen, Socialists, and the republic. By the late 1920s, this discontent led to rural terrorism and violent confrontations between the farmers' movement and the government. These events, best described in Hans Fallada's contemporary novel *Farmers, Political Bosses, and Bombs,* turned the farmers into a force for radical change. Rejected by urban voters, the Nazis decided to concentrate on the countryside.

Romantic nationalism, strong religious beliefs, and anti-Semitism in these rural districts, along with economic problems, made rural populations perfect targets for Nazi propaganda. Playing upon an existing proclivity toward *völkisch* nationalism, the Nazis emphasized that the peasantry had a special status as the true nobility of Germany, because they were the purest form of the *Volk* and in essence the racial backbone of the nation. The Nazis claimed that Jewish bankers and capitalists, and the Marxists that controlled the government, were threatening the economic existence of this group. The Nazis promised the peasants agrarian reform, massive tax relief, and the elimination of indebtedness.

Such propaganda was part of an intensive recruitment drive in rural areas and small towns, where the Nazis kept up a constant pace of activity. They saturated most districts with parades and demonstrations, presented countless

lectures aimed at specific economic problems or local issues, organized entertainment events, and showed Nazi-oriented and patriotic films. The major
political parties had never paid such attention to the peasantry, and sympathy
for the Nazis increased accordingly. Another successful tactic was Nazi infil-
tration of various rural social, patriotic, and political associations. The Nazis
then worked to reorient these groups toward national socialism and gradually
turned many of them into political instruments of the party.

In the small towns, the Nazis presented themselves as allies of the traditional German right and not as revolutionaries. Their stated goal was the
rejuvenation of Germany, and they relentlessly attacked the government
and other parties as pawns of the Allies who had kept Germany as a slave
among nations. Their previous Socialist rhetoric was quickly downplayed, as
they portrayed themselves as the defenders of the middle classes and private
property, threatened by Marxism, big business, and foreign financial control. Nazi anticapitalism, they explained, was directed only against the large
corporations, the Jews, and international finance. Nazi speakers addressed
middle-class problems, exploiting the fears and prejudices of this class, while
propagandists saturated the towns with posters and leaflets. The Nazi tactic of
penetration proved as successful in the towns as it was in the countryside, and
they continued to infiltrate various organizations and to nazify them. They
also managed to penetrate numerous middle-class professional, business, and
student associations in the larger cities. The drive to attract middle-class individuals was partially due to Hitler's desire to staff the party organization with
more intelligent and more competent bureaucrats. The influx of educated
members of the middle class into the party in the late twenties showed the
positive results of this aspect of the recruitment campaign, just as continual
growth in membership from the countryside was an encouraging sign for
the rural strategy. However, it would become clear only in late 1929 that
the National Socialists had finally found the right political strategy and had
been able to identify the groups that would provide the foundations for mass
support.

A series of events in 1929 rapidly changed the political climate to the
advantage of the Nazis. The first development in this direction came with
the rightist campaign against the Young Plan, which was to establish a new
schedule for German reparation payments. Although the plan contained
significant concessions to the Germans, it still required that they continue to
pay reparations for fifty-nine more years. To the right, this was further proof
that Germany remained the victim of Versailles and that the "November
Criminals" in control of Weimar were engaging in treason. In the summer
of 1929 an alliance of big business, nationalist organizations, and rightist

political parties was formed to fight the plan. These groups cooperated in agitating against the Young Plan and in sponsoring a national referendum to prevent its ratification. The central figure in this campaign initially was Alfred Hugenberg, the new leader of the German Nationalist party and a wealthy industrialist. An extreme nationalist, Hugenberg sought the destruction of Versailles, Weimar democracy, and the power of the German left; thereafter, he intended that Germany would be governed as a conservative authoritarian state. Hugenberg viewed the national uproar over the Young Plan as an opportunity to recoup the great losses sustained by the right in 1928.

After some hesitation, Hitler joined this rightist coalition. Upstart radical Nazis and reactionary industrialists again became temporary allies. Hugenberg and Hitler each intended to exploit the other for his own purposes. Hugenberg headed an established and well-financed party with political and social respectability, but one that suffered from lethargy and declining popularity. Hitler represented a rising, dynamic, new movement with the potential to muster widespread support. Having little faith in the ability of the Nazis to acquire power or to govern, Hugenberg wanted to use Hitler as a "drummer" to win back the masses to the rightist cause. In Hitler's eyes, Hugenberg was a key to national attention, to respect among middle-class voters, and to financial resources from big business.

The Nazis waged an energetic and vicious campaign, attempting to aggravate popular discontent and to fire hatred wherever possible. Their finely tuned political machine now operated for the first time with money supplied by big business and rightist groups. It was a nationwide campaign on a popular national issue, and the aggressive Nazis quickly moved to the forefront of the rightist resistance movement against the Young Plan. In most places, Hitler was no longer legally banned from speaking, and his speeches were a major factor in attracting and inspiring enthusiasm in crowds across the country.

Though the referendum held in November 1929 turned out to be a failure, with less than 14 percent of the voters in favor of rejecting the Young Plan, the Nazis benefited tremendously. Not only would the Nazis have access to greater financial resources in the future, but they had at last achieved national recognition. Hitler was no longer a relatively unknown regional figure, remembered only for the Beer Hall *Putsch*; he was a politician of national stature who appeared to have the confidence of Hugenberg. Hitler had been found acceptable as an ally by prestigious and respected members of the German political and business elites. His movement had received national publicity for almost a year through the mass media owned by Hugenberg and other rightists throughout Germany. Both Hitler and the Nazis had thereby acquired a greater degree of respectability in the minds of at least part of the middle and upper classes. Finally, the Nazi campaign itself had given the party a reputation for organizational effectiveness, dynamism, and determination. Concrete results for the party were immediately evident. The NSDAP almost doubled in size during 1929, and by the end of that year the strength of the SA, now with 100,000 fighters, equaled the size of the German army.

After the failure of the referendum against the Young Plan, Germany did not return to the state of quiet and order it had known for several years. A new and more critical national problem was about to create a sense of desperation and fear that the country had not experienced since the early twenties. With it came another wave of antirepublican hostility. A slowdown in business activity occurred in 1929, and the number of unemployed surged to 2 million. The worst was yet to come. On October 24 the New York stock market crash signaled the beginning of a worldwide depression. The international economic crisis had an immediate effect on Germany, because its economy was heavily dependent upon foreign loans and investments and because it was burdened with substantial reparation debts. An almost endless stream of business failures followed for the next few years. Another million were added to the unemployment rolls in 1930. One year later the total number of unemployed reached 4 million, and by 1932 the figure went beyond the 6 million mark. It has been estimated that at the peak of the Great Depression, as many as 20 million people out of a population of 65 million were living on public assistance.

A climate of despair set in as millions of men remained idle and without hope, losing confidence in themselves and the republic. This situation created a reservoir of discontent that could be tapped by those offering radical solutions. Although the bulk of the workers, employed and unemployed, did not desert the left for the Nazi party, they did become more radicalized. Increasing numbers turned away from the reformist and democratically oriented Social Democratic party and followed the Communist path of revolutionary action. Thus, one of the major pillars of the republic, the SPD, would lose part of its strength to the extreme left that sought the overthrow of Weimar democracy. Those workers who remained loyal to the SPD demanded that it take a more radical stand on economic issues.

The beginning of the Great Depression caused an almost spontaneous panic among the middle classes. They had not forgotten how the Great Inflation of 1923 had wiped out their savings and undermined their economic and social status. They also remembered the breakdown of domestic order and the revolutionary efforts by Communists during Weimar's early years. Many felt that a prolonged economic crisis would eventually mean the loss of their jobs or businesses; they were also fearful that the radicalization of the unemployed would end in a Communist revolution. Some were quite susceptible to the argument that Versailles and reparations were responsible for the depression in Germany. The small businessman saw himself trapped between the competition of larger corporations and department stores on one side and the demands of powerful labor unions on the other. Resentment toward big business on the part of the lower-middle class, especially white-collar workers, had been growing for some time. The middle class, for the most part, lost faith in the DNVP and DVP, because in the economic sphere these parties tended to represent the interests of big business. The middle segment of society became more insecure and radical in its sentiments with each year of the depression.

Throughout this period, the Nazis made a concerted effort to recruit members and sympathizers from among the unemployed as well as from those who believed that they might be the next casualties of the economic crisis. A percentage of unemployed workers joined the NSDAP, but most of these were either young or the chronically unemployed. The unemployed of the lower-middle class flocked to the party. Both groups were won over by the apparent Nazi concern for their plight and with vague promises of decisive political and economic change. In many cases, membership in an SA unit meant relief from the idleness and alienation of their daily existence. Eventually, a large portion of the NSDAP consisted of the unemployed.

When appealing to the middle class as a whole, the Nazis usually resorted to fear tactics in an attempt to increase the degree of panic. This was accompanied by a litany of charges that Versailles, reparations, democracy, Marxism, big business, and the Jews were ruining the middle classes. Only the Nazi movement stood up for the "little man" and could protect him and the nation from certain disaster. Notable by their absence in Nazi propaganda were specific proposals for economic reform and recovery. Emotional tirades about the Marxist danger and the selfish interests of big business and Jews were far more effective in the psychological atmosphere of the time. And, of course, the lack of concrete economic programs allowed Hitler to continue to assure his wealthy financial backers from industry and business that the Nazi propaganda against them was merely a tactic for rallying mass support.

The economic crisis struck Germany just as the man who symbolized the period of stability and prosperity passed away. Yet the death of Gustav Stresemann on October 3, 1929, was more than symbolic; it was a major political blow to the republic. Stresemann's leadership had been largely responsible for the progress made in Germany between 1924 and 1929; the country was left without any comparable figure to replace him. This loss was quickly felt when worsening economic conditions created a political deadlock within the government. The "Great Coalition" government formed in 1928 rested upon the cooperation of the Social Democrats and the conservative DVP. It had been prosperity and Stresemann's political skill that had made it possible for these antagonistic parties to share power, but by the end of 1929 both of these necessary elements were gone, and the coalition split along the lines of class and economic interest. The immediate issue was how to handle the problems of growing government deficits and rising expenditures for unemployment insurance. The Social Democrats, as the party of labor, fought for higher taxes and more government spending to meet the needs of the millions of unemployed. The DVP, representing the business community, countered with demands for lower wages, extensive reductions in unemployment benefits, and the elimination of various social programs. By March 1930, the "Great Coalition" collapsed.

It was in this atmosphere of economic panic, popular anxiety and radicalization, party strife, and paralysis within the parliament that the so-called presidential system was born. The introduction of this system did not involve constitutional changes; it meant only a more extensive use of those constitutional powers already available to the president, though the constitutionality of many aspects of this system would remain debatable. Under the presidential system, a new government would be formed consisting of a chancellor and cabinet ministers who would govern with the confidence of the president, have the national welfare in mind, and stand above the special interests represented by political parties. This government would rely less on parliament and more on the authority and leadership of the president. It was believed that such a presidential government, supported by the army and state bureaucracy, would provide Germany with the strong leadership and stability it needed in this time of economic and political turmoil. This system was originally viewed as a means of compensating for the ineffectiveness of parliamentary rule in Weimar and of preventing a seizure of power by the extremists of the right or left.

The underlying assumption of the presidential system was that in times of crisis the president had the obligation to take extraordinary action to protect the security and welfare of the nation. If necessary legislation was not forthcoming from the parliament because of party strife, then the president had the right to govern through the emergency powers granted him under Article 48 of the Weimar constitution. According to Article 48, a president could take "necessary measures," including the temporary suspension of certain parts of the constitution and the use of the army, when public order and security were seriously threatened. The purpose of this clause was to provide a means for defending the state and constitution under conditions of crisis. All measures had to be directed at this expressed objective. The Reichstag had the authority to rescind any emergency decree, and the constitution had to be reinstated in its original form after the restoration of order and security. The first president of Weimar, Friedrich Ebert, had invoked Article 48 on numerous occasions during the early years of turmoil. In the short history of Weimar this article was used approximately 250 times in defense of the republic, and without such action the German democracy probably would have failed sooner than it did.

Given the experiences of the early republic, many Germans were willing to accept stronger presidential action and the broad use of Article 48 when confronted with a new round of crises beginning in 1930. This view was by no means universal, because many suspected that the presidential system was the first step toward dismantling democracy in Germany and the start of a dictatorship. Their fears were increased by the fact that the exact nature and limits of presidential authority under Article 48 were not clearly defined. Throughout Weimar, legal experts debated Article 48 without arriving at a consensus. Concerned about possible abuse leading ultimately to the end of democracy, a majority of legal experts argued that presidential authority must remain limited and that a law must be passed describing precisely what measures a president could take under Article 48. They were opposed by those theorists who felt that the president must retain broad authority and a substantial degree of flexibility to handle a wide variety of unforeseen and unpredictable emergency situations. The latter held that the constitution had in fact granted the president such extensive authority and that any attempt to restrict his powers would be contrary to the original intent of Article 48 and would defeat its purpose. This controversy became more intense once the presidential system was instituted in 1930.

The leading figure in the decision to experiment with a presidential government was General Kurt von Schleicher. Although he belonged to no political party and initially held no political office, Schleicher was very much a political animal. Well informed of political developments within and outside the government, he became a master at behind-the-scenes maneuvering. At times, the fate of chancellors and cabinets rested in his hands. Schleicher's influence could be attributed mainly to his role as confidant to President Hindenburg, who trusted his advice until the end of 1932. Schleicher was not a reactionary and stood in opposition to the right-wing radicalism of the German Nationalist party. Like Stresemann, he had come to accept the existence of the republic, and his major concern was its stabilization. He hoped that the presidential system would achieve this objective.

The theoretical and legal justifications for Schleicher's plans were provided by Professor Carl Schmitt, one of Weimar's most renowned political and legal thinkers. A specialist in constitutional law, Schmitt was a major authority on Article 48 and presidential power. Throughout the 1920s he had favored a broad interpretation of presidential emergency powers and opposed attempts at placing limitations on, or describing precisely, such authority. In 1929 Schmitt declared that the Weimar constitution had designated the president as the "defender of the constitution." From Schmitt's perspective, the presidency was the only stable force in the entire Weimar political system. The president was directly elected for seven years and thus remained independent of fragile and shifting party coalitions in the Reichstag. He could overcome the paralysis of parliament by dissolving that body and calling new elections, and his presidential oath obliged him to defend the constitution. Schmitt argued that Article 48 and control of the army gave the president sufficient power and authority to stabilize the republic and defend the constitutional order. After Schmitt became a legal adviser to Schleicher in 1930, the concept of the "defender of the constitution" became an essential theoretical foundation for the presidential system.

Heinrich Brüning, the first chancellor to head a presidential government, was personally selected by Schleicher. A conservative nationalist and leader in the Catholic Center party with experience in financial matters, Brüning appeared to be someone who could attract a broad political following. When he was appointed chancellor on March 28, 1930, he made it quite clear that he was heading a presidential government that stood above political parties. He was willing to work with parliament, but his cabinet was not formed through compromises with various political parties. He was prepared to bypass the Reichstag through the use of Article 48 if this became necessary. When the Reichstag rejected his budget in July, Brüning instituted his economic programs through presidential emergency decrees under Article 48. The Reichstag then exercised its constitutional authority under the same provision and rescinded these decrees. Brüning's determination and the true nature of the new presidential style of government became immediately evident from the events that followed.

Under normal circumstances, the Brüning government would have fallen after such a parliamentary defeat, but the new presidential government considered itself above parliamentary politics. So long as it did not violate the constitution, this government felt justified in remaining in office and in acting in what it considered to be the national interest. Instead of resigning, Brüning had the president dissolve the Reichstag and scheduled new elections for September 14, 1930. In the meantime Brüning continued to govern Germany and reinstituted his economic programs through Article 48; these measures could not be rejected, because a new parliament was not yet in existence.

Brüning hoped that large numbers of Germans would be encouraged by his decisive leadership and would elect a new parliament that would support his presidential government. He had greatly miscalculated. It was a mistake to hold elections in the midst of a worsening economic crisis. The election campaign of 1930, one of the most intense in German history, was conducted in an atmosphere of fear and hostility. The government was held responsible for the economic collapse and, at the same time, accused by the left and many moderate republicans of violating the constitution through its dictatorial use of Article 48. Others saw the government as the problem rather than the solution; they were looking for a fresh alternative. And the radicals of the left and right stood ready to supply the desperate with hopeful alternatives. The climate was ripe for exploitation by the Nazi political and propaganda machine.

The improved financial situation of the Nazi party allowed it to wage an effective political campaign on a nationwide scale. As they had done in the agitation against the Young Plan, the Nazis again saturated the country with parades, rallies, leaflets, and posters. The energy of the Nazi party seemed limitless, and the other parties were incapable of matching its dynamism. The highly trained Nazi corps of speakers fanned out through the country to strengthen the campaign at the regional and local levels, while Hitler tirelessly flew back and forth across Germany, no longer restrained by legal prohibitions or confined to addressing regional audiences. Using the airplane as a political tool, Hitler was now able to sway crowds everywhere, and he became one of the most decisive factors in the election.

The audience that was susceptible to Nazi rhetoric had greatly expanded over the past year. The NSDAP continued to tighten its grip over rural areas and small towns and to recruit the young, the unemployed, and new voters. But now they decided to try to capture the support of those segments of the middle and lower-middle classes that normally voted for traditional right-wing parties, such as the DVP and DNVP. Repudiating his former political alliance with the old German right, Hitler began attacking these parties and competing for their voters. Compared to the dynamic Nazi party, the DNVP of Hugenberg appeared old, lethargic, and reactionary. Weimar democracy, Versailles, and communism were common enemies, but the Nazis were more extreme in their denunciations and more forceful in promoting themselves as the party of change. The DNVP had the additional disadvantage of being the party that represented the special interests of big business, whereas the

Nazis projected the image of a party of the little man, whether he be worker, middle class, or farmer.

At a time when loyalty to the traditional conservative parties had been dissipating for years, the Nazis found a vulnerable audience in these now rootless constituencies. Indeed, within the new *Zeitgeist* of popular panic and despair, increasing numbers of such former conservative voters became, ironically, susceptible even to Nazi social revolutionary rhetoric that had distinctly antibourgeois overtones. In a psychological cauldron of contradictory feelings of traditional longings and new desperation, the Nazi populist rhetoric and mobilization channeled an array of resentments against the DNVP. The Nazis depicted the DNVP as the defender of established hierarchies and entrenched interests standing in the way of urgently needed change. The Nazi hatred for the so-called reactionaries once again highlighted the revolutionary nature of this party and the role that populist dynamism played in their rise to power by mobilizing the masses below. In such confusing times, an antibourgeois message proved effective among the bourgeoisie itself.

The Nazis emphasized the well-known failures of the government and criticized the programs of other parties, while they themselves resorted to vague promises and avoided specific commitments that could be challenged. Other parties had had their chance and failed; the presidential government could offer only more sacrifice; but Hitler adopted an optimistic tone. He offered hope in the midst of widespread pessimism and despair. Once his party swept the enemies of the German people from power, he claimed, the new era of national rejuvenation and economic recovery would begin.

Hitler knew that the more desperate the situation, the more people there would be who would want to believe such rhetoric. Therefore, the Nazis did their best to exaggerate conditions, painting the bleakest possible picture of the future under the Weimar system. They also tried to highlight the weakness of the republic by taking control of the streets through massive and often disruptive demonstrations. These activities, along with attempts to provoke opponents and interfere with their campaigns, sometimes ended in violent street battles. This left the middle classes with the impression that the government could not maintain public order and security. It also enhanced middle-class fears that Communists, who tried to match Nazi violence, might launch a revolution. Although many middle-class citizens abhorred such violence and disorder in general, many believed the Nazi claim that it had been incited by Communists. The revolutionary rhetoric of the Communists was as extreme as anything emanating from the Nazi camp, and Communist propaganda about destroying middle-class oppression played into the hands of the Nazis.

It had become a Nazi objective to polarize the country and force the middle classes into a situation where they would have to choose between the right and the left. When the Nazis positioned themselves as the defenders of the middle classes, of nationalism, and of Christian culture and religion, willing to confront the Communists in the streets if necessary, the choice became easier for many citizens. Such Nazi appeals appear to have been increasingly effective with women. Although membership of women in the NSDAP still remained at only 7.8 percent, female electoral support for the Nazis rose appreciably and consistently. Voting patterns even suggest that by the end of Weimar more women voted for the Nazis than did men.

The elections of 1930 were a major breakthrough for the Nazis. Their opponents were stunned by the magnitude of the Nazi victory; Hitler himself was taken by surprise. Because of the state of the economy, gains by the radicals were anticipated, but even the most optimistic expectation of the NSDAP—to acquire seventy seats in the Reichstag—was greatly exceeded. The NSDAP became the second largest party in parliament, rising from twelve seats in 1928 to 107. Since most of the Nazi gains were made at the expense of the rightist parties, it was immediately clear that the NSDAP had finally won over large portions of the middle class. The DNVP had lost almost half its seats to the Nazis and, along with other moderate and rightist parties, had experienced the beginning of a rapid political decline. Overnight, it seemed, the Nazis had emerged as the dominant political force on the right. Although the Social Democrats remained the largest party, the Communist party increased its representation from fifty-four to seventy-seven seats, making it the third largest party. The Nazi goal of polarizing society was closer to realization. The middle of the political spectrum, on which the future of the republic depended, had been substantially reduced.

In addition to increasing their longstanding lower-middle-class constituency, the Nazi success had emanated primarily from middle-class Protestant voters in towns and rural areas. Equally significant, this so-called middle-class breakthrough had also included noticeable support from new middle-class voters in the cities. This was a crucial turning point in the development of the Nazi middle-class constituency, for the evident breakdown in middle-class allegiance to the traditional conservative parties in the 1930 elections left a fertile area for Nazi political exploitation in the future. Despite the failure to lure substantial working-class or Catholic voters, the new Nazi electoral strategy and campaign techniques had proven immensely effective. The Nazis had finally expanded their constituency beyond the lower-middle-class voters that had characterized their electorate for the past decade.

With success came political momentum for the National Socialist movement. A rush to join the party brought in close to 100,000 new members within a matter of months. This trend would continue until after the Nazi seizure of power in 1933. Over these three years of the Great Depression, massive unemployment, and hopelessness, an increasing number of workers joined the NSDAP at a faster rate than did members of the lower-middle class. Although this tendency once again indicated the broad-based appeal of the Nazi party, it was not sufficient to dispel the notion among most workers that the NSDAP remained the party of the middle classes. This image was reinforced by the fact that, despite these changes in recruitment, workers were still proportionately underrepresented while both old members and new recruits from the lower-middle class were significantly overrepresented among the rank and file. In addition, more and more individuals from the middle classes and elites joined the party throughout this period. Membership rose greatly among owners and managers of small businesses, upper-level civil servants, and those with higher education. The need for more specialized expertise and administrative competence to run this vast national party apparatus and sustain electoral effectiveness had also led Hitler to recruit more university-trained elites and professionals for leadership positions. While resented by the "old fighters" and the lower-middle-class types that were still predominant within the Nazi hierarchy, these newly recruited elites made an important contribution to the Nazi success during the rise to power and during the Third Reich.

FIGURE 5.I
Reichstag Seats: 1928–1930 Elections

Elections: May 1928   Elections: September 1930

After 1930, a part of the German business community, the leaders of giant coal and steel industries in particular, was more willing to make additional financial resources available to the Nazis. With the decline of the traditional rightist parties, these industrial and business groups apparently hoped to use Hitler to defend their interests. Hitler had no intention of being controlled by the leaders of big business and was willing to exploit them to further his political cause. He downplayed the anticapitalist propaganda of the party, refused to take a stand on specific economic proposals for the future, and prevented Nazi deputies from advancing anticapitalist legislation in the Reichstag.

The Nazi victory shattered Brüning's hopes for the election of a supportive, or at least submissive, Reichstag. It also created a dilemma for the Social Democrats and other moderate republicans, who considered the presidential system a serious breach of the constitution. The large Nazi and Communist blocks in the Reichstag made it politically impossible for Brüning to form a government based upon a coalition of a majority of deputies. This problem left the government in a worse predicament than it had faced before the election. Brüning had no choice but to form a minority cabinet and continue governing Germany through the presidential system. He was tolerated by the SPD and moderates, opponents of the rule by emergency decrees, because they feared that a collapse of the Brüning government would result in new elections and even greater gains by the Communists and Nazis.

FIGURE 5.2
Growth of Nazi Membership

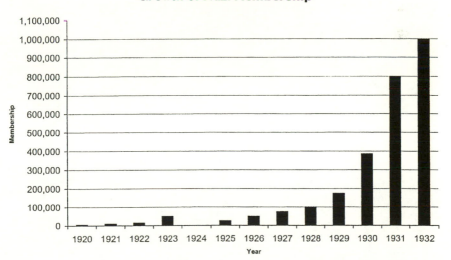

Until the spring of 1932, Brüning ruled Germany through a presidential government. For all essential purposes, parliament played a minor role, overshadowed by the exercise of presidential authority. In the end, Brüning neither solved Germany's problems nor slowed the momentum of the Nazis. Throughout 1931 the Nazis waged a relentless campaign against Weimar and the presidential system in the Reichstag, the press, and the streets. They also capitalized on their momentum and financial resources to keep up the pace of their recruitment drive. In 1928 membership was estimated at 100,000; by the beginning of 1932 the party would have approximately 450,000 members, and that figure would almost double before the end of that year. Equally impressive, the SA grew to several times the size of the German army itself, and Hitler could bring 100,000 of these dedicated shock troops to a single demonstration. To Hitler it seemed only a matter of time before he became the master of Germany.

CHAPTER 6

Hitler's Legal Path to Power

For two years after the elections of September 1930 the Nazis continued to follow the dual strategy they had devised for conquering Germany. They did everything possible to discredit and paralyze the existing government and to undermine the republican legal and political system, while they tried to use the democratic constitution and electoral process to win control over that very same system of government. They persisted in their scare tactics to frighten the population with the specters of economic ruin, social chaos, and Bolshevism. They intimidated their opponents, they created disorder in the streets and then charged that the government was incapable of providing public security, and they kept themselves in the public eye through parades and demonstrations by thousands of uniformed followers.

Inside parliament, they used obstructionist tactics to hamper the governmental process. Nazi deputies disrupted parliamentary sessions with catcalls and unnecessary debates on points of order, and they opposed every attempt at serious legislation. The Nazis made a mockery of parliamentary government itself. This party, which opposed the constitution, even took up the cause of defending the constitution as a tool to destroy democracy. The Nazis claimed that the presidential government of Brüning and the rule by Article 48 were flagrant constitutional violations. At one point the entire Nazi delegation marched out of the Reichstag and began a boycott against the parliament on the grounds that the Brüning government was illegal and therefore without constitutional authority. Despite such activity, Hitler repeatedly declared that the National Socialists were pursuing the legal path to power, and he demanded constitutional protection for his party.

Until 1932 Hitler was convinced that so long as his party remained free to organize and campaign the NSDAP would continue to win electoral victories until it had a majority in the Reichstag. Then the Nazi revolution would begin. But the events of 1932 caused Hitler and his followers to question the effectiveness of the dual strategy that had, until that time, worked so well. The government seemed incapable of turning the tide against the Nazi movement or of solving the national crisis, and Brüning became an easy target for Nazi propaganda assaults. Unemployment reached 6 million by 1932 as Brüning's budgets and policies only worsened economic conditions. The unpopularity of the "Hunger Chancellor" reached a new peak. However, these factors did not produce the quick collapse of Weimar, and the shift of popular support to the Nazis, though great, never approximated Hitler's expectations. While 1932 was a year of impressive electoral gains and growth in Nazi party membership, it was also one of political setbacks and frustrations for the Nazis. The party remained in a state of internal tension, often on the verge of splitting apart, and Hitler himself was uneasy and often indecisive.

The first indication of how far the Nazis were from acquiring the backing of a majority of Germans was evident in the presidential elections of 1932. Neither Hitler nor Hindenburg wanted to participate in an election when the president's term expired in the spring of 1932. At eighty-four, Hindenburg agreed to run again only after his advisers convinced him that the welfare of the nation rested on his control of the presidency. Hitler, on the other hand, was reluctant to challenge such a formidable national figure as Hindenburg, a war hero who, in the popular mind, had been the major stabilizing factor in German political life since 1925. Fearing that defeat might reveal a weakness in the Nazi movement or slow its momentum, Hitler did a good deal of agonizing before deciding he had no choice but to represent the NSDAP in the election. Although he was the leader of the second largest party in Germany and one of the most significant politicians of the era, Hitler was making his first attempt to run for public office. Until this point he did not have German citizenship. This legal obstacle was quickly removed when the Nazis in the state government of Brunswick had Hitler appointed to a government post, which automatically conveyed German citizenship on this former Austrian and stateless person.

The election of March 13 pitted Hindenburg against the candidates of the major antirepublican parties. The Nazis ran Hitler, the DNVP Theodor Duesterberg, and the Communists their party leader, Ernst Thälmann. Hindenburg was not the candidate of the right as he had been in 1925 but a figure supported by the republicans. Viewing the election as a showdown over the future of German democracy, the SPD, Catholic Center party, and moderate elements among the middle classes rallied behind the president. The intensity of the campaign surpassed that of 1930, particularly where the Nazis were concerned. Again, they set their political and propaganda machine into motion. Parades, demonstrations, exhausting speaking tours by Hitler and the party speaker corps dominated the German political scene. With larger numbers in the party and better financing, the Nazis saturated the country with more posters, pamphlets, films, and recordings than ever before. Unconcerned about contradictions, the party appealed to the special interests of every economic group, urging local party units to emphasize issues of pressing importance to constituents in their particular area. They were for the middle classes in one district and for the workers in another—at times nationalists and at times Socialists. The primary message, of course, was that Hitler remained the last hope of Germany.

Although the Nazi campaign resulted in an increase of 5 million votes over what the party had in 1930, it was not sufficient to bring them even close to victory. Hindenburg fell less than 1 percent short of receiving the absolute majority, whereas the Nazis were far behind with barely 30 percent of the vote. Clearly rejected by most Germans and with party morale rapidly declining, Hitler tried to save the situation by challenging Hindenburg in the required run-off election. This time Hitler had more powerful allies, as the rightist parties dropped their candidates and transferred their support to Hitler. This resurrection of the old rightist-Nazi alliance, originally created during the anti–Young Plan campaign, was made possible by rightist disappointment that Hindenburg was the candidate of the Social Democrats and Catholics. Thus Hitler's chances were greatly improved. The Nazis altered their campaign strategy only to the extent that they now gave up hope of winning worker and Catholic votes and directed their attention to the middle classes. Nonetheless, Hitler was handed another decisive defeat, as Hindenburg won the presidency with 53 percent of the vote. That the Hitler-rightist alliance acquired less than 37 percent was evidence that even in the midst of the depression, a majority of Germans refused to hand Hitler the power of the state. But the Nazi defeat did not mean that the republic was safe, for the 10 percent won by the Communists combined with Hitler's total showed that almost half of German society was willing to accept a radical alternative to Weimar.

Almost immediately the Nazi party experienced additional setbacks. On April 14, 1932, Hindenburg placed a ban on the SA, dissolving one of the party's most potent forces and creating discord within the NSDAP over whether this paramilitary group of 400,000 should resist. Wanting to avoid a fight with the police and army, Hitler managed to get the SA to accept this prohibition, but discontent remained at a high level. In the same month, the Nazis launched two sweeping campaigns during the state elections in Bavaria and Prussia. Again, they made substantial gains without coming close to winning a majority. Questions were raised about whether to abandon the strategy of pursuing electoral majorities. Frustration and disappointment brought internal party bickering and rivalries to the surface, and Hitler had difficulty controlling these disputes. Furthermore, the party had expended its financial resources, moving from solvency to major indebtedness after three campaigns. At this point, Hitler was willing to discuss negotiations with other parties and the government in order to give the NSDAP time to recover and reassess its position.

From the perspective of the government, however, the Nazis were still a major force, and it was concerned about how long the radical SA, now four times the size of the German army, could be restrained if the legal path to power were closed. There was also the problem of ensuring the future viability of the presidential system, since Brüning had obviously proven a failure. As before, the decisive figure on the government's side was Schleicher, who now planned to contain the Nazis by forming a non-Nazi rightist government that would be tolerated by Hitler. This toleration would be won by granting certain concessions to the Nazis, including some cabinet posts, though real power would remain in the hands of Schleicher and other conservatives. Brüning's replacement, new Reichstag elections, and a repeal of the SA ban were carrots Schleicher held out to the Nazis. Hitler agreed to tolerate a new government if these conditions were fulfilled. Although this strategy was a grave mistake and would soon backfire, Schleicher was convinced that such compromises were necessary to avoid civil war. Overconfident in his ability to handle the Nazis and in his plan's potential for success, Schleicher persuaded Hindenburg to replace Brüning with the rightist politician Franz von Papen. Schleicher intended Papen to be a mere figurehead whom he could control behind the scene. Schleicher expected that Papen, an almost fanatical advocate of the conservative nationalist cause, would help win back rightist support for the presidential government, and that new elections would increase the strength of the traditional right and weaken the Nazi appeal. After Brüning's forced resignation on May 30, Papen became chancellor, the Reichstag was dissolved, and new elections were set for July 31, 1932. The other concession to the Nazis was fulfilled on June 14 when the government lifted its ban on the SA.

Hitler's preference for new elections at this time indicated that he believed the Nazis could win a Reichstag majority, and the psychological atmosphere in which the elections were held clearly favored the Nazis. This period was characterized by escalating levels of political violence and a growing feeling on the part of the general public that the existing government was incapable of maintaining law and order. Waves of Hitler's uniformed shock troops returned to the streets after the repeal of the SA ban. The very presence of thousands of SA men was bound to create disorder, and clashes between groups of Nazis and Communists made street battles an almost daily occurrence in many parts of Germany. Civil war was a real possibility, and the police had tremendous difficulty keeping the situation under control. The highest number of casualties was in the state of Prussia, where within a month after the removal of the SA prohibition ninety-nine men were killed and 1,125 seriously wounded. Shortly before the election, a shootout between Communists and Nazis in Hamburg-Altona ended with seventeen dead and 285 wounded in a single Sunday afternoon.

Three days later, on July 20, 1932, the anti-Nazi Prussian government was removed from office and martial law declared throughout the state under emergency decrees issued by the Papen government. Although this was done in part to keep the powerful Prussian police from falling into Nazi hands and to prevent the outbreak of civil war, Papen had also acted out of personal political motives. He wanted to destroy the power of the Social Democrats in Prussia and show that his government, so far quite ineffective, could take decisive action. He believed that this would improve his chances of winning rightist support in the approaching elections. But only the Nazis benefited. The republican factions felt that Papen's action in Prussia was clearly unconstitutional, and they were left demoralized because they no longer believed that the government could be depended upon to uphold the constitution. The absence of any overt resistance to the Papen takeover also led the Nazis to conclude that the republic was easy prey for a pseudolegal seizure of power.

The electoral campaign had, in fact, rejuvenated the ranks of the Nazi party. Overcoming the financial problems and malaise it had experienced in the spring, the NSDAP again unleashed its political machine in anticipation of complete victory. The now familiar techniques of parades and propaganda posters, unrealistic and contradictory promises, and denunciations of opponents and the government rallied additional millions to the National Socialist side. Hitler's flights around the country on another exhaustive round of speaking engagements again proved effective. The first signs of middle-class support in the cities during the 1930 elections had greatly expanded and included those circles previously considered too respectable to vote National Socialist. Some wealthy voters, high-level civil servants, upper-middle-class Germans, and university students joined the urban middle classes in the big cities in voting for the Nazis. On July 31, 1932, the Nazis made their most impressive showing to date and their greatest ever in a free election, becoming the largest party in the Reichstag.

Yet total victory still eluded the Nazis. They won more than 37 percent of the vote and 230 parliamentary seats. The number of pro-Nazi voters had doubled since the last Reichstag elections. But the elusive majority was not in sight. The Nazi hopes of becoming a truly national party transcending traditional social, economic, and religious divisions had not materialized. They had not, as their propaganda claimed, overcome the class and religious identity of their party. Nazi attempts in 1932 to draw votes from desperate workers suffering from three years of the Great Depression had failed yet again. Radicalized and distressed workers left the SPD for the Communists and not the NSDAP. Catholic support faltered but remained firm. Furthermore, the broad constituency the Nazis had attracted was not as loyal or stable as were those voters who identified with the SPD and Center party. The Nazis had put together a very diverse electorate by exploiting the fears and resentments of various segments of society. The Nazis temporarily filled a vacuum left by the collapse of support for the traditional conservative parties but had not acquired the trust of their former voters. The contradictions and divergent interests of their broad constituencies were likewise causing rifts within the party and its leadership. How soft and fickle the middle-class Nazi electorate was would become quite apparent just a few months later.

At this point, Hitler once more faced crucial choices. Many Nazi leaders thought the party should enter a coalition and then gradually usurp all power after they were in the government. Others, especially in the rank and file of the revolutionary SA, were less patient and agitated for direct seizure of power. Hitler, too, was impatient and wanted complete control, but he was skeptical of any illegal or overt action, realizing that the guise of legality had prevented the suppression of the movement. He also knew that his hand had been greatly strengthened by his party's tremendous gains and the fact that the elections had placed the parliamentary system in a state of complete paralysis.

Indeed, the government was trapped in a constitutional as well as a political dilemma. After the elections the two extremist parties were in a position from which they could legally hinder attempts at governing Germany through either the parliament or the presidential system. Together the Nazis and the Communists (who now held eighty-nine seats) controlled the absolute majority of 52.4 percent in the Reichstag. Although these violent enemies could not cooperate in forming a coalition government, they could paralyze the entire system by preventing the formation of a parliamentary majority. The NSDAP and KPD also could undermine a presidential government by using their majority to reject chancellors through a vote of "no confidence" and by rescinding presidential emergency decrees issued under Article 48. Since this authority was constitutionally guaranteed to the parliament, the anticonstitutional parties could now abuse these rights to destroy constitutional government.

Within days of the election, a confident Hitler began to make demands. Hitler told Schleicher that he wanted the chancellorship for himself, all key cabinet ministries for Nazis, and an enabling act allowing him to rule by special decree. Hindenburg adamantly refused to grant Hitler such total power over the state, urging him to cooperate with other parties in forming a coalition government. When this rebuff was made public, the SA again showed signs of restlessness. Many Nazis felt that the elections had given them a greater right to govern than any other party and that if power were now denied to them, they should seize it by force. Although Hitler was outraged over his public rebuke and power had been kept from him, his anger and impatience did not lead him to discard the strategy of legality. For the moment, he rejected the options of sharing power in a coalition government and of revolutionary action. He waited for the opening of parliament in September, knowing that the government's dilemma remained.

In the meantime, the government desperately sought a solution. Discussions within the government had become complicated by the fact that Schleicher had developed serious reservations about Papen, who was now even more unpopular than Brüning had been and had no major party behind him. Schleicher also was concerned about the political course advocated by Chancellor Papen, who proposed to exploit the crisis to reform the constitution and replace the republican form of government with an authoritarian state. According to the Papen scheme, the Reichstag should be dissolved for an indefinite period and the constitution revised in the interim. Fearing the reaction to this unconstitutional plan, Schleicher, with Hindenburg's support, successfully resisted this proposal throughout the summer and fall of 1932. The government finally decided its only reasonable alternative was to risk new elections. The Reichstag would be dissolved at its first session before the radicals could paralyze that body or bring down the presidential government of Papen with a vote of no confidence.

The Nazis saw the new elections as an effort to deny them the fruits of their electoral victory and to destroy their ability to keep the government trapped in its constitutional dilemma. When the Nazis and Communists tried to use a vote of no confidence to prevent Papen from dissolving the Reichstag on September 12, a theatrical showdown ensued. Papen claimed that parliament had been dissolved, while the Nazis and Communists charged that Papen had no authority, since he was no longer chancellor after the no-confidence vote. The radicals finally accepted the dissolution of the Reichstag, and began to prepare for the November 6 elections.

Almost from the start of this campaign most Nazi leaders realized that the party was in for a difficult time, and as the election came closer, their worries appeared to be well founded. Hitler remained confident and did his best to instill confidence and a spirit of enthusiasm in his followers, though he was aware of the concern and anxiety within the party leadership. The reasons for the rapid shift from jubilation in early August to a mood of doubt were diverse. Nazism had its greatest appeal in the panic and fear that accompanied worsening economic circumstances, but by early winter 1932 these conditions had changed. The depression seemed to have passed its worst point, and there were signs of economic improvement. The public mood, while not especially optimistic, certainly was less pessimistic than at any time since 1930. Moreover, after years of repetition, the vague and contradictory promises and rhetoric of Nazi propaganda had lost some of their power of persuasion and were more open to question. After several costly major campaigns at all levels of government in less than one year, the party showed signs of physical, psychological, and financial exhaustion. The NSDAP had thrown everything it had into the July elections, and another effort of this magnitude so soon thereafter was impossible.

Under these unfavorable circumstances, the party waged a major campaign. While the NSDAP did have more members than ever before, the organization's efforts were hindered by internal dissension between the party old guard and the newcomers. Most important was the lack of adequate financial resources. Contributions had dropped off significantly as middle-class Germans and industrial leaders became uncertain about what a National Socialist takeover would mean. They were alarmed by the violent activities and radical behavior displayed by the SA in the aftermath of the July elections and by Hitler's claim to absolute power. The earlier fears about whether nazism was a revolutionary and anticapitalist movement were revived. Doubts were reinforced by the Nazi campaign itself, which was directed against the "reactionary" policies of the Papen government and which had strong anticapitalist overtones. The image of Nazis as social and economic revolutionaries, even Bolsheviks in disguise, was one held by many after the Nazis joined the Communists in support of a transit strike in Berlin shortly before the election.

The election results of November confirmed the fears of the Nazi leadership, for they clearly established that the party had passed its peak and had lost much of its political momentum. Although it remained the largest party, the NSDAP had lost 2 million votes since July and thirty-four seats in the Reichstag. Subsequently, the Nazis suffered similar losses in state and local elections. The Hitler movement no longer appeared invincible. This critical setback indicated that the strategy of acquiring power by winning an electoral majority was no longer viable.

Although Hitler's confidence had been shaken by this reversal of fortune, he refused to change his course. His demands to the government remained essentially the same, including the office of chancellor for himself. This unrealistic attitude aggravated tensions within the Nazi hierarchy. Gregor Strasser argued that the Nazis should participate in a coalition government and attempt to enter power through the "back door." This disagreement, along with party infighting and restlessness, brought the organization to the verge of a split. As a result, Hitler was forced to devote a good deal of his time and energy to reasserting his authority within the party and to holding the organization together.

The Nazi losses by no means solved the problems of the government. The economy had improved, but the country was still in the midst of a severe depression. Millions were unemployed; and the Papen government commanded little respect and the public had no confidence in it. Despite the elections, the Nazi party remained a strong and dangerous foe, backed by almost a third of the nation and in control of a paramilitary force of 400,000 SA troops. Certainly a revolutionary situation existed. That millions of Germans strongly favored radical political action was evidenced not only by the large number who continued to cast their ballots for the Nazis but also by the Communist vote that gave the KPD a hundred seats in the Reichstag. Finally, the constitutional dilemma had not been resolved; without Nazi participation it was impossible to form a majority coalition government from among the various parties in the Reichstag.

Papen seized the moment to push once more for his own reactionary solution. In essence, Papen proposed what many conservative intellectuals had called the "New State," one that would greatly reduce, if not eliminate altogether, the influence of political parties and place power in the hands of those allegedly best suited to govern. To accomplish this, the president was to declare a state of emergency, dissolve the Reichstag for an undetermined length of time, and perhaps even impose a ban on the extremist parties. The constitution would be revised in such a way that voting rights and the power of parliament would be restricted significantly, resulting in a powerful authoritarian state to replace the feeble democratic system of Weimar. Again, Schleicher vehemently opposed the plan as dangerous; he believed that such unconstitutional action would be opposed by the republican parties and trade unions and perhaps unleash a civil war at a time when the army was not strong enough to cope with a revolt by the Nazis and Communists. Schleicher was wary of allowing the army to be caught in a situation where it would have to defend the unconstitutional schemes of a chancellor who had no popular basis of support. Other alternatives, Schleicher held, must be attempted before considering such a dangerous breach of the constitution and challenging powerful political parties.

After years of behind-the-scene maneuvering, Schleicher now decided to accept personally the responsibility of political leadership and proposed that he replace Papen as chancellor and be given the opportunity to try a new

FIGURE 6.I
Reichstag Seats: July–November 1932 Elections

Elections: July 1932

DVP 7
DDP 4
DNVP 37
NSDAP 230
Center 75
SPD 133
KPD 89

Elections: November 1932

DNVP 52
DVP 11
DDP 2
NSDAP 196
Center 70
SPD 121
KPD 100

approach to the political predicament of the government. His plan involved the formation of a national front that would provide the government with widespread popular backing. He hoped that his support would extend from the Social Democrats, trade unions, and Catholics to the left wing of the Nazi party. He would discard the previous government's policy of confrontation with the parties in the Reichstag in favor of reconciliation and cooperation. Popular support also would be won through a massive program of social and economic reform, including public works projects, to alleviate unemployment and counteract the depression. Furthermore, he would attempt to capitalize on the potential split in the Nazi party and bring the leftist Strasser faction into his government. Horrified at the prospect of civil war and disturbed by the thought of violating his constitutional oath, Hindenburg agreed to allow Schleicher his chance. Nevertheless, the president dismissed Papen reluctantly, because he had by this time grown quite fond of him. The personal relationship between these two men would soon prove crucial in the final stage of the Nazi rise to power.

Appointed chancellor in early December, Schleicher knew before the end of that month that his plan had little chance of success. The Social Democrats and trade unions, suspicious of this intriguing general-turned-politician, could not be won over. By turning to the left with the offer of cooperation and Socialist programs, Schleicher also alienated the German right and powerful industrial groups. And he was unable to split the Nazi party. Hitler's heated confrontation with Strasser over possible Nazi cooperation with the Schleicher government resulted in Strasser's resignation from the NSDAP. The Nazi party, with Hitler as its undisputed head, remained united and in opposition to the government.

During these weeks, Papen continued to be politically active. Through personal negotiations, Papen was able to revive the old Nazi-rightist alliance. Hitler now was willing to negotiate with Papen and the right, because few legal options were open to him. A future electoral victory appeared remote, party members again were suffering from serious demoralization, and the party financial situation had become desperate. Not wanting to miss his chance, Hitler did what Strasser had urged throughout the year. He prepared to join a coalition government and come to power through the "back door." Ironically, the apparent purge of Strasser made it easier for Hitler to deal with the rightist parties, which were interrelated with big business, because it seemed that Hitler had triumphed over the anticapitalist wing of the NSDAP. And Hitler played up the anti-Communist stance of his party, presenting his movement as a bulwark against Bolshevism. To big business, cooperation with the Nazis was the lesser evil; certainly it was preferable to Schleicher's overtures to the left. On the surface, at least, the Papen plan would also keep the Nazis contained. For, though Hitler and Papen would share the chancellorship, most cabinet ministries would remain in the hands of conservatives, and the president could, of course, dismiss Hitler if this became necessary.

When Schleicher learned of the possibility of a Hitler-Papen government, he decided that only extraordinary action could keep the power of the state from eventually falling completely into Nazi hands. Therefore, he proposed that the president declare a state of emergency and place a ban on the Nazi and Communist parties. The Reichstag would be dissolved and elections postponed until economic and political stability was restored, and a presidential government, with Schleicher as chancellor, would rule through emergency decrees. The constitution would not be altered, but parts of it would be suspended temporarily. Although the plan would involve a temporary violation of the constitution, Schleicher felt that this was preferable to granting the Nazis the opportunity to usurp complete power once they were in the government.

In the summer of 1932, Schleicher's constitutional adviser, Carl Schmitt, published a book in which he argued that an anticonstitutional party should not be granted the "equal chance," available to other parties, to acquire power legally. No constitution, Schmitt stated, could provide the legal means for its own destruction. If necessary, individual parts of the constitution could be suspended temporarily in order to preserve the essence of the constitutional order as a whole and to deny the "equal chance" to those parties that had as their expressed goal the destruction of the constitution. To adhere to the letter of the constitution, while ignoring the perilous political threats to the constitution, would be suicidal. Schleicher was in general agreement with this perspective.

Hindenburg, however, took a very narrow approach to constitutional questions, as did many defenders of Weimar democracy. A breach of any part of the constitution would be opposed. The president considered his constitutional oath sacred, and he informed Schleicher that he had no intention of violating it by acting contrary to what was specifically stated in individual articles of the constitution. To Hindenburg, the defense of the constitution meant upholding the letter of that document. Hindenburg reminded Schleicher that his plan was similar to the one Papen had presented months before and which Schleicher had charged would lead to civil war. By this time, Schleicher no longer had the president's confidence, and Hindenburg rejected the plan for emergency action.

At this point, Papen's negotiations with the rightist parties and Hitler had come to fruition. Papen, who now had become Hindenburg's new confidant, could offer the president an option that did not involve a violation of the letter of the constitution. A Hitler-Papen government needed only presidential approval. Hindenburg remained skeptical of appointing Hitler chancellor, and the last week of January 1933 saw Papen engaged in personal efforts to overcome the president's reservations. Hindenburg was informed of Hitler's willingness to uphold the constitution. Even the president's son, Oskar, became an advocate of the Papen plan, and he had an influence on his father's decision. Similar pressure was brought to bear on rightist friends of Hindenburg (such as DNVP leader Hugenberg) who were to serve in the new cabinet. They tried to remove the president's doubts with the argument that a conservative-dominated cabinet would keep Hitler under control. Nonetheless, as late as January 28, the president held out against appointing Hitler chancellor of Germany.

Finally, unable to find another viable candidate to assume the chancellorship and under great pressure from trusted friends, the eighty-five-year-old Hindenburg gave in. On the morning of January 30, 1933, Hitler was sworn in as chancellor of the Weimar Republic. The letter of the constitution had been fulfilled, but its spirit clearly had been violated. Hitler came to power through the "back door" at a time when his movement was declining in strength and burdened by internal crises, and while a large majority of the

FIGURE 6.2
Reichstag Elections: Voting Trends, 1928–1933

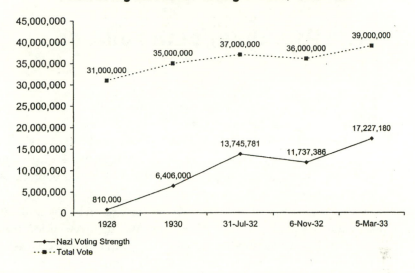

German people still opposed Hitler and national socialism. Hitler had accomplished through Papen's intrigues what he could not achieve through either elections or revolution. The full implications of this development were not yet evident to those who had helped place Hitler in this position. These conservatives believed that they had contained Hitler, pointing to the fact that eight of the most decisive cabinet posts were in their hands with only three ministries going to the Nazis. And, of course, Hindenburg could always dismiss Hitler.

Despite his pledge to Hindenburg to abide by the constitution, Hitler had no intention of letting this document interfere with the fulfillment of his political and ideological objectives. He had come to power legally and now would manipulate his legal authority to consolidate his control and to destroy the constitutional order of Weimar. The first sign of what the future held for Germany appeared on the very night of his appointment. For more than five hours, thousands of Nazis, along with groups from various nationalist organizations, paraded through the streets of Berlin in celebration, and the entire affair was broadcast over the radio across the nation. The Third Reich had begun.

CHAPTER 7

The Pseudolegal Revolution

Hitler's appointment was not the culmination of the national revolution, but merely the beginning of it. The actual Nazi revolution was yet to be realized and would not be completed until August of 1934. It was brought about in stages and through a series of legal, pseudolegal, and clearly illegal maneuvers. The first step had been Hitler's acquisition of the office of chancellor, followed by the usurpation of more power by the NSDAP. Hitler then used the power of the state now at his disposal to consolidate his control, eliminate potential opposition, and institute a revolution from above. In essence, he pursued the same dual strategy of legality and illegality that had been so effective in weakening the republic and bringing the chancellorship into his hands. The mask of legality was crucial in allowing Hitler to usurp more and more power, in getting the German population and state authorities to follow his directives, and in making it exceptionally difficult for his opposition to resist.

Hitler's immediate concern following his appointment was to retain his pivotal role in the government and in his own party. Initially, his position was not as secure as one might have assumed. His party had not overcome its internal problems; a few months before, it had come close to splitting into hostile factions. Many of the impatient radicals within the NSDAP wanted a quick revolution, and their demands could have undercut Hitler's legal strategy. A majority of the population still rejected national socialism, and Hitler was dependent upon the support of the conservatives around Hindenburg and in his own cabinet. Therefore, Hitler concentrated on consolidating and expanding his control and did not seek the immediate fulfillment of the goals of the Nazi ideology and Party Program.

Hitler again proved to be a shrewd and cautious politician. He managed to keep under control the most radical tendencies of his movement while allowing the conservatives with whom he was cooperating to believe that they had him contained. As vice-chancellor, Papen harbored the illusion that he was sharing power with Hitler, and other conservatives in the cabinet retained responsibility in important areas of government. During the national celebration at Potsdam on March 21, 1933, Hitler appeared in formal dress rather than his party uniform, and the tone of his speech was moderate, emphasizing

German traditions and the need for national unity. He sounded very much like a conservative and led many to believe that perhaps he had been tamed; his previous revolutionary zeal seemed to have been mere political rhetoric. This image was reinforced by the deference he showed to Hindenburg and the German army, two symbols of the old Germany. During this early phase, Hitler also played upon the theme of Christianity, trying to remove the doubts of churchmen. He presented his movement as the defender of Christianity and morality against atheistic Bolshevism and cultural decadence.

Simultaneously, Hitler tried to outmaneuver the conservatives and to eliminate the need for their support. In their audacious propaganda and image-building campaign, the Nazis even successfully usurped the conservative Prussian tradition that had been monopolized by the old right. The Nazis now appeared to be the ones embodying, and more likely to realize, the values of duty and sacrifice presumed to characterize the "true German." In their successful appeals to mass audiences, the Nazis had, as one historian noted, triumphed as the "self-appointed guardians of the national heritage," with which so many Germans intuitively identified.

Hitler's first victory over conservatives occurred on January 31, 1933, when he overcame their opposition to new elections. The Reichstag was dissolved and a new round of elections were scheduled for March 5, 1933. The conservatives wanted to continue governing in a presidential system where Hindenburg's authority would remain decisive, whereas Hitler anticipated a Nazi majority in the Reichstag that would enhance his power. As a majority chancellor, Hitler would be less dependent upon the conservatives and the president; under such circumstances it would be more difficult to contain him. The elections were also a part of Hitler's overall legal strategy, since they would provide him with a popular mandate for his party rule and the political course he sought to pursue. A Nazi majority could legally turn National Socialist policies into law, which the state authorities would be required to enforce and citizens obliged to obey.

Conducted in an atmosphere of anxiety, intimidation, and fatalism, the elections fell short of being a free and democratic affair. Using the power of the state to assist in their campaign and hinder that of their opponents, the Nazis had a tremendous and indisputably unfair advantage. Under previous chancellors, presidential emergency decrees were often instituted to keep the Nazis under control, but now the NSDAP was free from such constraints, and Article 48 became one of Hitler's most important weapons. Although the president alone could issue such decrees, it was Hitler who determined the need for particular emergency measures and their selective application. In early February 1933, decrees were instituted that greatly limited freedom of the press and assembly. While Nazi publications and public meetings remained unaffected, the Communist campaign was almost completely disrupted by these government measures and by arrests of many KPD leaders and members. Political functions of even the SPD and Center party were disturbed. One of the most effective political tools of its day, the radio, was for all practical purposes monopolized by the Nazis, and broadcasts of Hitler's speeches became mandatory throughout the country.

Although financial support from big business contributed significantly to the effectiveness of Hitler's political machine, the Nazis benefited as well from terrorist acts. Opponents were intimidated and their activities disrupted through physical attacks by Nazis. The victims of this political violence found there was little protection provided by the law and legal authorities, since the police administrations in many states had already been brought under Nazi pressure or control. In Prussia, Germany's largest state and the one that contained the capital, the problem of harassment and lack of legal protection was particularly acute, because thousands of SA and SS men had been appointed as auxiliary policemen. The entire election was a striking example of the Nazi reliance on both legal and illegal methods.

As the elections approached, unexpected developments worked to the Nazi advantage. On the night of February 27, a week before the elections, the Reichstag went up in flames. The Nazis immediately claimed that this was the beginning of a full-scale Communist revolution, since a former Dutch communist, Marinus van der Lubbe, had been arrested at the scene and charged with arson. For a long time, historians generally agreed that the Nazis started the fire, but now most have concluded that the source of the fire remains unknown. Hitler recognized the political value that could be gained by exploiting the fear of communism, and his party used the mass media to increase public anxiety about a Bolshevik revolt. The mythical Communist revolution also was used as a pretext for tightening Nazi control throughout the country and for harsher actions against political opponents. By February 28, Hitler had convinced Hindenburg that the Communist menace required another emergency decree to defend public order and security. This decree suspended most civil liberties and allowed the Nazis to suppress what was left of the Communist press and to arrest several thousand KPD activists and some prominent leftist intellectuals. As before, the activities of other parties also were restricted and disrupted. Presenting themselves as the bulwark against communism, the Nazis had a psychological advantage going into the elections.

In the election of March 5, 1933, the Nazis made substantial gains, indicating that they had a stronger popular following than in 1932. But a majority of Germans still rejected the National Socialist alternative, leaving the Nazis with 43.9 percent of the vote. The increase in Nazi votes was due to the restrictions on the opposition parties, the renewed momentum and respectability that followed Hitler's appointment as chancellor, the millions of new voters attracted by hope and Hitler's charisma, and defectors from the KPD who felt that the Nazis were revolutionaries and would introduce radical economic and social change. Hitler still lacked the legal majority to implement his revolution from above. Legally Hitler would still have to rely upon the conservative forces in the Reichstag, whose 8 percent of the vote was essential for a parliamentary majority. This apparent dependence reinforced once again the illusion of continued conservative control over the National Socialists, though Hitler moved quickly to escape this dependency by claiming victory and declaring that the nation had granted him a popular mandate. The Nazi propaganda machine emphasized that the elections constituted a national revolution, while SA and SS contingents in various parts of the country demanded that Nazi flags and symbols be placed on public buildings and that local and state governments conform to Nazi policies.

The most crucial step in establishing the Nazi dictatorship came with the Enabling Act of March 24, 1933. This act, which required a constitutional amendment, would grant Hitler greater emergency powers than those provided under Article 48 and, in essence, would destroy the remaining aspects of a constitutional form of government in Germany. Its passage was nothing less than a political revolution that finally ended the Weimar Republic. The justification for such exceptional authority was that it was necessary to restore public order, provide a stable political system, initiate programs for economic recovery, and start the general process of national rejuvenation. In seeking this legislation, Hitler had the support of his conservative allies, who had always been antirepublican and favored an authoritarian state to replace Weimar. But opposition from other parties in parliament was an obstacle to achieving the necessary two-thirds majority required for a constitutional amendment. After the arrest of the Communist deputies, the Nazis still needed the cooperation of the Catholic Center party. Through intimidation and pressure, along with verbal guarantees about preserving parts of the Weimar constitution, the Nazis convinced the Center party to vote for the Enabling Act. The Center party capitulated because it felt that Hitler was determined to have such authority one way or another and that it could best protect Catholic institutions and interests in Germany by cooperating with the new regime. They also feared that their party might meet the same fate as the Communists if they resisted. This decision by the Center party, formerly one of the pillars of the republic and a defender of the constitution, was further evidence of the effects of Nazi domination of the political and psychological climate even before Hitler received dictatorial powers. The only major group that had the courage to oppose this legislation was the Social Democratic party; many of its members later suffered and died in concentration camps.

Lasting for four years, the Enabling Act eliminated the separation of powers by allowing Hitler to pass laws without the consent of the Reichstag. Not only could laws deviate from the constitution, but such emergency legislation could not be rescinded by the Reichstag, as had been the case with Article 48. The other rights of the Reichstag and the power of the president could not be infringed upon, leading many conservatives to believe that Hitler could still be restrained or even removed when necessary. In reality, only the president could act as a check on Hitler, since the president could dismiss the Nazi leader from the office of chancellor and would maintain control over the army. But the aging president, with greatly diminished physical and mental capacities, never exercised this authority, and it soon became apparent that Hitler would not need his conservative allies or their votes in the Reichstag for very long.

The Enabling Act put Hitler in a position from which he could legally transform the state and German society. An important aspect of this revolutionary process was described as *Gleichschaltung*, or coordination. The policy of *Gleichschaltung* would assist Hitler's expansion and consolidation of power, as well as the realization of the Nazi revolution, by forcing state and social institutions to submit to the will of the party and the ideological goals of national socialism. It was directed at destroying those potential centers of resistance and noncooperation that remained and assuring the Nazis an eventual monopoly in German society and politics. Up to this point, Hitler had acquired control over the central government, but the state governments, the bureaucracies, the trade unions, and political parties stood outside his grasp. Until these institutions were eliminated or nazified, dictatorial rule and the National Socialist revolution would be incomplete.

To prevent united opposition to his consolidation of power, Hitler instituted the policy of *Gleichschaltung* gradually and always under the guise of the legal authority conferred by the Enabling Act and the popular mandate of March 5. Although by this time the Nazis exercised extensive influence in most state governments, in many cases having direct control, Hitler wanted to complete and to legalize this takeover to ensure compliance with his policies. A law was passed on March 31 dissolving and reorganizing the state governments without elections. These new governments could thereafter pass laws without the consent of the state legislatures and could deviate from the state constitutions. A "Second Law for the Coordination of the States with the Reich" of April 7 further empowered Hitler to appoint Reich commissars to oversee state governments. For all practical purposes, state governments were no longer autonomous, and resistance from state governments became impossible.

The Nazis legalized the purge of the bureaucracy they had started earlier. A new civil service law abolished the security of tenure for bureaucrats and was used to legitimize the dismissal of Jews and those of democratic and leftist political views. In this way, the bureaucracy, an essential institution in the machinery of the modern state, was brought into line by the Nazi party and could then be used to facilitate the introduction of a dictatorship. The civil service law was also employed to purge Jews and unreliable political elements from the schools and universities, since German teachers and professors were civil servants. Thousands of civil servants, teachers, and professors, many of them among the most talented and distinguished in Germany, lost their positions for ideological or racial reasons. The nazification of the German educational system began with this phase of ideological and institutional *Gleichschaltung*.

The lack of any significant opposition to the imposition of such measures was partially the result of the mood of resignation and fatalism among large segments of the population, who felt helpless in the face of Nazi power, brutality, and legal authority. Whatever voices of opposition remained were overshadowed by the growing opportunism and enthusiasm found in other sectors of the society. Fearing for their careers, futures, and security, many Germans became silent, while others opportunistically jumped on the Nazi bandwagon to further their own interests. Many teachers, professors, and bureaucrats joined the NSDAP, not out of political or ideological conviction, but in order to protect their jobs or to advance their careers. Few civil servants took a moral or political stand and resigned voluntarily; some of those purged actually tried to get back their old positions. Many intellectuals, including the renowned philosopher Martin Heidegger and the brilliant legal theorist (and former Nazi opponent) Carl Schmitt, announced adherence to the new regime after the Enabling Act. Public support also was displayed by hundreds of university professors and major professional organizations. Much of this action was taken under pressure from the Nazis and Nazi student groups that took control of the universities, demanding the removal of leftist, uncooperative, and Jewish professors. However, there was also real enthusiasm on the part of many Germans. Between the time of Hitler's appointment and early spring, the NSDAP acquired about a million new members. Although the party old guard complained about the influx of opportunistic newcomers, called "March violets," the general increase in membership, like the expressions of public support by associations and prominent individuals, added credibility to Hitler's claim to a popular mandate. It also tended to discourage Nazi opponents, who felt that this popular wave had already shifted the country a long way in the direction of national socialism and who had the impression that the Nazis were much more powerful than they actually were at this stage.

The two institutions that might have offered organized and overt resistance, the army and the trade unions, took no action. Loyal to Hindenburg, anti-Communist and antirepublican in sympathy, the army would remain neutral so long as the Nazis did not encroach upon their interests or the presidency. The trade unions, on the other hand, were staunchly republican and had earlier saved the republic by defeating a rightist *Putsch* in 1920 through a general strike. With more than 6 million members, the various trade unions would have been a formidable force if their leadership had been willing or able to mount a successful general strike once again. Unfortunately, the trade unions had been greatly weakened by the depression, massive unemployment, defections, and the mood of resignation of the population as a whole. Although a general strike under these circumstances was unlikely, Hitler could neither tolerate the continued existence of the unions nor risk forcing them into action against him. He waited several months, gaining strength before confronting this problem, and when he did move against the unions, his actions involved a deceptive gesture of compromise and reconciliation followed by sudden and brutal suppression.

In dealing with labor Hitler cleverly turned again to the Socialist aspect of the Nazi ideology. During his first months in office he had tended toward the right, the middle classes, and capitalists; the major political targets of his early attacks had been the left. By late April he made it appear that he was shifting direction by making vague overtures to the working classes and creating the impression in the minds of some workers that perhaps the Nazi movement did have a strong Socialist component. Some began to think that if given a chance Hitler might introduce far-reaching economic and social reforms as called for by the Party Program of 1920. Quite unexpectedly, Hitler fulfilled a long-standing goal of German workers to have May 1 declared a paid national holiday. Historically, May Day had been the most important celebration of labor and the left throughout Europe, though even under Weimar it had never become a national holiday. Claiming that May Day would be a day of unity among the NSDAP, other nationalist groups, and labor, Hitler organized massive parades and celebrations across Germany for May 1, 1933. On that day SA and SS units, workers, and employers marched in the same parades. Later, they listened to Hitler and other party functionaries speak of national unity among all Germans and of the elimination of class distinctions within the new Nazi *Volksgemeinschaft*. Workers were told that their needs would be met in the new order through a type of true "German socialism," its exact nature vague and undefined.

Uncertain about Hitler's next move and unsure of what action it should take in view of this Nazi initiative, the workers and their leadership momentarily were paralyzed. The very next day Hitler's duplicity became clear to all, as the SA and SS followed a well-prepared plan to crush the trade unions. All assets, presses, and offices of Socialist unions were seized and many leaders arrested. Confused, fatalistic, without their leadership, and caught off guard by this swift action, workers offered no resistance. Other unions acquiesced thereafter by voluntarily submitting to a Nazi takeover of their institutions. A law enacted on May 10 dissolved all trade unions and replaced them with the Nazi-organized and -controlled German Labor Front. Although in theory the German Labor Front was to integrate all workers into a single national union and represent the interests of labor in the NSDAP and economic life in general, it mostly served as nothing more than a means of controlling labor and a tool for indoctrinating workers with the National Socialist spirit. Within a matter of days Hitler had removed a significant obstacle in the path to totalitarian rule.

Hitler's next major objective was the introduction of the one-party state at the expense of the multiparty system of the republic. Hitler's move against one of the last remnants of Weimar was made easier by the hatred of the left felt by the middle classes. Also, the conservatives, who disapproved of all political parties except their own, collaborated with Hitler. Before Hitler's rise to power, many conservatives had sought the destruction of the KPD and SPD. The KPD had already been decimated, and the destruction of the SPD was facilitated by a deep rift that occurred in that party after the repressions in May. Many SPD leaders had fled abroad and were calling for resistance on the part of the left and labor in Germany, whereas those leaders who stayed in the country intended to pursue a strategy of remaining as the legally elected opposition party within the Reichstag. The position of the SPD leaders who remained in Germany was the result of underestimating the determination, radicalism, and dynamism of the Nazi movement. They had expected the Nazi experiment to fail rather quickly and wanted to preserve their organization in preparation for political action after the collapse of the Hitler regime. This rift not only weakened the SPD further but also handed Hitler a pretext for legally suppressing the SPD on the grounds that its members abroad were engaged in treason. In banning the SPD, Hitler could count on the support of his conservative allies. But soon it was their turn and these conservatives then found themselves confronting the Nazis alone. With the SPD officially dissolved on June 22 and more of its leaders arrested, the conservative parties, like the more moderate parties, did not hold out long against Nazi pressure. Within a matter of weeks, all remaining parties dissolved themselves, leaving the NSDAP with a monopoly on political power.

The end of the Weimar party system signaled the failure of the conservative strategy of containing Hitler. With republican and leftist opposition crushed, the Nazis again revealed their true revolutionary nature. The "national revolution" was clearly now a "national socialist revolution." The German heritage and Prussian tradition, earlier touted with such fanfare, would be preserved only if subsumed usefully into the revolutionary transformation of society forcefully pursued by the Nazis. By the spring of 1933, the Nazis unleashed a vigorous and brutal two-pronged campaign of propaganda and violence against conservatives. Nazis condemned the conservative traditions and heritage of the German bourgeoisie and its values as "reactionary," ridiculing even the memory of the Kaiser era that so many Germans still yearned for. Meanwhile, the SA ferociously attacked the DNVP. This wave of Nazi political violence against the right matched their earlier attacks on Communists and Social Democrats. Unable to retaliate in the face of Nazi-controlled state power, the right likewise succumbed to fear and fatalism; opposition appeared futile.

Hugenberg, the man who had brought Hitler to the center of national politics in 1929 with the intention of manipulating him for the nationalistic cause, was forced to resign from the cabinet on June 26. Hugenberg's belief that the president would back him against such Nazi pressure, like his belief that Hitler still needed the votes of the DNVP in the Reichstag, was unfounded. The president did not interfere with his dismissal, and the following day the German Nationalist party dissolved itself. Meeting the same fate as the left, the conservative movement ceased to exist as an organized political force. The rise of new political organizations was prohibited by a law of July 14, legalizing the Nazi monopoly on power by making the NSDAP the only party in Germany. The one-party state had become a reality.

Hitler also was successful in acquiring an important degree of legitimacy and respect for his regime through an agreement with the Catholic Church. Negotiations with the papacy in Rome during June and July culminated in a Concordat between the Hitler government and the Catholic Church. The papacy recognized the Hitler regime and relinquished the rights of Catholic institutions and clergy in Germany to engage in political activity. For these concessions, the church was guaranteed protection for freedom of faith, as well as for Catholic schools, institutions, and property within Germany. Concluding that resistance was futile, the Catholic hierarchy decided that compromise with the Nazis was the only means of defending Catholic interests. The Concordat was a major triumph for Hitler; he had been recognized by one of the world's most important moral and religious forces, and the possibility of opposition from Catholic Germans was no longer a problem. The submission to the Nazis of this symbolic moral force made it much easier for millions of others to submit and compromise with Germany's new masters.

The destruction of Weimar and the success of political *Gleichschaltung* during the first half year of the new regime had placed tremendous power in Hitler's hands, yet his position was by no means secure. Hitler's second year in power was a time of crisis and much more difficult than his first. Although the president and the army had so far done little to stem the Nazi tide, they still were forces with which Hitler had to contend. The events of 1934 created a good deal of anxiety in Hitler about whether their noninterference would continue. For the most part, the crisis emanated from within Hitler's own party. Demands and actions by certain segments challenged Hitler's absolute control and his political course.

By 1934 the inherent contradictions within the Nazi movement, which had been downplayed in favor of party unity during the conquest of power, brought the organization to the point of internal war. Large segments of the party had taken the Socialist, revolutionary, and anticapitalist aspects of the Nazi ideology quite seriously and had expected a social and economic revolution to follow soon after the seizure of power. After July 1933, Hitler wanted to temper the revolutionary fervor of the party, consolidate its gains, and begin the development of the new order under conditions of stability. The radicals remained dissatisfied and sought to continue the revolution until their Socialist goals were met. They began to agitate for a "second revolution" that would include the nationalization of large corporations, the elimination of debts for small farmers, and programs to protect the farmer and small businessman against the power of big capital.

At the forefront of the movement for the "second revolution" was the SA. Many of its members were committed to the Socialist program and felt betrayed by Hitler's alliance with conservatives and industrialists. Others were men who had spent years fighting for the national revolution but had not yet profited by acquiring jobs or offices. This discontent was vocalized quite strongly by SA leader Ernst Röhm, who had emerged as a powerful force with more than a million organized Storm Troopers under his control and a few million more in the SA reserves. The problem of the SA went beyond social and economic issues, since Röhm also demanded that the SA serve as the basis for a greatly expanded new army under his leadership.

The demands for economic revolution and a Nazi army were contrary to Hitler's intended political course. He had never been a strong advocate of the Socialist goals of nazism and feared that any attempt to introduce such changes at this point would disrupt the economy. Hitler realized that his success depended in part on his ability to counteract the depression and thought that this could best be accomplished by mobilizing the existing economic system. A good deal of his support came from big business and industry, and he did not want to alienate them since he needed them to bring about rapid economic recovery and expansion as a prelude to his planned rearmament program. The creation of an economically strong and rearmed Germany to carry out his foreign policy took priority over the promises he had previously made to protect the little man. His position on the army issue was similar, as he believed that the army officer corps was far superior to those leading and staffing the SA. The new Nazi army would be resisted by the old one and could topple Hitler from power. Even in the unlikely event that the army did not act, a new army of several million men under Röhm would make the SA leader a powerful competitor to Hitler for control of the Nazi party.

Since July 1933, Hitler had unsuccessfully tried to quell the agitation of the SA. The winter and spring of 1934 only brought more unrest in the form of numerous massive SA demonstrations and parades, along with public criticism of the current state of political affairs. Hitler's anxiety about this large uncontrollable force was shared by the army, Hindenburg, and substantial parts of the German population. An atmosphere of anticipation developed, creating fear among conservatives, in particular, of a radical social revolution. There were even rumors that Röhm was planning a revolt against Hitler.

The SA problem became complicated by renewed political initiatives from the conservative camp. The gangsterism and excesses of the Nazi party, the unruly and radical behavior of the SA, and the general tone of the Hitler regime finally prompted Papen and other conservatives to act. They sought a solution in the restoration of the monarchy upon the death of Hindenburg as a way of saving traditional German society and the state from Nazi barbarism. Papen, the intellectual Edgar Jung, members of the Catholic Action Group, and others began to express criticism of the new order and managed to get Hindenburg's support for their monarchist plans, though the president's backing of a monarchist restoration had not been made public. The views of the conservatives corresponded to a change in popular attitudes; the earlier mood of resignation by some and enthusiasm by others had given way to a sense of dissatisfaction. Feelings of anticipation were heightened by rumors that General Schleicher was again politically active. Then on June 17, 1934, in a speech at the University of Marburg, Papen openly criticized the dangers posed by the changes in German political and social life over the previous year. It was nothing less than a guarded attack on the Nazi revolution.

After remaining indecisive and uncertain for a period of months, Hitler reacted to these developments with swift and brutal measures. Using the excuse that Röhm was plotting a revolt, Hitler secretly prepared for the suppression of the SA leadership by his loyal elite guard, the SS. The army not only condoned this purge but supplied the SS with the arms used to destroy its competitor in the military sphere. Between June 30 and July 2, the SS struck in all parts of the country, arresting SA leaders and murdering almost two hundred. Among the most prominent Nazis killed were Röhm and Gregor Strasser, Hitler's former competitor for leadership of the NSDAP and an exponent of German socialism. During this "Night of the Long Knives," the SS murdered several innocent people and extended the killing beyond the list of alleged conspirators. The murdered included members of conservative circles as well. Schleicher, his wife, and his political adviser were shot, as were Papen's associate Edgar Jung and several other conservative and Catholic figures. Papen himself was placed under house arrest. The conservative opposition and the radical wing of the NSDAP were decimated.

Reactions to these purges and murders were mixed. On the one hand, the brutality and cold-bloodedness of the Nazis could no longer be denied. Attempts at hushing up the affair failed, and Hitler felt compelled to justify his actions. Once again resorting to the abuse of the principle of legality, Hitler had his cabinet pass a law on July 3 justifying the purge as a legal act in defense of the state. This was followed by the *Führer's* speech before the Reichstag on July 13. Hitler claimed he had acted to defend the country against a revolt, declaring that in the moment of extreme danger to the nation, he became the highest judge. Nonetheless, the citizens of Germany were shocked by the executions without trial and particularly by the murder of innocent people. But on the other hand, there was a sense of relief that the radical wing of the party had been tamed. Business interests and the middle classes as a whole no longer had to fear a social and economic revolution or an armed struggle within the NSDAP. The reaction of the army was similar. Although it was disturbed by the murder of Schleicher, the army was consoled by the fact that the purge of the SA had left the army as the sole force in military affairs. Military leaders now looked forward to the restoration of the old army to its former height of power and prestige; they also thought they would remain to a large extent free from political interference in internal military matters.

With the army placated and Hindenburg on the verge of senility and death, there was nothing in the way of Hitler's final consolidation of power.

When the president died on August 2, 1934, Hitler immediately announced that the office of president would be combined with that of chancellor. Thereafter, he would be the sole head of state and of the armed forces. This act was a violation of both German law and the Enabling Act, which protected the office of the president. But by this time, law was something to be manipulated or disregarded by the Nazis as their needs required, though Hitler continued to mask many of his actions with the cover of legality. On the day of Hindenburg's death, for example, all officers and troops in the military had to swear a legal oath of total obedience to Hitler. This oath was the final symbolic act in Hitler's establishment of an absolute dictatorship. It took fourteen years for him to rise to power and almost two more before he could grasp total control, but now he was truly the uncontested *Führer* of the German *Volk*.

1. Nazi Storm Troopers on parade. (National Archives)

2. Nazi mass rally at the Berlin Sportpalast. (National Archives)

3. NSDAP Standard: "Germany Awaken." (National Archives)

4. Hitler as charismatic orator. (National Archives)

5. Reich propaganda minister Josef Goebbels. (National Archives)

6. Storm Troopers advancing with Nazi colors. (National Archives)

7. (Left to right) Deputy *Führer* Rudolf Hess, Hitler, and *Gauleiter* Julius Streicher. (National Archives)

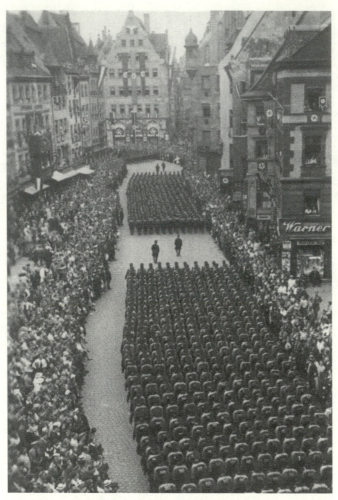

8. Nazi parade through Nuremberg. (National Archives)

9. The annual Nuremberg party rally. (National Archives)

10. Nazi propaganda poster: "Yes, *Führer*, we will follow you!" (U.S. Holocaust Memorial Museum Photo Archives)

11. Nazi women greet Hitler. (National Archives)

12. The Hitler Youth. (National Archives)

13. Members of the German Girls' League performing domestic chores. (National Archives)

14. A standard-bearer of the German Girls' League. (National Archives)

15. Hitler's motorcade through Nuremberg. (National Archives)

16. Hitler meets with German workers. (National Archives)

PART THREE

The Nazification of German Society, 1934–1938

I believe that one can no longer find anyone in Germany who doubts that the 30th of January has begun a new epoch in German historical development. . . . National Socialism is a worldview and it is only a question of now realizing its theories. . . . We want to undertake a fundamental change and are ready to implement a reform of every root and branch.

> —Josef Goebbels, Berlin Sportpalast, February 1933

The goal of our movement was to mobilize men, to organize men, and to win them over to the National Revolutionary idea. . . . The *Gleichschaltung* between the revolutionary government and the *Volk* will require an unflagging effort.

> —Josef Goebbels, speech to the press, March 1933

CHAPTER 8

The Total State
versus the
Dual State and Polycracy

The slogan *"Ein Volk, Ein Reich, Ein Führer"* left an indelible mark on the minds of most Germans who lived through the Nazi years. It appeared on countless posters and in publications; it was heard constantly in radio broadcasts and speeches. This concept of one nation, one empire, and one leader reflected the longstanding Nazi desire to transform Germany into a homogenous racial community, their ideal *Volksgemeinschaft*, led by the *Führer*. The Nazis proudly proclaimed that their Reich would be a total state, a society in which the party and its ideology would permeate every aspect of public and private life. In an attempt to institute this total state, the Nazis sought to penetrate existing state and public institutions, as well as to destroy or nazify all private organizations of the society. When Hitler emerged triumphant from the political struggles of 1934, it seemed on the surface that nothing could prevent the introduction of the total state, but the transformation of Germany into a totalitarian society remained incomplete. Although the breadth and depth of nazification was quite extensive, the Nazis failed to destroy many of the traditional institutions, patterns of behavior, and values of the old Germany. In various areas the Nazis found it necessary to make ideological and political compromises for reasons of economic expediency or to avoid the rise of opposition. Plagued by intraparty rivalries and incompetency, the Nazi power structure itself hindered the efficient implementation of totalitarianism. Consequently important existing institutions, laws, class distinctions, and values remained unchanged by the national revolution.

The Third Reich has been accurately described by Ernst Fraenkel as a dual state. During these years, Nazi ideology and institutions coexisted with many traditional institutions and beliefs. This relationship, however, was not an equal one. The Nazis might have failed to nazify certain institutions, but they had the power to intervene when necessary, and they never relented in their efforts to achieve the total state. Although the dual state existed until the end of the Third Reich, no institution was unaffected by nazism, and as time passed, Nazi penetration continually increased in many of those areas that resisted a complete Nazi takeover. Nazi totalitarianism was limited by the failure to capture the hearts and minds of millions of Germans or to change many beliefs and behavioral patterns, but the Nazis did exercise totalitarian political control over the life of every German. In the political sphere, the total state was a reality.

Totalitarian control was not exercised by a unified or centralized authority within the state or the party. The Third Reich was, in essence, a polycratic regime. The German people were affected by forces emanating from a variety of party and state offices. Outside of Hitler, there did not exist any central authority in charge of administering, governing, or reforming German society. In theory, the *Führer* state was one in which law was the will of the *Führer*; in practice, Hitler's word was absolute. But Hitler did not concern himself with the day-to-day business of governing, leaving this to subordinates. Hitler's directives were often vague, and often he did not address certain pressing issues of law, administration, or political authority. Below Hitler there were no clear lines of authority precisely defining the responsibilities and areas of control of each party or government office. The party never established a Nazi constitution or any coherent scheme of government organization, political authority, or law. Many state offices from the previous government structure remained intact and to these were added countless party offices. The duties of many of the offices overlapped, as did their authority; the result was duplication of function, bureaucratic struggles, inefficiency, and general confusion.

Clear directives from Hitler would be followed by all. Yet when these required interpretation, which was often the case, or when no directives were forthcoming, each state or party official had to decide for his own agency. Given the number of overlapping offices, conflicting interpretations and uncoordinated, sometimes contradictory, policies and laws were the norm during the Third Reich. The Nazi new order was not a paradigm of Germanic order and efficiency, with selfless party officials devoting their lives to the common interest or the goals of national socialism. The exact nature of national socialism and the policies necessary for its realization remained issues for dispute within the NSDAP. Government in the Third Reich was characterized by jealousy and bureaucratic empire-building. Party officials more often than not tended to view the will of the *Führer*, the welfare of the nation, and the goals of the ideology from the perspective of their own ideological orientation, career advancement, or the narrow interests of their particular organization. Party officials engaged in bureaucratic wars to expand their power and the area controlled by their organizations at the expense of other party or state offices, as well as to repulse jurisdictional encroachments by rival organizations. Recent research has indicated that the problems the Nazis later faced in occupied Europe forced greater cooperation among these polycratic institutions and centers of power. Nonetheless, the polycratic nature of the Third Reich did impede party-imposed totalitarianism on the Germans and the efficiency of the regime. Polycracy also begat endemic corruption, one of the worst characteristics of that party, state, and society.

To a certain extent, Hitler was personally responsible for the problems created by this organizational maze and polycracy. He rejected all attempts to institute uniform organizational structures or legal rules, for this would have added some structure and consistency to his personal exercise of power. Hitler preferred to maintain absolute power, unlimited even by rules that he himself would create. The will of the *Führer* was to remain something unstructured and spontaneous, subject to change and arbitrary decisions. The diffusion and overlapping of authority below Hitler assured the continuation of his absolute power and unchallenged leadership. Through favoritism, personal appointments, and the creation of new offices, he could acquire the allegiance of newly appointed high officials and reward old ones for their past loyalty. The competing and overlapping jurisdictions of different organizations served a similar purpose, as this situation prevented any single organization or its leader from emerging as a rival to Hitler.

Among the more important unresolved problems hindering the efficiency and unity of the Third Reich was the relationship between the Nazi party and the state apparatus that was in existence when Hitler came to power. In this area, the presence of a dual state was clearly evident. Although Hitler was the legal head of both the Nazi party and the German state, the two remained separate entities. Many higher Nazi officials, such as theorist Alfred Rosenberg, wanted to penetrate the state apparatus and reduce it to a mere instrument of the party, but their attempts met with only partial success, and even this took several years. Certain institutions of the state were nazified completely quite early; for example, Wilhelm Frick became minister of the interior and Walther Darré, minister of agriculture, while new ministries of state created by the Nazis went to such figures as Goebbels (propaganda) and Göring (air). However, until late in the Third Reich, many significant state offices were held by non-Nazi conservative bureaucrats and experts. The ministries of economics and finance were headed by such professionals as Hjalmar Schacht and Count Lutz von Schwerin-Krosigk, respectively, while the army was under the direction of Defense Minister Field Marshal Werner von Blomberg, and Constantin von Neurath served as foreign minister.

Constant struggle took place among many of the conservative ministers, who defended the independence of their agencies against party interference, and party leaders, who wanted to expand Nazi influence in these ministries. Party officials pressured the state offices headed by conservatives to appoint and promote members of the NSDAP and to bring the activities of these ministries into line with party policies and the goals of national socialism. Special efforts were also made to have civil servants join the party, thereby facilitating Nazi influence in the bureaucracy.

The legal and judicial systems became a major battleground between the old Germany and the Nazi new order. The Nazi Party Program had called for the introduction of a new legal system based upon a National Socialist version of an undefined type of Germanic law. But to a surprising degree, the existing legal system resisted Nazi attempts at completely revolutionizing German law and the courts along the lines of Nazi ideology. The complexities of a modern industrialized society, even within a totalitarian state, required established legal structures and procedures. A revolutionary transformation of the entire legal system would have been too disruptive to the social and economic order of Germany; it might also have elicited an adverse reaction from powerful sectors of the economy, whose assistance Hitler still needed for economic recovery and rearmament. Thus the Nazis tolerated much of the old legal system. In turn, the defenders of this system of justice recognized the realities of National Socialist power. They acquiesced in important changes in law and the judiciary demanded by the Nazis, while trying to salvage as much of the old system as possible. The concessions made by both sides resulted in a dual system of law for the duration of Nazi rule.

The traditional court system, like many laws and established procedures, remained in effect to a large extent. Next to this legal system there emerged a National Socialist system of law, which in some cases merely influenced the former and in other ways superseded it. In the long run, this second system, and the pressure it put on the first, did lead to substantial nazification of important areas of law and to a perversion of justice itself. Civil law was not drastically altered, particularly where the rights of private property were involved. In these areas, and even in many criminal cases, judges applied existing laws, adhered to due legal processes, and rendered just sentences. But judges now were bound by newly enacted Nazi laws as well; this meant the enforcement of such things as new civil service and racial laws, which violated the legal rights Germans had previously enjoyed. Though they might have done so reluctantly in many cases, judges now were assisting in the nazification of German society by ruling in accordance with new laws. Judges also were often under pressure to decide cases according to the will of the party, which made its position known in particular cases. The Nazis frequently subjected the courts and individual judges to public criticism in the press for their decisions.

The one sphere of law that the Nazis dominated directly was political crimes. In early 1933, special courts were established to handle such cases, which were then removed from the jurisdiction of the regular courts. The rights of defendants, including that of appeal, were greatly restricted in these special courts, which gained a reputation for swift judgments and harsh penalties, though not for justice. In 1934 the infamous people's court was founded to try cases of treason and crimes against the state. Its decisions were frequently based upon political considerations, party pressure, and prejudice rather than evidence of actual legal violations. Together, the special courts and the people's court represented nothing less than the politicization of justice; they were among the most effective means of suppressing and controlling the German population.

The principle of rule by law was more severely violated by Gestapo interference in legal matters. Certain decisions of even the special courts were disregarded by the Gestapo, which acted in violation of laws and procedures established by the Nazis themselves. In many instances, individuals were acquitted by the special courts only to be arrested and imprisoned by the Gestapo.

The limits of the total state were best illustrated by the degree of independence maintained by the army and economy. The *Wehrmacht*, with its conservative officer corps, was a bastion of traditionalism. Although members of this institution were disdainful of the upstart Nazis and the Bohemian corporal who was now their leader, they had tolerated the Nazi seizure of power, thereafter submitting to the authority of the Nazi regime. They pursued this course with the expectations that Hitler would bring about a national rejuvenation in Germany and that the army would regain its lost power and prestige. German generals assumed that the *Wehrmacht* would not only play an important role in German society but remain free of party interference. Rearmament, along with the elimination in 1934 of the SA as a competitor in the military sphere, seemed to indicate that these assumptions were correct. Hitler did not trust his generals; they were a part of the reactionary Germany he had struggled against for years, and they were probably the only force that had any realistic chance of toppling him from power. Nonetheless, he allowed the army a substantial amount of autonomy because he needed its leadership, expertise, and experience for the creation of a powerful modern war machine to back up his foreign policy. The army was not nazified.

For many years, military affairs remained the prerogative of the army, which successfully resisted direct party control. The significance of the independence of the *Wehrmacht* during the first half of the Third Reich went beyond its ability to defend its institutional interests against party encroachments. The army symbolized the traditions and values of the old Germany that conflicted with the Nazi ideology, as well as with the crude, often barbaric behavior and policies of the NSDAP. To many Germans, the army stood as a bulwark against the total nazification of German society and culture; many, in fact, looked to the army as a refuge from the barbarism spreading across the country.

Autonomy did not mean the army was entirely free from Nazi penetration or influence. The oath to Hitler sworn by every officer compelled the army to follow Hitler's directives, and, as a self-proclaimed expert in military affairs, the *Führer* often disputed the judgment of his generals. With each passing year the generals encountered a growing number of Nazi sympathizers within the rank and file of the *Wehrmacht*. This subtle influx of National Socialist sentiment, which tended to counterbalance the aristocratic values of the old officer corps, was a natural consequence of an expanded army. The reintroduction of a military draft in 1935 brought hundreds of thousands of new recruits into the *Wehrmacht*, many of whom were believers in nazism or had been greatly influenced by years of Nazi propaganda and indoctrination. Thus an ideological duality between the old Germany and the new existed even within this relatively autonomous institution.

Hitler made a similar pragmatic compromise in the economic sphere, where he sacrificed important ideological principles and goals in order to achieve other important objectives. Consequently, many of the Socialist and anticapitalist planks of the Party Program, like many of the promises the NSDAP had made to its middle-class supporters, would not be fulfilled by the new regime. Ideology played a secondary role in Hitler's economic policies compared to expediency in producing rapid economic recovery, autarchy (economic self-sufficiency), and rearmament. For reasons of expediency, Hitler did not attempt to nazify the economy. Instead, he left the actual running of the economy to experts in big business and industry, while instituting a large amount of control from above to force cooperation and compliance with his economic objectives. So long as they cooperated, big business and industry profited by this relationship, though the Nazis could, and did, interfere in the economic realm whenever necessary. In essence, the German economy under Hitler was neither totally free nor totally controlled.

Until 1937, Hitler placed the direction of his economic program in the hands of a non-Nazi, Hjalmar Schacht, president of the Reichsbank and minister of economics. Although Schacht tried to achieve German economic recovery and rearmament on the basis of sound fiscal policies, Hitler's demands forced greater state interference in the economy with each passing year. Schacht had to balance Nazi objectives with economic realities and powerful corporate interests. Big business and industry thrived but found their flexibility restricted by government regulations. The state set production objectives and quotas; it controlled prices, wages, and profits. Taxes were high, dividends were limited by law, and corporations were forced to buy large amounts of government bonds. These policies encouraged reinvestment and economic expansion, as well as providing the huge amounts of capital and government revenue necessary for rearmament.

Since massive unemployment had contributed so significantly to Hitler's political success, he knew that the credibility of his regime rested in part on a solution to this problem. The alleviation of unemployment in the first phase of the Third Reich resulted as much from a revival of capitalist confidence and investment as from Nazi-sponsored programs to create jobs. To Hitler's good fortune, Germany had already passed through the worst of the depression by the time he was appointed chancellor, and economic conditions showed gradual improvement in 1933. Although business confidence and recovery, which began to reduce unemployment, started before Nazi policies took effect, Hitler received credit for this. It cannot be denied that Hitler's policies were largely responsible for the elimination of unemployment within just a few years. By protecting business against the socialization demanded by leftists within the party, by encouraging business expansion, and by instituting rearmament, Hitler contributed further to business confidence and provided stimuli for economic recovery.

The Nazis also intervened directly to solve the unemployment problem by introducing various public works projects, but these were so limited in nature that they did not place a major financial burden on the government or alarm the business community with a specter of Nazi socialism. In actuality, the first state-supported public works projects begun in 1933 did not originate with the Nazis; they had been planned by the Schleicher government. These programs consisted of creating jobs by government-financed improvements in agriculture, housing construction, and street repair. To these were added a variety of other public works projects; among the most important were the *Autobahnen* (superhighways). The *Autobahn* project had a three-fold purpose: reduce unemployment, stimulate economic activity through government spending, and improve Germany's strategic position by greatly facilitating the rapid movement of troops and supplies from one part of the country to another.

Although Nazi expenditures for these projects were never as great as the society was led to believe, such action did help to legitimize the regime in the minds of millions of Germans. The Nazis seemed to be taking quick, effective measures to solve Germany's economic ills. Tens of thousands of jobs were created through public works, an expanded economy produced work for hundreds of thousands of others, and unemployment rates continued to drop. By 1934 the number of unemployed had been reduced to 3 million from its high of 6 million at the depth of the depression in 1932. The start of rearmament and the reintroduction of a military draft in 1935 absorbed the rest of the unemployed. By 1936 Germany had full employment, something that had never been achieved under Weimar's democracy, and Hitler could point to the elimination of unemployment as proof of the determination and effectiveness of his rule.

Concern for the plight of the unemployed was not the primary motivation for Hitler's economic policies. As evident in *Mein Kampf*, his main economic goals were rearmament and autarchy. Realizing that the acquisition of *Lebensraum* could be achieved only through war, Hitler wanted to rearm the nation as quickly as possible and at the same time reduce Germany's economic dependence on the outside world. Rearmament began slowly in 1933 but steadily picked up momentum with each year. In 1936 Hitler informed the party and army leadership that Germany must be prepared for war within four years. To accomplish this, Göring was placed in charge of a Four Year Plan that would give top priority to military needs; it would also ensure that the necessary production and raw material quotas would be met on schedule. Germany shifted production away from consumer goods and toward armaments, with tens of billions of marks (more funds than in any other nation) provided for military expenditures. Priority was also granted to achieving autarchy so that Germany could sustain itself in time of war, when imports might be cut off.

Schacht and big business did their best to accommodate themselves to Hitler's program, but until the middle of World War II, Germany did not have a totally mobilized war economy. Total mobilization was not Hitler's objective, since he envisioned a series of short wars against single opponents. However, even his more limited goals for war production and autarchy were never realized. Rearmament and autarchy required the importation and stockpiling of strategic materials on a huge scale. Approximately 80 percent of Germany's oil and iron ore, all of its rubber, and even part of its food supply came from abroad. Since these demands were beyond Germany's available foreign exchange, Hitler pressured industry to produce synthetics. While Germany eventually became self-sufficient in rubber through the use of synthetics, it never came close to its needs in other areas, particularly oil. The exceptionally high cost of synthetics and imports also continued to burden the Germany economy.

These problems were further aggravated by bureaucratic rivalries, corruption, and lack of sufficient coordination among various parts of the economy. The shortage of capital, raw materials, and labor led to competition among different economic sectors for these scarce resources. Thus it was impossible for many industries to meet their established quotas. Different industries, like many Nazi agencies, were often more concerned with their own interests than they were in cooperating for the common good or national objectives. Also, too many different Nazi agencies were involved in directing one aspect or another of the rearmament program and the economy. Although Göring had established a central office to coordinate these agencies and different industrial sectors, he proved to be inept. Neither a coherent systematic plan nor centralized control over the war economy materialized during the first Four Year Plan. In the end, German rearmament was quite impressive, but the war economy and autarchy envisioned by Hitler remained beyond reach. Unrealistic goals and bureaucratic muddling were perennial problems. By the outbreak of war, it would be clear that the German military machine and the war economy that supported it suffered from serious deficiencies. Certainly the German economy did not fit the Nazi image of a unified total state.

The major beneficiaries of Nazi economic policies were the Hitlerian state, the army, and large corporate enterprises. While a strong state and army were in keeping with the nationalistic aims of nazism, the preponderance of corporate power and other economic developments ran counter to many of the social, economic, and *völkisch* tenets of the National Socialist ideology. The Party Program had "demanded" profit sharing for employees of companies, the abolition of income not earned by work, and the nationalization of large corporations. Yet, under Nazi rule, corporate giants such as I. G. Farben, Krupp, and Siemens not only grew but accumulated more economic power and wealth, to the detriment of labor and smaller businesses. While big business and industry benefited most, employers and managers in general acquired increasingly greater incomes, creating a widening gap between the portion of the country's wealth shared between owners and employees.

Workers in the Third Reich lost most of their freedoms and rights, though historians disagree about whether their standard of living declined substantially. With their unions destroyed, workers had no say in their wages and conditions of employment, which were now regulated by the state. Despite economic recovery, real wages never rose to what they had been in 1928. Taxes were high; the cost of many consumer goods such as clothing and beer increased. Eventually, many workers lost the right to decide where they would live and the type of work they would do, since the government wanted to shift workers into regions and industries that needed labor.

On the other hand, workers were not cast into a condition of deprivation. To a certain extent, workers were pacified by what the Nazi state did provide. Full employment was an impressive accomplishment; job security, even at lower wages, and undesirable jobs were certainly preferable to unemployment. Workers usually compared their wages with the lower ones of the depression era rather than with the much higher rate of 1928. From this perspective they were enjoying a marked improvement in their lives. Skilled workers and youths gained much more under the new economic program. A serious shortage of skilled labor created by economic expansion and rearmament led to even higher wages and better working conditions for those who could meet these needs of industry. Working-class youths benefited from state-promoted vocational training and job placement. The rising cost for certain consumer goods was counterbalanced by a decline in the price of others, as well as by state subsidies in special areas and controls on rents and heating costs. Workers received additional benefits in the form of paid holidays, subsidized tours and vacations, and party-sponsored recreational and social activities. Workers did not become devoted followers of national socialism, but neither were they driven to revolt out of economic dissatisfaction with the new regime.

The lower-middle class and farmers, from whom the Nazis had originally drawn most of their support, gained the least from Nazi economic policies. White-collar workers maintained their class status above laborers, and they increased in numbers under the Third Reich because of economic expansion and bureaucratic proliferation. Like the working classes, they received security rather than economic or social advancement. Many older white-collar workers, in fact, had to accept working-class jobs. The average small businessman, shopkeeper, and artisan found that his position either did not improve or deteriorated, despite Nazi propaganda about protecting the little man. Some did benefit from economic expansion and government contracts. Others, however, found it difficult to survive the high taxes, wage-price regulations, and strong competition from big business, which was usually favored by government policies.

The continuing economic decline of small farmers indicated more than just a reneging on political promises. It directly contradicted many essential elements in the Nazi *völkisch* philosophy. From the late twenties through the Third Reich, Nazi propaganda presented the German peasant and small farmer as the racial backbone of the nation. They were idolized as the purest form of the *Volk*, who had remained close to the soil from which German culture had grown, retaining their strength through hard work and their moral vitality through adherence to ancient Germanic values. This *völkisch* core had not been tainted by the moral decadence and physical weaknesses caused by modern ideas, urbanization, and industrialization. They were the nation's future, not its past. Nazi theorists insisted that eventually most Germans would be resettled on the land; these same theorists lambasted big cities and industrial life as major factors in the decline of the race. Trends toward moral and physical decadence had to be counteracted by preserving small farms and by stopping the migration from the countryside into the cities. Nazi policies, however, promoted just the opposite.

Industrialization was a fact of life and the foundation of Germany's power. For this reason, industry received top priority in Hitler's calculations. Early in the Third Reich, conditions did improve for the small farmer, but as the war economy made greater demands on the resources of the country, he fell further behind and received a declining share of the nation's wealth. Nazi programs to assist farmers were insufficient and quite limited compared to the programs implemented to expand large industrial enterprises. As time went on, the struggle for survival intensified for the small farmer, whose position was made more difficult by the shortage of labor. Here again Nazi economic policies undermined *völkisch* goals. Tremendous labor demands in industrial sectors drew hundreds of thousands of workers from rural areas into the cities. Nazi policies encouraged rather than slowed this migration. In this respect, the creation of a strong economy and war machine was achieved even at the risk of a further decline in the purest of the racial stock the Nazis cherished so much.

Such ideological compromises for the sake of expediency precluded a social and economic revolution in the Third Reich. Much had changed in the new order, yet much had remained the same. Workers were still workers; small businessmen and farmers continued to confront longstanding economic problems. For neither of these groups had the Nazis ushered in a new era of prosperity, and no drastic alteration was made in the relationships between economic and social classes. The Nazi revolution had not swept away reactionary groups and the upper classes to make way for a better society for the little man. Reactionary aristocrats continued to play crucial roles in the army, and conservatives still staffed most of the bureaucracy; the status and social prestige enjoyed by both had remained unaffected. Upper-class families and corporate leaders retained their central place in economic affairs, receiving a disproportionate share of the country's wealth. Most Germans remained as class-conscious as they had been under Weimar.

Despite the failure to destroy the traditional class and economic systems, the Nazis never abandoned the vision of a *Volksgemeinschaft*. In their propaganda, speeches, and writings, they continually emphasized the need for *Gemeinschaft*. Although Germans belonged to different classes and had different jobs and incomes, they were all considered *Volksgenossen* (racial comrades), united by blood and a common national destiny. Society might be organized as a hierarchy of talent, wealth, and occupation, but all Germans had equal social status by the mere fact that they were a part of the German race and worked for the general good of the total *Gemeinschaft*. The Nazis were relentless in their efforts to downplay class consciousness and replace it with a national consciousness. They encouraged workers to view themselves as the social equals of other classes, and many of their policies were aimed at breaking down traditional class barriers. To a certain extent, there did exist greater social mobility in Nazi Germany than under any previous regime. The Nazis also introduced a new dimension to German social relationships. The Nazi party itself, which had millions of members and played a pervasive role in German society, almost approximated a new social class. Membership in the party, especially at the higher ranks, automatically conveyed special social status regardless of one's class origins. Even those in the lower ranks had achieved a certain status, distinction, and honor by the fact that they were a part of organized national socialism.

These changes notwithstanding, the Third Reich was not a *Gemeinschaft*. Class identity and class consciousness remained strong. It is doubtful that many aristocrats or upper-class Germans ever really accepted the upstart Nazis as their social equals or viewed the workers and peasants as their comrades. And though many lower-class Germans might have been susceptible to Nazi propaganda about equality of worth and status, it is questionable how many felt equal to those above them. Similarly, century-long religious and regional differences were not eradicated by efforts to instill the sense of national identity required by a true *Gemeinschaft*. Nazi Germany might have been "One Reich," but within it there were many who still thought of themselves as Bavarians and Prussians, Berliners and Rhinelanders, Catholics and Protestants, workers and aristocrats.

The dominant group in German society during these years was the Nazi party. For various reasons it compromised certain ideological tenets and did not nazify every segment of society and economics. As the dominant force, however, it could interfere whenever necessary, and with certain significant exceptions it was usually successful in imposing its will on issues of importance to the party. Each year saw greater Nazi interference in German life and institutions. In this regard, the years 1937 and 1938 were a turning point in the nazification of Germany. In January of 1937, a new civil service law required all bureaucrats to be members of the NSDAP. They also had to swear an oath to Hitler personally and display enthusiasm for national socialism. Party influence over the bureaucracy was extended further by the fact that Hitler would now personally appoint members of the upper echelons of the civil service. With such changes the Nazi goal of making the civil service a tool of the party was closer to realization. Later in the year, the planning and direction of the economy was taken over by the Nazi leadership when Schacht resigned as minister of economics. Göring filled this position for about a year before handing it to Nazi press chief Walter Funk. Hitler's decision in 1938 to tighten his control over the army and the execution of foreign policy was even more important. The German generals and conservative foreign minister Constantin von Neurath expressed serious reservations about Hitler's course in foreign affairs, which they feared would lead to war at a time when Germany was still unprepared. Therefore, Hitler removed Neurath and gave his post to the self-proclaimed Nazi expert on foreign affairs Joachim von Ribbentrop, who was mostly concerned with pleasing his *Führer* rather than providing realistic advice on foreign policy. Along with the removal of Neurath was a purge of the top army command. Field Marshal von Blomberg was accused (wrongly) of dishonoring the officer corps by marrying an alleged prostitute, and General von Fritsch was undermined by false testimony about homosexual activities. Blomberg was forced to resign as war minister and Fritsch lost his post as commander of the army. Thereafter, Hitler appointed himself commander-in-chief of the military.

By 1938 the top positions in the civil service, army, and foreign ministry were in Nazi hands. These changes did not eliminate the dual state, because the army was never nazified and most professional civil servants, despite their required party membership, were still conservative in their ideological orientation. But the conservative counterweight to Hitler's reckless economic, political, and military course, which up to this point had existed at the upper levels of government, was removed. The cautious and realistic counsel of these conservative former top leaders was replaced by the advice of more submissive figures. The new generals and old party guard Hitler gathered around him were reluctant to dispute the will or judgment of the *Führer*. Subsequent events would show how disastrous these changes would be for Germany.

CHAPTER 9

Political Biology, Culture, and Society

The concept of the total state implied that every aspect of German cultural and social life reflect the tenets of the Nazi *völkisch* ideology. Before coming to power, the Nazis had anticipated a complete social and cultural revolution, but class and economic systems did not undergo a revolutionary transformation, and Nazi social policies often contradicted their ideology. Nonetheless, the Nazis did introduce far-reaching changes in German society, and the effects of their cultural policies were truly revolutionary. This is particularly so concerning Nazi racial ideology. Despite its polycratic tendencies, the regime was, in policy and practice, unified by a political biology that became the fundamental principle of the Third Reich. Its societal and cultural goals emanated from racial beliefs.

For the first time in history, a group holding political power was able to create a racial state. It was to be a society in which biology was destiny. The presumed biological makeup of the German race would affect all aspects of private as well as public life. Supposedly, national characteristics, levels of intelligence, and social behavior were determined not by culture, environment, or history but by the genetic pool created by the long process of natural evolution that had created the distinctive races of man. The Aryan or Nordic race had evolved with unique traits that placed it at the top of the racial hierarchy as the creator of higher civilization. The survival and future advance of this civilization thus depended upon the continued domination of the great race that had created it. To achieve this goal, the Aryan race must protect its purity, expand in size, and prove powerful enough to triumph over competing races in the eternal struggle for survival. It must ensure its own racial homogeneity and vibrancy by preventing the dilution of the strength of its genetic pool from within and without. Internal racial degeneracy could be inhibited by a eugenics program. The external biological threat could be combated by averting inbreeding with inferior races.

Within months of the seizure of power in 1933, the Nazis initiated a series of racial hygienic laws and policies that would be expanded over the next decade into a full-scale eugenics program. These were directed at Germans who, due to an alleged hereditary physical, mental, or behavioral deficiency, threatened the racial vibrancy of the *Volksgemeinschaft*. Deemed of "lesser racial value" than healthy and hereditarily sound Aryans, these Germans were subject to compulsory sterilizations and abortions mandated by the law and enforced by the courts. These included people with physical deformities, hereditary blindness and deafness, manic depression and schizophrenia, feeble-mindedness, and even chronic alcoholism. The Nazis sterilized over 300,000 of these alleged racial defectives. To ensure healthy offspring, all couples had to acquire health office fitness certificates before they could marry.

While Nazi sterilization policies and practices, like the later euthanasia program, elicited mixed reactions from the German population, even resistance from the churches, the regime's broader campaign of racial and social purification often had broader public support. Since racial theorists attributed particular "asocial" behavior to hereditary causes, racial science often masked mere social prejudice. Thus not only could the Nazis invoke the authority of science and alleged medical necessity, but they also could rely on deeply entrenched social biases, concerns, and fears. The social groups the Nazis targeted for condemnation and suppression had already been persecuted throughout history and been social outcasts in pre-Nazi Germany. Some groups had been restricted by earlier laws as well as socially stigmatized. The Nazis gradually radicalized such prejudices from social disdain and legal suppression to the point of systematic murder.

Vagrants, the chronically unemployed, habitual criminals, homosexuals and lesbians, or just those who deviated from commonly expected lifestyles could face roundups, preventive detention, sterilization, or later death in concentration camps. Women were particularly susceptible to classifications of inherited mental illness and asocial behavior. Promiscuity, illegitimate children, merely appearing to be a problem child, or being someone neighbors found socially troublesome or unacceptable could result in a "scientific" judgment for court-ordered sterilization of women. But all lesser members of the race needed to be identified, contained, and restrained from propagating so that only the "healthy" and "fit" could multiply and flourish.

Although Hitler clearly shared the antihomosexual attitudes of that era, he had little interest in homosexuality as a policy issue. Other leaders, however, notably the extremely homophobic Himmler, were obsessed with homosexuality. Outlawed since 1871, homosexuality was nonetheless more publicly expressed in the culturally tolerant big cities of the Weimar republic, where legal enforcement was lax. Conservatives and religious groups had condemned such open homosexuality, like abortion, as evidence of Germany's catastrophic cultural degeneration caused by the sexual license of decadent Weimar society. The Nazis cleverly exploited such issues and channeled this discontent into their overall campaign against modernist trends in artistic expression and social values. Having promised to save German decency and morality from such decadence, the Nazis, once in power, integrated antihomosexual attitudes into their racial ideological panorama. Though lesbians were also viewed as culturally decadent, male homosexuals were the primary focus in the masculine-minded world of national socialism, where manly and militaristic values predominated against the presumed femininity, weakness, and cowardice of homosexual men. Himmler personally believed that homosexuals were pederasts and a danger to young Germans. But, in general, anything other than heterosexuality was a violation of the natural order of the universe on which Nazi political biology was based. Such unnatural behavior would sap the essential vitality of the *Volk*. Homosexuality and abortion would hinder Germany's recovery from its demographic losses in World War I, as well as slow the expansion of the Nordic race crucial to Hitler's visions of a continentally dominant Third Reich.

Stricter enforcement of existing antihomosexual laws was followed by the establishment in 1936 of the Reich Central Office for the Combating of Homosexuality and Abortion. Ridiculed in Nazi publications as "enemies of the state" and abhorrent, abnormal beings, homosexuals found themselves under surveillance by police and informants. They were arrested in larger numbers until some eight thousand were convicted in 1938. By that time, most of those incarcerated went to concentration camps instead of prison. Of the fifty thousand convicted of homosexuality, approximately ten to fifteen thousand suffered the indignity and inhumanity of the camps. Given traditional societal prejudice and Nazi ideological derision, those forced to wear the "pink triangle" were among the most vulnerable of camp inmates. Scorned as reprehensible deviants not only by guards but by fellow prisoners, they were often singled out for abuse, death-inducing labor, or systematic extermination by the SS. In search of a cure for homosexuality, Himmler personally ordered medical experimentation on these helpless men.

To promote their racial vision for society, the Nazis employed scholars, scientists, and institutions to conduct racial research justifying and elaborating their claims to the scientific validity of their ideas. While established institutes and academics lent credibility to Nazi racial doctrine, the regime created new racial offices to coordinate such work and publicize it widely. Such research provided the necessary data for Nazi eugenics planning at home and later for their racial policies in conquered Europe. Equally important, it advanced Hitler's desire to convince the German people to accept a new societal consensus based upon an all-pervasive racial theory.

A primary goal of those Nazis who dealt with cultural affairs was to mobilize the German people in support of the new regime and to instill a National Socialist consciousness that would ensure loyalty as well as an enthusiastic commitment to the racial cause. Nazi ideologues believed that they were engaged in a cultural struggle that would determine the future of the German race. Therefore, they could no more tolerate freedom in the cultural realm than they could accept opposition or independent forces within the political sphere. The counterpart to the political total state was a homogeneous total racialist culture.

In waging this cultural war, the Nazis relied heavily upon a narrow and distorted sense of morality. Every idea, style, and mode of thought or expression that did not conform to the *völkisch* perception of life was considered immoral and decadent. True German culture was that which grew out of the blood, traditions, and spirit of the *Volk*. It was a reflection of the very soul of the people and must be free of foreign influence. Since *völkisch* culture embodied the traditional values of family, fatherland, morality, heroism, and strength, anything that challenged these values was condemned as a danger to the well-being of the race. The major threat, according to the Nazis, came from Jewish influences and from those German intellectuals and artists associated with the general cultural trend known as modernism. In fact, modernism itself was viewed as a foreign influence brought to Germany by the Jews and other enemies, who were trying to undermine the moral fiber of society, thereby weakening the country from within. Modern architecture, expressionist art and music, aspects of popular culture such as modern dancing and jazz, and literature critical of German traditions were all categorized as cultural bolshevism. Hitler frequently referred to these as a moral plague poisoning the German people; he called for a cleansing of the culture in all fields. Individual freedom of expression, he stated, must be secondary to the preservation of the race and its moral vitality. In the Third Reich, culture would be tightly controlled and regulated to guarantee that every manifestation of it would be in the interest of the total *Gemeinschaft* as defined by the Nazis.

The cleansing of German culture and the creation of the proper National Socialist spirit were to be brought about by a process similar to the one employed in grasping total political power. The Nazi cultural revolution began with the extension of the policy of *Gleichschaltung* to cultural and social institutions. The emergency decrees of early 1933 had already greatly restricted the free press and given the Nazis almost a monopoly over the radio medium.

Fear of legal action by the Nazi-controlled state or of political reprisals had produced a certain degree of compliance with the wishes of the new regime. Thus the shift toward cultural conformity had started quite early. With the creation of the Ministry of Propaganda under Goebbels in March of 1933, Germany entered a new phase of state-enforced discipline, regimentation, and censorship in all areas of publishing. Thereafter, the Nazis could control the flow of most information to the German people and manipulate the minds of millions with distortions, half-truths, and lies. Nazi interpretations of events would go unchallenged, and their one-sided views would be spread by an ever-expanding Nazi publishing network.

Another landmark in achieving total control over German culture came in September of 1933, when a Reich cultural chamber was established granting Goebbels authority to reorganize and regulate virtually every facet of German cultural life. Every artist, writer, musician, and performer had to join a cultural chamber in his particular field in order to practice his profession. Goebbels used this authority to enforce ideological conformity by purging or refusing membership to anyone who deviated from the narrow themes, modes of expression, and standards the Nazis found acceptable. Jews, leftists, and those experimenting with new styles no longer had an opportunity to engage in their professions; others were faced with the alternatives of conforming or meeting a similar fate to those already excluded. The result was a tremendous loss of talent, a stifling of free intellectual activity, and an end to one of Germany's most magnificent periods of creativity, one that had made Weimar culture so rich and of such enduring value. In its place there arose a cold, mostly sterile culture dominated by *völkisch* themes and Nazi-dictated styles.

Starting in early 1933, a steady stream of intellectuals left Germany for various parts of the world. They became exiles out of protest against the new regime or because the Reich cultural chamber had prevented them from practicing their professions. Among the more than two thousand intellectuals that would eventually go into exile were Nobel Prize–winning novelist Thomas Mann, physicist Albert Einstein, playwright Bertolt Brecht, and Erich Maria Remarque, author of *All Quiet on the Western Front*. This migration was welcomed by the Nazis, who saw this as the beginning of the purification of German culture. When these emigrés began criticizing the Hitler dictatorship from abroad, the Nazis reacted by charging them with treason. In the eyes of the Nazis the activities of the emigrés proved that they had been a threat to the state and that, in fact, these intellectuals had never been true members of the German nation.

Behind the charges of disloyalty launched against the emigrés stood a general anti-intellectual sentiment. From his earliest years, Hitler despised intellectuals, and his hatred was shared by many within the NSDAP. Most Nazis did not value thought and cultivation of the intellect, but preferred action and a reliance upon instinct; abstract thinking was degraded as a Jewish characteristic. The repercussions of this anti-intellectualism were apparent quite early. On May 10, 1933, SA men and Nazi students across the country lit huge bonfires in which thousands of books were publicly burned. Jewish, liberal, Socialist, and other so-called un-German works were thrown into the flames before cheering crowds. The treasonous intellectuals had been banished, and now their ideas had to be erased from the German memory.

The book burnings were only a part of the general cultural revolution that took many different forms. Not only were certain writers prohibited from publishing, but extensive blacklists were compiled of works to be purged from libraries. Many newspapers also were closed, while those that remained in business had to impose upon themselves a large degree of censorship to please the propaganda ministry. To withhold criticism of the Third Reich was insufficient; publishers had to display the proper tone supportive of the new regime. Journalists and publishers received lectures from the propaganda ministry on the role of the press in the new society, and they were usually informed on how to deal with particular news items.

The impact of this new trend in publishing had a particularly devastating effect on German literature. The vacuum left by the purge of many of the works of Germany's literary masters was filled by publications of a nationalistic or *völkisch* orientation. Hans Grimm's 1926 book *People without Space* enjoyed enormous success during the Third Reich because its theme was in tune with Nazi thoughts on *Lebensraum*. In place of the stimulating poetry of Heinrich Heine there appeared poems by Nazis, such as Hanns Johst and Baldur von Schirach, the leader of the Hitler Youth. Johst, who dedicated one of his books to Heinrich Himmler, once said, "Whenever I hear the word *culture*, I cock my pistol," and Schirach proclaimed that there was only one essential book, *Mein Kampf*, from which all strength would flow for the struggle for Germany. There were countless works in the genre known as "blood and soil literature," which usually idolized the life and character of the purest of the *Volk*—the peasantry. Other works stressed German racial superiority or heroic leadership. Books dealing with the dedication and heroism of German soldiers during World War I were especially favored by the party. There were exceptions, of course. One of Germany's most gifted writers, Gottfried Benn, continued to be productive for some time, but only because he publicly supported the Nazi regime in its early phase. And an abundance of general literature of an apolitical and noncommittal nature was produced and tolerated by the party so long as it did not deviate from the new standards of cultural conformity.

The decline of the German educational system was no less drastic than that of the quality of literary creativity. While the purges of the universities sent some of Germany's best minds into exile, those professors who remained found their activities closely scrutinized by the party. The cherished ideals of freedom of instruction and research, along with rigorous academic standards for students, which for generations had made the German university a model for the rest of the world, rapidly disappeared. As Nazi educator Ernst Krieck put it, the *völkisch* university no longer recognized a private sphere of existence for students and faculty; there was only public service. Each university instructor had to join the Nazi Lecturers' Association, which gave the party control over appointments and promotions. Few professors were willing to endanger their careers by pursuing research that might be disapproved.

In certain politically sensitive areas, the Nazis dictated the trends and results of research. The Reich Institute for the History of the New Germany, headed by Walter Frank, was organized to rewrite history from the perspective of the Nazi racial ideology. Objectivity and rigorous historical methodology gave way to ideology; the picture of the past became greatly distorted, if not totally invented. Research was also hampered by the ban on the use of Jewish works and ideas. It became virtually impossible to deal adequately with those fields of scholarship in which Jewish researchers had made substantial contributions. Even the politically neutral area of natural science became a center of ideological controversy. Nobel Prize winner Philipp Leonard, an advocate of pure "German physics," argued that scientific thought was conditioned by blood and race. It was his contention that research by Aryans alone had furnished the foundations of modern science, but that this achievement was now being undermined by a type of "Jewish science" that was not based on truth. Leonard accused the eminent German physicist and Nobel recipient Werner Heisenberg of teaching "Jewish physics" because of the latter's use of Einstein's relativity theory. Subsequently, Heisenberg was attacked in the *Völkischer Beobachter*, and the SS paper *Das Schwarze Korps* called him a "White Jew" who must be banished like the Jews. Although Heisenberg survived this criticism and scientific progress was made in the Third Reich, the climate was hardly conducive to free inquiry, and advances in science came at a much slower pace than previously.

It was difficult to replace those removed from universities with scholars who were both highly talented and acceptable to the Nazis. Positions of importance were granted to many who would never have been considered under the old system. Reinhard Höhn's appointment to a prestigious chair of public law at the University of Berlin was not due to his scholarship in jurisprudence, but to his position as an SS officer in the Security Service. Pressures from the party and Nazi student organizations also led to a dramatic lowering of university admission standards, producing a corresponding drop in performance among students and in demands by professors.

Part of the problem faced by the university system was caused by the deterioration of conditions in the primary and secondary schools. Recognizing that the future of Germany depended upon the young, the Nazis were particularly concerned that the minds of the nation's youth be molded according to the dictates of national socialism; entire sections of *Mein Kampf* had been devoted to the question of education. In nazifying the school system, the party concentrated mainly on control of teachers, changes in curriculum, and establishment of special elite schools. The collaboration of teachers was acquired without exceptional difficulty. Many teachers were nationalistic and conservative by nature; indeed, a large number of teachers had been supporters and members of the NSDAP. And like other segments of society, most non-Nazi teachers quickly fell in line as *Gleichschaltung* proceeded. Membership in the Nazi Teachers' Association became mandatory, and this institution served as an additional means of party influence. Teachers were obligated to undergo special training to indoctrinate them in National Socialist educational goals and methods. The effectiveness of teachers was greatly undermined by the general anti-intellectual climate of the Third Reich, a growing hostility toward teachers shown by pupils, and the preoccupation of pupils with the outside activities encouraged by Nazi youth organizations.

The level of education suffered equally from curriculum changes. The cultural purge included the destruction of many textbooks with which the party disagreed, so a shortage of books existed. The traditional classical education, which had formerly prepared the best pupils for entry into a university, was de-emphasized in favor of history, biology, and the German language. While history courses were designed to provide a proper National Socialist consciousness of the past and of politics in general, biology was a means of teaching racial doctrine. Not only were pupils taught Nazi racial theories about the hereditary behavioral characteristics of different groups, but they were instructed in how to identify various racial "types," such as Nordics and Jews, by measuring their skulls. Competitive sports and physical education received special priority, since Hitler considered the development of the body and strength more essential to the future of the race than academic studies.

The creation of elite institutions such as Adolf Hitler Schools to train and cultivate the future leadership of Germany served a similar ideological purpose. They did not stress development of the intellect, and admission was not determined by brilliance. A basic educational curriculum existed in these schools, but they dealt mostly with ideological indoctrination, military discipline and training, and rigorous sports activity. Entry was reserved for those who had the purest racial characteristics and who displayed leadership, strength, devotion, and courage.

In general, pupils received an inadequate education and one that left them with a distorted perception of life and the world around them. Many pupils had difficulty passing courses, and university professors complained that the new generation of students was not prepared for higher education. University students were particularly deficient in foreign languages and knowledge of scientific research methods.

Völkisch theories of education were matched by Nazi ideas about the arts. Hitler's artistic pretensions, peculiar tastes, and strong opinions on the subject meant that the arts would be given particular attention. Since Hitler regarded modern art as decadent, many of the most impressive creations of Weimar culture became objects of ridicule and were destroyed by the Nazis. Only realistic, neoclassical, and *völkisch* themes and styles were acceptable. The Reich chamber of fine arts prohibited modern artists from continuing to create, and their existing works were displayed only in exhibits for "Degenerate Art"; these works were removed from museums and galleries. Literally thousands of works were confiscated, and over four thousand pieces were publicly burned in 1939. The new art was to be a reflection of the heroic and *völkisch* perception of reality. Sculptures and paintings of Nordic nudes and heroic soldiers were created in neoclassical style, since Hitler considered classical models to be the highest standards of beauty. The new style was a type of National Socialist realism, in which figures and scenes were depicted in detailed and easily comprehensible forms, as opposed to the abstractions in the works of many of Weimar's expressionists. The most clearly *völkisch* art was romanticized depictions of the purity and stability of peasant life in an idyllic country setting.

In the minds of the Nazis there was nothing inconsistent with the mixture of neoclassical and Germanic themes and styles. Nazi racial theorists claimed that the original ancient Greeks were Nordic, and Hitler himself stated that the highest culture, which he was struggling to preserve against Judaism and Bolshevism, was a combination of Hellenic and Germanic civilizations. Like education, Nazi art projected a false picture of life, for little of the new art mirrored the modern industrial and urban existence of most Germans.

Hitler's personal influence in the arts was greatest in the field of architecture. He considered architecture more than any other form of expression the most powerful and enduring manifestation of a culture and civilization. He had a penchant for architecture on a monumental scale built in neoclassical style. Only such gigantic structures made of large, heavy stones could truly represent the overwhelming power and greatness of a Reich that would found the most magnificent civilization in history and last for a thousand years. Since Nazi architects catered to the *Führer*'s tastes and desires in their writing, planning, and creations, monumental architecture became the norm for public buildings. As a self-proclaimed expert in architecture, Hitler helped design several public structures with his personal architect Albert Speer. One of Speer's most impressive achievements was the design of the parade grounds, arena, and congress hall in Nuremberg where the annual party rallies were held. Built to accommodate hundreds of thousands of participants and spectators, the huge outdoor structures were made of large stones and illuminated by searchlights that created a mystical, Wagnerian atmosphere during evening programs. The feeling of power and of a unified *Volksgemeinschaft* reflected in these rallies was due in no small measure to this architectural setting.

While monumental architecture in the major cities expressed power and unity, the styles used in housing in some towns and suburbs were a manifestation of the *völkisch* tradition. Since peasant culture was allegedly a direct, untainted outgrowth of Germanic blood and soil, peasant cottages became a model for a kind of pure *völkisch* architecture. New homes were constructed in half-timber style with thatched roofs so as to resemble a romanticized version of peasant existence. This was a nostalgic attempt to resist the modern world by creating new homes in the style of an age that had long vanished.

Antimodernism and racism had a similar impact on Nazi policies toward music. A ban on Jewish musicians and their works was only a part of the tragic destruction of Weimar's golden age of music. All modern themes and styles were attacked. Atonal music was considered Jewish, and jazz was called "Negro noise"; both were found contrary to the cultural foundations of national socialism. Even those pieces by classical German composers who the party felt were partially influenced by Jews had to be rewritten or reinterpreted. As in other areas of culture, there emerged in music racial studies to support Nazi demands for purification. Works such as *Music and Race* by Richard Eichenauer laid the foundations for an entire field of racial music theory. Some students of this theory claimed an ability to identify distinctly Jewish sounds and forms. The new cultural climate opened the way for a renaissance in German folk music and a revival of the romantic songs of the youth movement. To these were added countless popular songs about national socialism, honoring the heroes and martyrs of the party and the national revolution. The most famous Nazi work of this type, of course, was the "Horst Wessel Song," which served as the party anthem. In a similar way, the rejuvenation of a nationalistic and militaristic spirit in the Third Reich meant a greater emphasis on military music and marches.

Under the circumstances, classical music fared quite well, despite the loss of some of Germany's foremost conductors and the ban on numerous works. One reason was ideological. The masterpieces of Beethoven, Mozart, and Schumann were seen as additional proof of Germanic cultural superiority. However, like most Germans, the Nazis also showed a basic pride in the nation's rich artistic heritage, especially in classical music. Göring and several other top leaders in the party flattered themselves by acting as patrons of the arts, which ensured substantial government support for concerts, operas, and musicians. A mixture of national pride, artistic appreciation, and ideology granted the music of Richard Wagner special status within the Third Reich. There was much in the work of this nineteenth-century musical and theatrical genius with which the Nazis could identify. Quite extreme in his nationalistic sentiments and statements, Wagner had sought to inspire a Germanic cultural rejuvenation through his work. The romantic myths of ancient Germanic gods and medieval heroes contained in his operas fit in perfectly with the Nazi *völkisch* consciousness. Wagner was also a vehement anti-Semite who claimed that the Jews were incapable of creating music or poetry and were corrupting German art with their money. During the Third Reich, Wagner's music was played at cultural and social events. From the beginning, his music was an integral part of the Nazi party rallies at Nuremberg. The annual Wagnerian Bayreuth Festival in Bavaria was soon transformed from a national event into a National Socialist cultural phenomenon faithfully attended by the *Führer*.

Reuniting Germans with their mythological past was one intention of the *Thingspiel*, the only unique Nazi cultural innovation. A *Thing* was an ancient Germanic tribal assembly. The Nazis tried to re-create the spirit of these gatherings through an outdoor theatrical performance known as a *Thingspiel*. Heroes and action, evil spirits and ancient oaths, elaborate ceremonies and powerful choruses provided the contents of the *Thingspielen*, which were held in specially constructed amphitheaters called *Thing* places. These amphitheaters were built directly into the hills outside towns and cities in order to bring the audience into a unity with nature and the Germanic soil. Since a major purpose of the *Thingspiel* was to inspire a feeling of *Gemeinschaft*, audience participation was often a part of a performance. About forty *Thing* places were constructed in various parts of Germany using monumental and neoclassical architecture. The largest ones could accommodate several thousand people. Although many exponents of "blood and soil" theories considered the *Thingspiel* the ideal medium, and the *Thing* place the perfect setting, for such revivalistic *völkisch* celebrations, most Germans did not find them a lasting attraction. Some early success was followed by public apathy, and the *Thingspiel* turned out to be a failure.

Public apathy was a serious problem for the Nazi regime. The Third Reich had millions of enthusiastic supporters who were thrilled by the excitement and fanfare of the parades, rallies, and public ceremonies of the new order. But the oppressive nature and regimentation of Nazi Germany left millions of others in a state of depression. They wanted their entertainment to offer an escape. Not surprisingly the most popular form of mass entertainment was the cinema, and movie attendance increased most dramatically during the Nazi years. Since Goebbels realized this escapist need within the population, he did not turn German cinema into a major vehicle for propaganda. The overwhelming majority of films in Nazi Germany were produced mostly for entertainment rather than to convey a political or ideological message. Comedies, love stories, and adventures were in demand, but because of the lack of freedom and of talent, Nazi cinema did not match the achievements of Weimar film. Some of Germany's most talented directors and actors were now living abroad, and an awareness of the threatening hand of the party was always present. Producers and directors had to take care not to offend Nazi moral, social, or ideological sensibilities.

Goebbels had not abandoned cinema as a propaganda tool, but used it with care so as to make it a more effective political instrument. The most talented directors, producers, and actors in Nazi Germany were used to make political films. Consequently, films dealing with war and Germany's great historical leaders were among the most elaborate and successful productions in the Nazi era of cinema. Preference also was given to films with *völkisch* plots and characters and to films designed to incite hatred toward the Jews. Perhaps the most vile of all Nazi anti-Semitic films was *Jew Süss*, which depicted the torture and rape of an innocent Aryan girl at the hands of a crafty and vengeful Jew. Yet some films and directors from this period earned lasting international recognition. Leni Riefenstahl's *Triumph of the Will* won the grand prize at the 1937 International Exposition of the Arts in Paris, and as late as 1974 she was honored at a Film Festival in Colorado. A documentary of the 1934 Nuremberg party rally, *Triumph of the Will* was an impressive piece of artistic propaganda, glorifying Hitler and portraying the Nazi party as a unified, powerful movement that had rejuvenated the nation. The film's renown was due not to its content but to its technical innovations and superb editing. Riefenstahl, Hitler's favorite filmmaker, also directed *The Olympiad*, a film on the 1936 Berlin Olympics, considered by some the best sports documentary ever produced. In the final analysis, accomplished artists like Riefenstahl helped sustain the Third Reich through their work despite their later claims that they were apolitical. They were better instruments of propaganda precisely because their films were so artistic and innovative. Their work enhanced the self-image of the Nazis while hiding the true nature of the regime.

A similar deceitful circumspection sanitizing the true Nazi purpose were the documentaries made in collaboration with those medical practitioners involved in the Eugenics Programs of sterilization and the secret practice of euthanasia. These documentaries aimed at justifying Nazi eugenic policies by portraying the mentally ill as dehumanized beings warranting drastic medical procedures. But in this genre, too, the subtleties of the emotional feature film elicited more sympathy for Nazi goals. *I Accuse*, the moving story of a scientist whose sincere love for his incurably ill wife leads to a "mercy killing," received a very favorable response among non-Catholic audiences.

One facet of popular entertainment about which the Nazis were particularly concerned was its moral content. The sexual liberation of the Weimar era was now taboo, as the Nazis closed cabarets and nude shows in order to purge the society of this immorality and decadence. There was a general clampdown on pornography and public prostitution. It was no longer possible for writers and movie directors to treat moral questions such as sex and prostitution in a realistic social context. Sex did not disappear from the Nazi screen, but it was greatly restricted; sex had to be used to convey a stern moral lesson and could never transgress the standards of purity that the Nazis had proclaimed for German women. In films it was foreign women who were portrayed as lacking the proper moral restraint; German women were depicted as chaste and noble. The fate of any German girl who violated this moral code was usually suicide by the end of the film.

The Nazi attitude toward the treatment of sex in literature and film was a reflection of the movement's general view of women. Every traditional bias about women that existed in European society was shared by the Nazis. Women were supposedly weak, emotional creatures, intellectually inferior to men, who required the protection and guidance of male society. Working women were frowned upon, because they allegedly neglected their families, became susceptible to moral corruption, and took jobs away from men, who could perform the work much better. It had been a grave mistake, the Nazis argued, to allow these basically irrational beings into the professions and politics. Antifeminism was a noticeable trait in nazism from its earliest years, when a 1921 party directive excluded women from leadership positions in the NSDAP. Several Nazi women's organizations existed, but these were always subordinate to the male-dominated party structure. Their purpose was never the advancement of women in the party or German society; it was to provide auxiliary support for the policies and activities of the party as a whole and to spread the National Socialist spirit among women.

When the Nazis took power in Germany, they attempted to impose their attitudes toward women on the entire society. Although the proposals of some ideologues to remove all married women from the workforce were never instituted, restrictive measures were placed on women. New policies discouraged them from becoming teachers and from entering universities; married women could no longer serve in the bureaucracy or practice medicine. The Nazi press and other party institutions tried to convince women that their natural place was in the home and their true vocation child rearing. Hitler himself stated, "The goal of female education must invariably be the future mother." Necessity, however, forced the Nazis eventually to compromise on this issue. The tremendous demand for labor created when so many men were drafted into the army, especially after millions of them went off to war, resulted in a continual and significant influx of women into the workforce. Even before the outbreak of war, almost 40 percent of women were working. Nonetheless, ideology remained a factor. The Nazis still tried to keep women out of leadership positions, and it was only under the desperate wartime circumstances of 1943 that the party finally decided to mobilize most available women for work. Ironically, while late in World War II the Nazis had abandoned their own ideological dictates to protect women and society from the detrimental effects of female work, large numbers of German women, particularly those in the middle class, evaded mandatory entry into the labor force.

Nazi views on women were interrelated with the *völkisch* ideology. Women were the breeders of the master race and the guardians of its purity and health. Hitler wanted a birthrate that would expand the German population from its then 65 million to 100 million, and to 250 million in the distant future. Therefore, women were urged to marry early and have large families. Procreation, like the care of children, was considered both an ideal and an obligation to the nation. Policies were instituted to assist rapid and extensive demographic growth. Motherhood and child rearing were promoted as being among the highest values of society, while individual fulfillment of women outside the home was condemned as a selfish concept. The party publicly honored those women who performed their natural function and patriotic duty by bearing several children. The greatest award, a gold Mother's Cross, was reserved for those who had eight or more children. The government also provided loans to newlyweds, child subsidies, and income tax incentives to encourage large families. Attempts were made to eliminate those things that might hinder the expansion of the race. Birth control was condemned, family planning centers were shut down, and harsh penalties were imposed for abortions.

In certain respects, several of these measures and incentives proved successful. There was a tremendous increase in the birthrate, adding a few million more people to Hitler's master race. But to what extent patriotic duty, a belief in Nazi ideology, and persuasive propaganda were the determining factors is still questionable; the size of the average German family remained essentially the same, because married couples continued to restrict the number of children they had. The population increase did not result from patriotic mothers bearing large numbers of children but from an increase in the number of families of average size. Nazi incentives and general economic improvement had made it easier for more young Germans to marry.

Similar contradictions in the goals of the Third Reich and the reality for women existed in other important areas as well. Contrary to Nazi aversion to women in politics and public life, the Nazis mobilized hundreds of thousands of women for all kinds of activities and functions throughout the Third Reich. Although these women would be powerless to influence policies decided by the exclusively male hierarchy of the party, they were able to exercise power at the grassroots level. German women were thus more involved in the public sphere of life and received more public recognition for this than in any earlier period. They held offices in and ran numerous Nazi women's organizations encompassing millions of women. They engaged in constant and extensive propaganda, social welfare, and educational activities that affected millions more women and children, greatly enhancing the esteem of Nazi women and establishing their competence throughout society.

If the future belonged to the young, Nazi culture had to prepare them for it through training and indoctrination. They would be raised as true believers in national socialism, willing to sacrifice themselves for the greater destiny of the *Volksgemeinschaft*. The Hitler Youth, under *Gauleiter* Baldur von Schirach, was the institution charged with this important task. By 1934 the Hitler Youth had expanded from 100,000 to more than 3 million members; a 1936 law made it the only legal youth organization, and all German boys between ten and eighteen years of age were forced to join. Similarly, girls were organized into the German Girls' League. These institutions granted the party unprecedented influence over the country's young and, in effect, contradicted the Nazi ideal of the family as the basic social unit. The Hitler Youth served a variety of political, military, and social functions. Nazi values and prejudices were fostered through lectures and study of the ideas of party theorists. Discipline, training, and regimentation prepared them for their future roles as soldiers and party members. At first, there was much in the Hitler Youth to attract the young. Idealism and the special attention the party leadership granted the young gave members a sense of purpose and importance. And the emphasis on sports, hiking, travel, and outdoor activities made the organization a social attraction. However, the impact of the Hitler Youth was not entirely what the party had intended. Although it no doubt created many devoted National Socialists and prepared many more for military duty, it also produced numerous social problems. Tension grew between parents and children over the freedom from parental control and the arrogance children learned in the Hitler Youth. Some sections of the organizations were known for their unruly behavior; many members eventually became bored and cynical; and the same class consciousness that pervaded society in general could be found in the Hitler Youth.

The control the party tried to exercise over the young, particularly over their free time and social life, was part of an overall attempt to control the lives of the population as a whole. Since the total state could not tolerate a vacuum in the social realm, leisure time and social activity had to be managed by the party as much as possible. The elimination or nazification of pre–National Socialist clubs and social organizations had started in 1933. This action, combined with control of the cinema, theater, and publishing industry, gave the Nazis substantial influence in German social life. Such influence over nonworking hours eventually extended into the very homes and apartments of most Germans as the Nazis capitalized on the radio. They encouraged radio listening, forced the installation of radios in most public places, and made inexpensive radios available for sale. When World War II began, more than two-thirds of all German households owned a radio. The specific type of entertainment, whether music, humor, or general programming, was limited to that approved by the party. Much leisure time was taken up with broadcasts of speeches by the *Führer* and other leaders, party programming (especially rallies and marches), and classical music.

Foremost among Nazi social institutions was *Kraft durch Freude* (KdF, or "Strength through Joy"), a very large organization created by the German Labor Front. "Strength through Joy" served a dual purpose of controlling leisure activities and of convincing the nation of the movement's sincere concern for the happiness of the average citizen. Essentially, control of leisure time was a political objective; however, many KdF activities were clearly designed for entertainment and relaxation. Millions of working-class Germans benefited from such programs, making "Strength through Joy" one of the most popular institutions of the Third Reich. KdF sponsored a massive number of concerts, cultural as well as sports events, hikes, adult education classes, tours, and even exhibits at factories intended to bring culture to the workers. Subsidized by the organization, these programs were either free or of minimal cost, though part of the expense was paid indirectly by the workers from their dues to the Labor Front.

The number of programs sponsored by KdF, like the number of participants, was quite astounding. Over 9 million people traveled through KdF programs in 1938; the party claimed that during a single year more than 35 million people participated in various activities within the greater metropolitan area of Berlin. A substantially higher proportion of German workers than ever before was able to spend a vacation away from home, and for the first time, thousands could take a sea trip abroad. Even though activities were planned by the party, closely monitored, and carefully regulated, most Germans seemed to enjoy them. One unfulfilled promise of the KdF was to provide an inexpensive automobile for every worker; this idea for a people's car had originated with Hitler. In 1938, KdF subsidized and built a new automobile plant for the so-called *Kraft-durch-Freude-Wagen*, which is known today as the Volkswagen, but the plant was soon converted to war production. The average German would have to wait until the end of the Third Reich to own his *KdF-Wagen*.

Of all Nazi cultural manifestations, the mass rally was the one phenomenon that most vividly and accurately expressed the essence of the Third Reich and its ideology. Whether on a local or national scale, rallies were a microcosm of the total state. At such events thousands of individuals were psychologically woven into a unified mass with a single consciousness. As Hitler described it, the individual is swept away by thousands of others into a state of intoxication and enthusiasm, leading to absolute conviction of the common truth held by all. Through what Hitler called the "magic influence" of *Massensuggestion*, the will and power of thousands are infused into the individual, who then becomes an integral part of the *Gemeinschaft*.

Like KdF activities and other cultural aspects of the total state, rallies were carefully prepared and controlled affairs in which participants followed a predetermined role. For the most part, interaction between speakers and general participants was limited to applause and other spontaneous responses to speeches. Party members participated as part of an organized group (Labor Front, SA, Hitler Youth, and so on) engaged in an activity specifically planned for it at a particular time. Even scheduled meetings were not actual conferences where discussions occurred and business was conducted; instead, they consisted mainly of speeches by party leaders. Enthusiasm and the feeling of *Gemeinschaft* were usually induced by the emotional nature of these speeches and by a carefully manipulated psychological atmosphere. Ceremony and semireligious ritual, flags and banners, floodlights and torchlight parades,

Wagnerian and martial music were all used to create the proper mood for mass suggestion and manipulation of the audience.

The Nuremberg party rallies were the most grandiose of all. Nuremberg had been selected as the site for these annual national celebrations because its Gothic architecture and medieval atmosphere seemed to be an ideal manifestation of *völkisch* culture. It was outside this city that the Nazis built gigantic monuments to their rule in the form of parade grounds, arenas, and meeting halls. After several renovations, the main outdoor arena could accommodate 400,000 spectators; the indoor congress hall could hold 30,000 people. The average number of people attending Nuremberg rallies was 500,000, with several hundred thousand party members often participating in a single event. The true dimensions of these rallies can be grasped only if one understands that hundreds of thousands of people were transported from all parts of Germany and that these rallies lasted for over a week.

The *Führer*, of course, remained the key element and focal point of every Nuremberg rally. Hitler delivered most of the speeches; he received most of the attention and honors; events seemed to be planned to impress him as much as the rest of the world. It might even be argued that the Nuremberg rallies were more of a tribute to Hitler himself than to national socialism. He was the high priest of nazism who blessed its flags with his touch and its followers with his salutes; he interpreted the ideology and the will of the *Volk*. More than anything else in the movement, it was the *Führer* who inspired religious belief and dedication in the masses. Speaking before hundreds of thousands at Nuremberg, while additional millions listened on the radio and hundreds of foreign correspondents waited to relate his message around the world, Hitler appeared to have turned his messianic fantasies into a reality. The Nuremberg rallies were not only a clear representation of the Nazi perception of *völkisch* culture and consciousness, they also left no doubt that the total state was definitely a *Führer* state.

CHAPTER 10

SS Terror, Anti-Semitism, and
Resistance to Nazification

The nazification of Germany created a strangely ambivalent psychological atmosphere of uncertainty, suspicion, and fear combined with a sense of normalcy in the everyday lives of most people before the war. One historian identified this as an interrelationship of coercion and consent. The new order was characterized by intolerance, repressive policies, and terror but also by a growing popular consensus. It was a time in which capricious actions, repressive policies, and persecution kept certain segments of the population, particularly Jews, in a constant state of anxiety. Although few Germans were potentially safe from the police state that was seizing control, most remained unaffected by it unless they contested the power and policies of the regime. Unwilling or unable to resist, most Germans acquiesced to—occasionally supported—the repression of those the regime had identified as political, racial, or ideological threats. In return the regime restored the country to normality, national prestige, and economic recovery after the chaos of Weimar, the oppression of Versailles, and the Great Depression. It was a growing consensus enhanced by clever Nazi propaganda regarding their efforts to reestablish law and order as well as to solve problems associated with moral and social deviance.

The terrorist aspect of the Third Reich was best exemplified by the SS, whose black uniforms, death's head insignia, and jackboots became symbols of unrestrained power, terror, and death. Founded in 1925 as Hitler's personal guard or *Schutzstaffel*, the SS continually grew in size and influence until it became the most powerful of all Nazi institutions. The expansion of the SS and the role it played in Nazi Germany can be attributed to Heinrich Himmler, who was appointed *Reichsführer-SS* in 1929. A fanatical racist and anti-Semite, Himmler was a ruthless and cold exponent of the most extreme version of the Nazi ideology. Although a weak little man without any of the so-called Nordic characteristics cherished by him and other party racists, Himmler was determined to develop the SS into the future racial elite of the nation. Within one year after becoming SS leader, Himmler had expanded the organization's membership from two hundred and fifty to two thousand; by 1933 there were over fifty thousand SS troops under his command.

In theory, the main criteria for acceptance into the SS were racial purity and ideological conviction. However, Himmler's desire for rapid expansion of his organization initially brought in many of dubious character and background. When requirements were tightened in the early phase of the Third Reich, thousands had to be expelled from the SS as unacceptable on grounds of race, homosexuality, political reliability, or social deviance. After 1935 all recruits had to prove their racial purity and that of their wives. Ideal candidates were supposed to resemble the stereotype of the pure Nordic man, who had blond hair, blue eyes, the proper physique, and the necessary racial features desired by the organization, though never precisely defined.

Under Himmler, the SS was transformed into an elite social caste separate from the rest of the nation, with its own esprit de corps, internal rules, and dynamics. Himmler often compared the SS to the medieval knights, and in order to enhance the elitist nature of his institution he made an effort, partially successful, to recruit members from the old German aristocracy and from among the university trained. It was an organization based on a hierarchy of rank and privilege, which remained shrouded in secrecy and mystery. The uniforms and symbols of the SS were specifically designed to project the image of power, mystery, and elitism. Closed to the rest of the society, the SS developed special tests, initiation rites, and rituals for entry as well as for advancement up through each rank of the hierarchy. Absolute obedience and unwavering loyalty to the organization were demanded; honor and duty were its highest ideals. Oaths to the *Führer*, devotion to national socialism, and the importance of defending the honor of the SS were given particular emphasis. In fact, SS men were eventually granted the legal right to defend their honor with their weapons, and the SS code of behavior demanded that they do so without hesitation. This organization was elevated above the laws and norms of the society; its members were not responsible to the state or the party courts. The actions of SS men were under the jurisdiction of the organization itself, and as an institution the SS was responsible only to Hitler.

As the SS grew in size and importance, it became diversified in structure and function. In 1931 an SS Security Service (SD) was established to handle party intelligence. The investigation of ideological suspects within the NSDAP and of Nazi political opponents was its initial purpose. A network of thousands of informers was created, and the information they collected was analyzed to determine appropriate action against enemies of the party. In this way, a tremendous amount of data on the politics, as well as the private lives, of countless public figures and average citizens became part of the secret SD files. Starting even before the Nazi seizure of power, this process greatly accelerated during the mid-1930s. The careers and lives of countless individuals were ruined by the use of this information in ideological witch hunts, many of which ended in the arrest and murder of the accused.

Reinhard Heydrich, a member of the educated middle class and former naval cadet, was selected to head the SD. Blond, blue-eyed, handsome, intelligent, and endowed with excellent athletic skills and a fine physique, Heydrich appeared to be a model of the Aryan racial ideal. He was not driven by ideology but by the pursuit and exercise of power; he was also suspected of having a Jewish grandmother. His lust for power and questions about his racial background, however, made him a perfect servant for Himmler. The SS *Führer* found in Heydrich an ambitious, exceptionally competent leader who had no moral scruples and would carry out the most devious plans of the SS. It is believed that Himmler used the suspicion about Heydrich's Jewish ancestry to keep him under control and to force him to fulfill the most extreme demands in order to prove his racial purity and devotion to national socialism. Some of the most barbarous policies of the Third Reich were instituted under Heydrich's direction; he was a notorious figure before his assassination in 1942.

One of Heydrich's ambitions was to acquire a monopoly for the SD over the police powers of the state. The police could then be used not only to purge ideological and political deviants from the party but also to ensure absolute compliance by the nation as a whole with the dictates of national socialism. The nazification of the various police forces in Germany began almost immediately after Hitler's acquisition of power. Himmler took control of the Bavarian political police in March 1933, whereas in April Göring established a secret state police, or Gestapo, in Prussia. Within a year all police forces in Germany were under Himmler. He then appointed Heydrich head of the Gestapo and expanded its authority to cover the entire country. In 1936 all police forces were centralized under the direction of the SS security department and made independent of all outside authority. Thereafter, Himmler's official title was *Reichsführer-SS* and chief of the German police. Such independent control of the police granted the SS enormous, certainly unprecedented, power in every aspect of society. Special sections were formed to collect intelligence on Marxists, emigrés, churches, economic groups, and intellectuals. Germany had been transformed into a police state.

The increasing power of the SS was felt from the very beginning of the Nazi regime. Early in 1933, SS troops served as auxiliary policemen in rounding up alleged enemies of the state, primarily Communists. Other SS units acted as the spearhead in the overt intimidation of political opposition during the first phase of *Gleichschaltung*. In 1934 it was armed units of the SS that launched the blood purge of the SA leadership, and in June of that year these SS troops took over sole command of the concentration camps. The SS units guarding the camps were later reorganized in 1936 into the "Death's Head Formations," consisting of about 3,500 men. The name of this group, like the camps it guarded, was symbolic of the terror and inhumanity of nazism in general and the SS state in particular.

The concentration camp system was born during the first phase of Hitler's consolidation of power for the purpose of containing the tens of thousands of political prisoners arrested by the Nazis. Originally, the numerous camps built in different parts of the country to hold Communists, Socialists, and labor leaders did not serve as death camps or large sources of slave labor. But their function soon went beyond the containment and isolation of political opponents. The camps, in effect, served as an effective instrument of terror; their very existence was sufficient to force large segments of the population into submission. When a German thought of the SS or the Gestapo, the image of the concentration camp and the horrible fate it offered immediately came to mind. The camps were beyond the jurisdiction of the courts and the law; the torture, degradation, deprivation, brutality, and general dehumanization that characterized the camps made them an object of dread long before the policies of genocide were instituted. Thousands died or were murdered in the camps even before the systematic mass murders began.

By the late 1930s, such unrestrained police powers made even Nazi leaders reluctant to challenge the SS. Himmler's power within the country and the party was further enhanced by the fact that, next to the *Wehrmacht*, the SS constituted the largest force of armed men in Germany. Yet the SS was far from reaching its peak of power or influence. In 1940 armed units of the SS, along with the "Death's Head Formations," were formally reorganized into the *Waffen-SS* (Armed SS) at a strength of about 100,000 men. Trained and equipped as a military force, the *Waffen-SS* distinguished itself by bravery, ruthlessness, and recklessness in battle. By 1944 the *Waffen-SS* had increased to almost a million men, constituting thirty-eight fully militarized SS divisions fighting alongside the regular army. They were dreaded not just by the enemy at the front but also by the prisoners of war they treated inhumanely and by the people in the occupied European territories, where German conquest brought with it the SS terror. Although officially under the command of the *Wehrmacht* at the front, the *Waffen-SS* retained a significant degree of autonomy in the occupied areas. It also served as a counterweight to the regular German army, since SS troops were loyal only to Himmler and Hitler. They could be relied upon to enforce the most extreme orders of the *Führer* in dealing with the political and racial enemies of national socialism; it was believed that, if necessary, they would defend the *Führer* against the army.

Before the outbreak of World War II, the SS was primarily concerned with alleged domestic enemies and waged a relentless, often vicious campaign against nonconformist individuals, groups, and institutions. While the secret police used intimidation and arrests against opponents, the SD publicly vilified those within and outside the party that it considered obstacles to the fulfillment of the National Socialist ideology. The pages of the SD newspaper, *Das Schwarze Korps*, were filled with attacks challenging the racial purity of certain party members and the ideological interpretations of others. The SD was particularly critical of opportunistic conservatives who had joined the party only in 1933 and who had attempted to water down the ideology. As institutions representing a philosophy of life contrary to nazism, the churches also were subjected to scathing attacks. Some of the most severe criticism was directed at the Roman Catholic Church; the SD viewed Roman Catholicism as a powerful foreign force and political Catholicism as a persistent threat to national socialism.

The Jews suffered the worst of the SS assault. Although most Nazi institutions were involved in one way or another in persecuting the Jews, the SS proved to be the most extreme advocate of Nazi anti-Semitism. Since a Nordic *Volksgemeinschaft* was the ultimate ideological goal, the SS, as the self-declared guardian of the racial and ideological purity of the *Volk*, was determined to make Germany *judenrein* (free of Jews).

Although Hitler had failed to fulfill many tenets of Nazi ideology, he would not compromise on his original objective of instituting a radical solution to the so-called Jewish question. Everything the Nazis detested and believed detrimental to Germany they identified with the Jews—capitalism and communism, modern culture and moral decadence had supposedly originated with the Jews. From the Nazi perspective, the Jews in Germany were a dangerous foreign race and not an integral part of the nation. In the Nazi mind, Jewish loyalty was not to Germany but to international Judaism. The Nazis believed in the myth of an international Jewish conspiracy and that Jewish predominance in German economic and public life was threatening the vitality and existence of German culture.

These notions were not based on fact. Jews did not constitute a distinct race in a biological sense, and by the twentieth century German Jews had undergone rapid and extensive cultural assimilation. Most German Jews had abandoned religious orthodoxy and their earlier identification with a culturally segregated Jewish community. Some had converted to Christianity, and there was a high rate of intermarriage between German Jews and Christians.

For most German Jews, Judaism was a private religious belief; in all other matters they viewed themselves as Germans. Adopting the cultural manifestations and lifestyles of the rest of the population, German Jews developed the same sense of national identity as that held by other citizens. They saw themselves as Germans first and were proud of the great German cultural tradition. During World War I, twelve thousand German Jews (out of a Jewish population of 600,000) died on the battlefields fighting for the fatherland they loved and thought was their rightful home.

The Jews were never in a position to control or manipulate the economic, cultural, or political life of Germany, as the Nazis charged. A sharp drop in the birthrate, along with intermarriage, had reduced the Jewish population and greatly accelerated the rate of assimilation by the time of the Weimar Republic. The 500,000 German Jews constituted less than 1 percent of the total population. The overwhelming majority of giant industrial corporations, which greatly determined the economic policies of the nation, were not owned or directed by Jews. In the area of finance, Jewish ownership of banks had declined to about 18 percent by the 1920s. Before the Weimar Republic, various social and legal obstacles also prevented most nonconverted Jews from entering the upper levels of the government bureaucracy, as well as from receiving university chairs and teaching positions. Although certain Jewish families, like many Christian families, had accumulated fortunes during the era of industrialization, most German Jews were middle class, and there were many poor Jews. Indeed, Jews had suffered as much from the economic problems of inflation and depression as any other segment of German society.

Since the late nineteenth century, many German Jews had enjoyed economic success. However, they tended to be concentrated in certain areas of business and professional life, rather than widely represented across the entire economy. Between 5 and 16 percent of persons in such professions as medicine, law, and journalism were Jews. The level of Jewish representation in the retailing and clothing businesses ranged from 25 to 30 percent; it was over 50 percent in the metal trade; and approximately 79 percent of department stores were Jewish owned.

In essence, the Jews, who were primarily middlemen, were not in a position to control the industrial and capitalist system of Germany. Nevertheless, their economic success produced resentment among those Germans who were economically insecure, especially members of the lower-middle class. The concentration of Jews in such highly visible areas of economic activity seemed to add credibility to the Nazi myth that increasing Jewish influence in the economy was at the expense of Christian Germans. To support their arguments, Nazi propagandists cited the Jewish-owned large department stores as enterprises that hurt the small shopkeeper. Nazis also could exploit the anti-Semitic sentiments that had been a part of European culture since the Middle Ages, presenting the stereotype of the Jew as the money-hungry, dishonest, and crafty businessman who lived as an economic parasite off the work of others. During the period of economic crisis, insecurity, and depression, many Germans became more susceptible to the economic anti-Semitism fostered by the Nazis. The Nazis manipulated traditional cultural anti-Semitism in a similar way. While the Jews regarded their major contributions to German intellectual and cultural life as evidence that they were an integral part of the nation, the Nazis viewed this as proof that German culture was being bastardized by Jewish influence.

The Nazis were convinced that a purified *Volksgemeinschaft* and the elimination of Germany's economic ills could be achieved only by removing the Jews from German society, but the Nazis did not come to power with any specific program to accomplish this. The anti-Semitic programs of the Hitler regime evolved gradually over a period of years and did not originally include plans for genocide. There was disagreement among various party factions over the proper approach. Goebbels and Streicher, backed by thugs in the SA, urged quick, drastic action to purge the Jews from German economic and public life, whereas Frick, Schacht, and even the SS favored a gradual, orderly policy.

Immediately after Hitler seized power, it appeared that the Nazis would try to apply radical means to eliminate Jews. SA troops assaulted Jews in some areas of the country, while the Nazi propaganda machine poured out a flood of vehement anti-Semitic publications and broadcasts. In April 1933 the Nazis tried an unsuccessful boycott of Jewish shops, followed by the purge of Jews from the civil service and universities. Anti-Semitism was legalized in the form of various laws that distinguished Jews from Aryans and excluded Jews from various occupations and roles in public life. A Jew was legally defined as anyone who had at least one Jewish grandparent. However, total exclusion of Jews from German life did not result. Most Jews retained their businesses, because Hitler wanted to avoid disruption of business and an economic backlash from abroad while he attempted to bring about economic recovery. Thereafter, Nazi prewar policy consisted of gradually implementing a series of legal restrictions on Jews and of encouraging Jewish emigration. Meanwhile, the anti-Semitic propaganda barrage continued; individual Jews were also harassed and beaten. A turning point came in the fall of 1935 with passage of the Nuremberg Laws that withdrew German citizenship from Jews and prohibited intermarriage between Aryans and Jews. The impetus for these laws was the anti-Semitic violence among rank-and-file local Nazis who were greatly distressed that the sweeping "National Revolution" they anticipated had not been fulfilled and Germany not yet cleansed of Jews. This grassroots radicalism jeopardized Hitler's gradual, legal, and centralized approach to the "Jewish Question." After forbidding such party street violence against Jews, Hitler appeased the radicals with the Nuremberg Laws, which also brought Nazi actions back into line with his policy of legal and orderly suppression.

The Nuremberg Laws further marginalized Jews, turning them into a problematic, alienated group with which other Germans could associate only by risking their own welfare and that of their families. They made it more difficult for non-Jews to empathize with the plight of Jews or to offer them assistance. And they allowed latent anti-Semitism to surface among those Germans who could now vent their prejudices with impunity against a people who were identified as enemies of their country. That one law was designated for "the Protection of German Blood and German Honor" again illustrates the racial motives and objectives of a regime with political biology at its core. Not only were new marriages and sexual relations among Jews and non-Jews outlawed but Jewish converts to Christianity and their descendants were legally categorized as Jews. The long-standing Christian goal of converting Jews and the traditional German conservatives' vision of solving the "Jewish Question" through assimilation were eliminated as the Nazi biological classification of races supplanted both religion and cultural identity as determining who was a German. Nazi authorities vigorously pursued the identification of converted Jews, subjecting them to the same legal restrictions (and ultimately persecution and death) as other "non-Aryans." Endangering racial purity by violating antimiscegenation laws meant imprisonment and in some cases death.

Existing mixed marriages were an embarrassment and *Mischling* (mixed race individuals) proof of the dangers of racial bastardization. Nazi leaders such as Goebbels ridiculed this racial degeneration, encouraging Aryans to divorce their Jewish spouses, and *Mischling* faced public as well as private ostracism. But as in other areas of Nazi society and law, inconsistency and lack of clarity existed in the interpretation and application of racial principles. Due to political expediency and concern for public opinion, the Nazis never formulated a coherent policy on *Mischling* or existing mixed marriages. Thousands of Jews with "Aryan" spouses lived in Germany throughout the war, and many *Mischling* survived the Holocaust.

Restrictions, the terror of the regime, and the persistent policy of the SS to keep up a steady pace of Jewish emigration produced the exodus of approximately 130,000 Jews from Germany between 1933 and 1938. Many Jews, however, underestimated the extremism of Nazism. They were reluctant to leave their homeland and risk the burdens of emigration in the midst of a worldwide depression that made most countries hesitant to accept Jews. Many viewed the Nazi experience in terms of the anti-Semitic restrictions they had endured for centuries; they had survived in the past and believed they would survive Hitler's dictatorship. The gradual pace at which Nazi anti-Jewish legislation was instituted, along with the fact that no massive violent assault on the Jewish community had occurred, tended to create an illusion of hope. During 1936, for instance, the Nazis toned down their anti-Semitic campaign because Hitler wanted to present a positive image to the world while the Olympics were held in Berlin. This temporary period of moderation and toleration again reinforced the hopes of German Jews.

In 1938 Nazi anti-Semitism reached a radical stage. When the Nazis occupied Austria in that year, they quickly imposed the same terrorist and legally restrictive system on the 200,000 Austrian Jews that they had only gradually implemented in Germany. In addition, newly enacted regulations made life even more unbearable for Jews in both countries. Jewish businesses had to be registered and publicly marked as Jewish. Jews had to assume the names of Sarah and Israel, and the letter J was stamped on their passports. More ominous still, the level of anti-Semitic violence increased significantly. Some synagogues were destroyed, and several thousand Jews were sent to concentration camps.

The clearest sign of the treatment the Jews of Europe would face within a few years occurred in the fall of 1938. Unknown to SS leaders, who still promoted a policy of gradual and orderly emigration, Goebbels had received Hitler's permission to launch a violent assault on the Jewish community. On the night of November 9, thousands of Nazis across Germany destroyed most synagogues and hundreds of Jewish businesses; thousands of Jews were beaten in the streets and in their homes and about one hundred were murdered; and approximately thirty thousand Jewish men were temporarily imprisoned in concentration camps. This was the infamous *Kristallnacht* or "Crystal Night" pogrom, labeled as such because of the tremendous amount of broken glass. While most of the violence was conducted by the SA, with most Germans definitely disapproving, a small (but larger than previously thought) number of average Germans were ritualistically involved in the event. At the local level, crowds cheered the assaults and jeered the Jews. And some passive members of these crowds subsequently joined in the looting of Jewish property. This pogrom was followed by more repression. Jews were forced to pay for the damage caused by this Nazi rampage and shortly thereafter were deprived of ownership of their businesses. Their hopes shattered, Jews rushed in large numbers to leave the Nazi regime of terror. Between "Crystal Night" and the outbreak of World War II, close to 200,000 Austrian and German Jews emigrated.

Even at this stage, however, the Nazi goal was not to exterminate the Jews, only to banish them from the German Reich. Despite the early reluctance of the SS to engage in violence to rid Germany of Jews, it acted as a major instrument of terror in conducting its anti-Semitic propaganda campaign, running the concentration camps, and enforcing anti-Jewish legislation. When a violent onslaught against Jews became a priority for Hitler, the SS obliged with ruthless inhumanity.

Nazi persecution of the Jews met with little resistance from the rest of society. This inaction did not mean that most Germans agreed with the anti-Jewish policies or that nazification had been so complete that opposition to the regime had been eliminated. Large segments of German society had not developed a National Socialist consciousness and were shocked by Nazi anti-Semitic violence. Nonetheless, numerous individuals, businesses, professionals, and institutions, including those without any previous indications of anti-Semitism, were complicit in accepting, even accelerating the Nazi persecution of Jews. Motivated by professional or economic interests, they benefited greatly from the purge of Jews from the professions, civil service, and certain businesses as well as eventually by the seizure of their economic and personal property. Non-Jews filled vacancies created by these racial purges or rose quickly up the corporate ladder. When the policy of "Aryanization" dictated the takeover of Jewish enterprises and other assets by true Aryans, German bankers, business leaders, insurance companies, and local officials exploited these opportunities to enhance the economic power and profitability of their own institutions or to promote the interests of their bureaucracies. They often did this on their own initiative or beyond what was required by the Nazi state. While noncompliance would certainly signal failure under the new regime, profiting at the expense of Jews was a temptation too many could not resist.

A similar relationship of coercion and consent existed between Nazi policies on the alienation and persecution of certain other social groups and the response of the German population generally. Acquiescence, support, and even popular pressure for such actions were more easily acquired regarding such groups than it had been for Jews. While the Jewish question had not been important to most Germans, moral degeneracy, crime, political subversion, and public order had been. These involved people for whom mainstream Germany had little sympathy and often manifested anxiety, prejudice, and hostility. The arrest of Communists was quite popular. So, too, was the campaign against so-called sexual deviants and those classified as asocial types, including homosexuals and Jehovah's Witnesses. Placing "work-shy" men, vagrants, and juvenile delinquents in work camps for rehabilitation met with similar popular approval. Harsh penalties were likewise expected for violent criminals and repeat offenders; under the pressures of war, public support for the death penalty increased.

The Nazis often publicized such roundups and the criminalization and punishment of social behavior. Even Nazi press depictions of concentration camps as places to isolate, punish, or rehabilitate such "social deviants" created favorable popular perceptions of such policies and institutions. Rather than encountering resistance to this social persecution, the Nazis often received assistance in the form of thousands of denunciations from average Germans of those whose social existence or behavior deviated from the expectations of mainstream society. Others turned in friends, relatives, and colleagues because they felt it was expected of them or feared charges of complicity or sympathy if they did not. There were also economic enticements as the construction and maintenance of various kinds of camps stimulated the local economy and reduced unemployment. Farmers near certain camps also found inmates a cheap source of exploitable agricultural labor. In certain cases, such as the Gypsies, local populations actually took the initiative in social persecution before the Nazis, still indifferent to Gypsies, had developed an interest in them. Complaints, legal restrictions, and police measures over decades had failed to eliminate or contain the Gypsy population across Germany. The public now pressured the Nazi state to develop repressive measures and take radical action to solve a long-term social problem. In doing so, this popular pressure brought the Gypsies into the Nazi policy sphere of social and racial deviance that dictated action against them. For most Germans, longstanding social prejudice or local issues prompted their initiatives or acquiescence. But often these coincided with, advanced, or justified the Nazi goal of the societal purification of biological and social deviants.

How longstanding societal intolerance of any group deemed odd or different coincided with Nazi insistence on total conformity and submission was perhaps best illustrated by the strong reaction against Jehovah's Witnesses, a numerically insignificant group. Consisting of a mere twenty to twenty-five thousand members, these sincere, Bible-reading believers appeared more numerous by their public, often door-to-door preaching, which irritated local Germans and struck established church officials as cultlike. To the Nazis, they were a minute but obstinate problem because, on religious principle, they renounced allegiance to any earthly government and their biblically based Christian pacifism led them to resist military service. While their pacifism defied Nazi militaristic culture, their refusal to give the *Führer* salute was an intolerable public affront to Hitler himself. After the Nazis outlawed the movement in July 1933, the Jehovah's Witnesses persisted in privately sustaining their circles. Some lost their children when, in retaliation, the Nazis took them from their "deviant" parents for "reeducation" as normal members of the *Volk*. Meanwhile, arrests mounted until some ten thousand ended up in concentration camps, wearing the "purple triangle" as a sign of devotion to their unshakeable faith. Estimates of Jehovah's Witnesses who perished in prisons or camps range from 1,200 to 5,000. These included around 250 who were executed for refusing military service. Their greatest defiance, however, came in the calm, nonresistant manner in which they submitted to the indignities of their persecution, incarceration, and for many, murder. Believing they were enduring this earthly torment because of their Christian faith, they humbly submitted to whatever task was required or inhumanely imposed upon them, so long as it did not violate their religious precepts. Nazi ideological dogmatists and oppressors, within a brutal regime sustained by domination, force, and death, had no answer for a small group of devotees willing to suffer martyrdom with saintly conviction and piety. Eventually, these rare human beings acquired a degree of respect even from their SS guards, who, knowing they would neither escape nor overtly resist, considered them trustworthy inmates available for labor outside the camps or personal SS work. The Jehovah's Witnesses stand as one of the most striking examples of heroic Christian resistance to Nazism.

The lack of widespread protests and efforts to save the Jews and others must also be evaluated in the context of general resistance to the Hitler dictatorship. The pseudolegality on which Hitler based his policies, the dictatorial power of the regime, and the terror of the police state made resistance exceptionally difficult and dangerous. After the successful introduction of political *Gleichschaltung*, most potential centers of organized resistance either had been destroyed or nazified.

Despite such problems, there did exist various types of resistance to Hitler's rule and to the nazification of all culture and society. Countless individuals paid with their lives for speaking out or for attempting to save others from Nazi tyranny. About five thousand Jews in Berlin survived the Holocaust because individual Germans kept them hidden. One of the most visible forms of opposition was emigration. Thousands of non-Jewish Germans, including many prominent artists and intellectuals, voluntarily left the country rather than submit to nazification. Many of those who wanted neither to risk political opposition nor to leave their country avoided involvement with the new order by joining the "inner emigration." Numerous writers, scholars, and scientists escaped into highly specialized, sometimes esoteric, fields of intellectual activity that did not attract the attention of the Nazi party and managed to keep alive a significant degree of intellectual creativity free from nazification. Writers such as Gertrud Le Fort opposed the new social order not by direct confrontation but by providing an alternative to Nazi culture in the form of works emphasizing moral and religious values. One of the most interesting cases of inner emigration literature was Ernst Jünger's *On the Marble Cliffs*, an allegory critical of the Nazi dictatorship that sold thirty-five thousand copies. For the average German, however, inner emigration meant merely a withdrawal from public life into silence.

While in general inner emigration pointed out the limits of a nazified total culture, silence and avoidance of nazification did very little to undermine the Nazi state or halt its repression and terror. The crimes of the dictatorship could be stopped only by overthrowing the regime, and this would require a highly organized resistance movement that was prepared to use violence. But the efficiency of the secret police, the suspicion most opposition groups had of each other, and the self-interest of different institutions prevented the rise of a unified popular movement of political resistance. Although at first remnants of the SPD and KPD tried to develop an underground resistance, these old foes could not overcome their longstanding political differences to form a united front against nazism. These disunited, small groups were eventually infiltrated by the secret police and crushed. Thereafter, only individual cells remained active, with no hope of developing the strength necessary to challenge the Third Reich.

The churches, on the other hand, were more successful in their opposition, though they never engaged in active resistance that was intended either to stop the persecution of the Jews or to undermine the dictatorship. The resistance of the Protestant and Catholic churches consisted mainly of defending their institutions against nazification and of opposing whenever possible Nazi destruction of Christian culture. The churches were able to defend their institutional interests only because they compromised with the new regime and did not challenge its political authority.

Historically very conservative and nationalistic, many Protestant churches initially welcomed the Nazi acquisition of power. They began to protest only when the Nazis tried to extend *Gleichschaltung* to religious institutions and theology. Using as a facade the German Christian Movement, a racist, pro-Nazi Protestant group, Hitler at first tried to unify the Protestant churches under a nazified Reich church headed by a Reich bishop. The Nazis also attempted to impose racist interpretations on Christian theology and to purge all non-Aryans from the churches. Protests from the churches and the formation of a Pastors' Emergency League (headed by Martin Niemöller) prevented these nazification efforts from being successful, and thereafter the German Christian Movement gradually declined into insignificance. Protestant churches later protested the Nazi euthanasia program, under which thousands of deformed, mentally ill, and incurably sick persons were put to death. Nevertheless, the churches continued to compromise; they did not take a stand on political issues or matters that did not directly involve Christians. There was no churchwide protest against Nazi treatment of the Jews, with the exception of some efforts to protect baptized Jews.

A similar type of compromise allowed the Roman Catholic Church to defend its institutional autonomy against nazification. After the 1933 Concordat between the Nazi state and the papacy, the Catholic Church limited its action mostly to trying to protect the rights it had received under that agreement against continual Nazi violations. The Catholic Church publicly protested the seizure of church property and the euthanasia program, but beyond seeking exemptions for Jewish converts to Catholicism, it never took a stand on Nazi persecution of the Jews.

Hitler temporarily allowed the churches to maintain their institutional and theological autonomy because he did not want to risk a showdown on the religion issue while he was preoccupied with more pressing problems at home and abroad. So long as the churches did not present an immediate threat by engaging in political opposition, they were able to avoid *Gleichschaltung* and integration into the total culture the Nazis wanted to impose. The survival of Christian culture and the fact that millions of Germans remained devoted believers in Christianity was yet another indication that the majority of Germans had not succumbed to the Nazi ideology. Some Christians, of course, saw no contradiction between their religious faith and Nazi doctrine. But Nazi leaders clearly recognized this as a contradiction; they regarded Christianity as an alternative worldview incompatible with National Socialist ideology and an obstacle to the realization of its tenets. Consequently, it was Hitler's long-range goal to eliminate the churches once he had consolidated control over his European empire.

In the meantime, this temporary, tenuous truce prevailed. The Nazis exploited every feasible political opportunity to undermine religion in society, while 95 percent of Germans still officially belonged to traditional Catholic and Protestant churches. Himmler's own father was a devout Catholic, and under familial pressure even many SS officers seriously committed to the Nazi cause nonetheless had their children baptized. Various Nazi restrictions on the public practice of Christianity were evaded. Outside the big cities, Christianity had its most formidable strongholds in rural mentalities and deeply embedded traditions that constituted the very social fabric and identity of these communities. Certain local party leaders backed down when faced with priests and pastors much more popular with their parishioners than Nazis were. Such popular responses led to the restoration of crucifixes in school-rooms in defiance of Nazi directives. Until restricted in the late 1930s, millions of Germans participated in church festivals and religious social events. When Nazi regulations eliminated most feast days as legal holidays, many peasants stayed away from work and celebrated nonetheless. And the Nazis never attempted to remove Christmas and Good Friday as legal holidays. Among other religious activities, Catholics continued with their processions and pilgrimages. Church attendance remained heavy, even increasing during the Third Reich. The exceptions were special masses for Hitler's birthday on April 20 and the official Mayday holiday where Nazi authorities took particular note of very sparse attendance.

Also noteworthy, Catholic and Protestant churchwomen involved in charitable and social welfare work offered a strong defense of traditional Christian culture and the role of religion in society against a Nazi state determined to usurp these functions. When the Nazis radically diminished or eliminated religious institutional control in these areas, Protestant churchwomen organized Bible study groups and a Young Mother's Circle to counteract the encroachments among the religious, especially young women, of Nazi cultural ideology. Catholic women upheld the virtues of virginity and worshipped St. Mary as the moral ideal for woman in direct defiance of Nazi political biology with its emphasis upon fertility and reproduction to facilitate rapid demographic growth of the master race.

Some Germans believed that morality and Christian duty required action beyond that of defending religious institutions. Individual laymen, ministers, priests, and nuns spoke out against Nazi anti-Semitic policies; many assisted Jews in hiding and escaping abroad. These activist Christians remained in the minority, however, and many paid heavily for taking these risks. Nazis reacted quickly and harshly, sending hundreds, including priests, nuns, and ministers, to concentration camps where many perished. The churches were intimidated by the Nazi response. Even while Nazis were exterminating millions of Jews, the pope and the Protestant churches remained silent. The only public proclamation by a German religious institution condemning the Nazi policy of genocide came from the Prussian Confessional Church in 1943.

In the complicated and fluctuating relationship of the Nazi state to religious institutions, sections of Protestantism in particular went beyond mere acquiescence into active promotion of Nazis ideas and initiatives regarding Jews. Traditional Christian anti-Semitism, often combined with German nationalism and *völkisch* racial ideas, led some Protestant clergymen and prominent theologians to invoke scripture and beliefs not only to stigmatize Jews as anti-Christian but as purveyors of the modernist currents that corrupted society and culture. The Institute for the Study and Eradication of Jewish Influence on German Religious Life sought to de-Judaize the New Testament and redefine Jesus as an "Aryan." The sentiments and activities of these Christians contributed to the legitimation of the Nazi worldview, while further alienating Jews from their fellow Germans, leaving them more vulnerable to their Nazi predators. The Nazi anti-Semitic fanatic Julius Streicher exploited such alleged compatibilities between Christianity and Nazism. He published numerous pictures in *Der Stürmer* of grotesquely caricatured demonic Jews gleefully crucifying Christ, often juxtaposed to Jews persecuting symbols of Germany or helpless Aryan women.

The only institution with the organizational network and power to destroy the Nazi dictatorship from within was the army. But, like the churches, the army maintained an ambivalent relationship with the Third Reich. Most officers detested the terror of the SS and the nazification of society, and the military leadership resisted Nazi encroachments on the army. The *Wehrmacht* held its traditional values and code of behavior as an alternative to National Socialist ideology. By the late 1930s, the army had become quite alarmed by Hitler's reckless foreign policy and thereafter by his conduct of the war. Still, the army was one of the major beneficiaries of the Third Reich. Hitler had placated the army through rearmament and universal conscription. Many of Hitler's accomplishments—especially the end of the Versailles system and the creation of a strong, united Germany with a rejuvenated national enthusiasm—were welcomed by the *Wehrmacht* leaders. Allowed to maintain its institutional autonomy, the army was reluctant to act against the *Führer*, who seemed to achieve one success after another in domestic and foreign policy. The military tradition of obedience to the state and its leader, reinforced by the oath to Hitler, also inhibited many officers from engaging in conspiracy.

Nonetheless, small pockets of resistance within the army began to form quite early. General Ludwig Beck, chief of staff until 1938, became the key figure in the army conspiracy against Hitler. Beck was assisted in his efforts by General Franz Halder, who replaced him as chief of staff. The officers who joined Beck's group worked closely with the civilian conservative resistance circles organized by Carl Goerdeler, former mayor of Leipzig. For years, Goerdeler traveled throughout Germany and abroad secretly expanding the network of conspirators. Eventually, the resistance circles included such prominent men as Ernst von Weizsäcker, head of the political department of the foreign ministry, and the German ambassador to Italy, Ulrich von Hassell.

As conservatives, these men did not seek the restoration of democracy. Their objective was the destruction of the Hitler dictatorship, and most of them envisioned a future Germany governed by some sort of conservative authoritarian system. A number of conspirators were motivated by the desire to spare Germany a catastrophic war; some also found the terror imposed on the German people by the SS and Gestapo intolerable. For certain individuals it was Christian morality that forced them to participate in the resistance movement, while for others it was an inability to stand by and watch their beloved culture replaced by the barbarism of national socialism. From the onset of the resistance to his execution by the Nazis in 1945, Goerdeler was deeply moved by the plight of Jews. He persistently acted to save German Jews, as well as to solve the problems faced by Jews worldwide, eventually favoring the establishment of a Jewish state in Palestine.

When an international crisis developed in 1938 over Hitler's demands for Czech territory, the conspirators tried to depose Hitler. Leaders of the plot attempted to convince the British to take a strong stand against Hitler on the issue of Czechoslovakia. If Hitler then threatened war, General Halder, supported by other officers, was ready to arrest Hitler and have the army seize control. But the British policy of appeasement, culminating in the Munich agreement, not only prevented a war but handed Hitler a major diplomatic victory that greatly enhanced his prestige in the eyes of many Germans. As a result, the army plot was never carried out.

Although this first attempt at overt resistance failed, opposition did not cease. Resistance circles within the army remained active and increased in size in subsequent years. The churches continued their struggle against Nazi interference in their internal affairs, and clandestine cells of Socialists and Communists existed. In some cases, it was circumstances, in others, lack of courage as well as institutional and personal self-interest that prevented anti-Nazi elements in the army and churches from taking more decisive action against the Hitler regime. Nevertheless, anti-Nazi sentiments in the army and churches, like those reflected by the "inner emigration" and by individual acts of heroism in defiance of the police state, showed that significant parts of the German population had not been infected with the National Socialist spirit.

17. Hitler and his generals ponder wartime strategy. (National Archives)

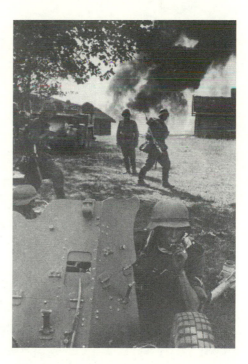

18. German troops on the eastern front. (National Archives)

19. Hitler in Paris after the swift defeat of France in 1940. (National Archives)

20. Triumphant German soldiers mock their Polish POW. (National Archives)

21. *Wehrmacht* tanks quickly advancing across the Russian steppes. (National Archives)

22. Russian winter halts the German offensive. (National Archives)

23. The *Blitzkrieg* bogged down in the Russian thaw. (National Archives)

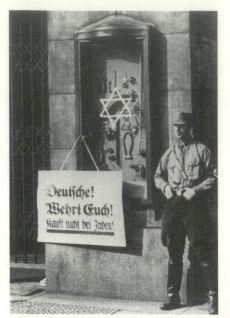

24. The anti-Jewish boycott of April 1933: "Germans beware! Don't buy from Jews." (National Archives)

25. An *Einsatzgruppen* member shoots a Ukrainian Jew at a mass grave. (Library of Congress, U.S. Holocaust Memorial Museum Photo Archives)

**26. SS *Führer* and architect
of the Holocaust, Heinrich
Himmler. (National Archives)**

**27. Hermann Göring and Rudolf Hess at the Nuremberg Trials. (National
Archives)**

28. Mass grave of Holocaust victims. (Julius Schatz, U.S. Holocaust Memorial Museum Photo Archives)

29. The Brandenburg Gate after the Allied bombing of Berlin. (National Archives)

PART FOUR

The Rise and Fall of the Nazi Empire in Europe, 1933–1945

Without the clearest knowledge of the racial problem and hence of the Jewish problem there will never be a resurrection of the German nation. The racial question holds the key not only to world history, but to all human culture.

And the end of Jewish rule in Russia will also be the end of Russia as a state. We have been chosen by Fate as witness of a catastrophe which will be the mightiest confirmation of the correctness of *völkisch* racial theory.

The fight against Jewish world Bolshevism requires a clear engagement against Soviet Russia.

—Adolf Hitler, *Mein Kampf*

CHAPTER 11

The *Führer* as Statesman:
Ideology and Foreign Policy

The triumph of national socialism in Germany represented only a partial fulfillment of the Nazi ideology. Hitler had always considered Nazi mastery of Germany as merely the prelude to the establishment of German domination in Europe. Many of his domestic policies, especially in the economic sphere, were formulated with foreign policy objectives in mind. Hitler made several pragmatic compromises in foreign affairs, as he had done in domestic policy, but these were made out of necessity and always remained temporary. Although at times diplomatic, economic, or military circumstances forced Hitler to act as if he had altered or abandoned the foreign policy goals stated in his early writings and speeches, he never lost sight of his ultimate ideological aim of a Nazi empire in Europe. More than anything else, it was ideology that determined Hitler's conduct of foreign affairs. He was motivated by his unshakable belief that "Germany will either be a world power or there will be no Germany." He was convinced that world power status could not be achieved by returning Germany to its pre-1914 borders or by the acquisition of a colonial empire. The foundation of such power for Germany would have to be in continental Europe; this required extensive territorial expansion, which could be achieved only through force.

Neither the idea of a European empire nor the concept of German world power status originated with the Nazis. Expansion and conquest in pursuit of empire had often occurred in European history. By the nineteenth century, Germany and Austria together controlled large segments of Eastern Europe, ruling over millions of Slavs and other ethnic groups who lived in these areas. The need to acquire even more territory was discussed by certain German politicians and writers before World War I. They argued that the traditional European nation-state was becoming obsolete, as its power was dwarfed by that of larger entities such as the British Empire, the Russian Empire, and the United States. The future belonged to the countries that had great land masses, large populations, and the extensive resources required to be a world power. Germany's survival as a great nation would depend upon its ability to achieve world power status by creating an empire in Europe that would provide it with the land mass, resources, and population necessary for it to compete economically and militarily with these larger territorial units.

Many of Germany's annexationist policies during World War I were intended to win world power status through the realization of the concept of *Mitteleuropa* (a German empire in Central Europe). The most extreme version of *Mitteleuropa* involved the annexation of parts of France, the Baltic, the Balkans, and Russian Poland. France, Belgium, Italy, and the Scandinavian countries would be reduced to vassal states and made part of a European economic confederation dominated by the Germans. Many of these goals received theoretical support from the new field of geopolitics that had been developed at the turn of the century. Geopolitical theorists emphasized the crucial interrelationship between geographical factors and politics. In essence, they argued that a nation's power depended upon its economic and strategic positions and that these were largely determined by the size as well as the type of territory it controlled.

Although Germany's defeat and the Treaty of Versailles ended the quest for *Mitteleuropa*, and at the same time greatly reduced Germany's territory, geopolitical thinking did not die out during the Weimar Republic. The field of geopolitics continued to grow and acquired a certain degree of respectability among German political theorists. The major exponent of geopolitical thought was Karl Haushofer, a Munich professor and mentor of Rudolf Hess. One of Haushofer's most important contributions was the theory of *Lebensraum* (living space). The cardinal principle of this theory was that a nation had the right to acquire the territory necessary to support its population.

In the early 1920s, Hess introduced Hitler to Haushofer's theories, and thereafter *Lebensraum* became a key element in the Nazi ideology. However, the Nazis transformed *Lebensraum* from a mere geopolitical concept into a racial one. Similarly, the notion of German world power status based upon an empire in Europe took on a new meaning for the Nazis. The acquisition of *Lebensraum* and world power status was necessary not only to secure the German nation for the future but also to fulfill the goals of the Nazi racial ideology. According to Hitler, the Germans, as the most creative race ("guardians of the highest humanity on this earth"), had a historic mission to preserve themselves and create the greatest civilization known to man. To achieve this goal, the German people must expand numerically as rapidly as possible and conquer the necessary *Lebensraum* to sustain this population. The Nazis interpreted *Lebensraum* in terms of their Social Darwinistic philosophy of the racial struggle for survival. The indigenous peoples in the conquered areas would have to be removed to make room for the racial empire of Aryans.

In *Mein Kampf* Hitler stated that *Lebensraum* would be acquired in Eastern Europe and Russia. This great land mass would greatly enhance Germany's strategic position as well as provide it with bountiful raw materials and agricultural land. From the late twenties through the Second World War, this scheme was developed into a grandiose vision of an empire extending from the Ural Mountains in Russia to the Atlantic. Europeans of Nordic stock (Danes, Norwegians, Austrians, and so on) would be reintegrated with their racial brothers, the Germans, and become a part of the *Volksgemeinschaft*. It was never precisely determined what would happen to the non-Nordic peoples in the West (e.g., the French and Italians), but certainly these nations would be reduced to subservience, with their populations living and working only for the benefit of the master race of conquering Nordics.

Nazi plans for the eastern territories were more explicit and fanatical. Hitler and Nazi racial theorists considered the Slavs as *Untermenschen* (subhumans); they were viewed as members of inferior races that could not create civilization and were actually a danger to it. Given their vast resources and enormous populations, the Slavic masses, with the assistance of technology borrowed from the West, could eventually overwhelm the numerically weaker Western nations. Since domination by these barbarians from the East would result in the decline of Western civilization, it was the obligation of the Germans to win this racial struggle for higher civilization and culture while time was still on their side. Hitler believed that the modern Russian state had been the work of the German elements in that nation, but that they had been destroyed by war and the Russian revolution. He was also convinced that the Bolshevik revolution had been led by Jews, that they now ruled Soviet Russia, and that such Jewish control had significantly weakened Russia's power. These fallacious assumptions led him to conclude that the conquest of Russia was possible in the near future.

Once Russia was defeated, the Nazis would implement their racial plans for the area. Leadership of the Slavic populations of Eastern Europe and Russia would be destroyed immediately; their land would be seized, and they would become laborers for the Reich. In the long run, some Slavic races would be decimated, while others would be forced to die out because they would be prevented from procreating. Societies consisting of tens of millions of people would vanish from the earth. Millions of Germans would colonize these eastern territories and establish a new society based upon small farms. The Germanic race would again return to the soil, thereby reversing the trend toward racial and cultural decline that had set in with urbanization. As *völkisch* writers since the nineteenth century had theorized, the *Volk* would regain its physical and moral vitality. With its racial foundations rejuvenated and with the necessary space and resources, the Germanic race would be secure for the future and could begin its great cultural mission.

These ideological perspectives led Hitler to pursue an Eastern-oriented foreign policy. Although Britain and France had been Germany's major enemies in World War I and most German nationalists continued to view these countries as Germany's major foreign policy problem, Hitler relegated them to secondary practical considerations in his ultimate quest for *Lebensraum*. Elimination of the Treaty of Versailles and the defeat of France would be just the first stage of his plan, since these actions would be taken primarily to free Germany for its conquest of Eastern Europe and Russia. In pursuing such policies, Hitler hoped at first that he could depend upon either the assistance or the neutrality of Britain, as he regarded the British as the natural ally of the Germans and the traditional enemy of the French. Hitler thought that so long as Germany did not challenge British supremacy on the seas or the security of her empire, neutrality, perhaps even an alliance between the two nations, was possible. It was in the self-interest of the British, as well as of the Italians, he argued, to side with Germany against France.

In achieving his foreign policy objectives, Hitler had no predetermined plan or precise timetable. He clearly worked toward general goals, such as the acquisition of *Lebensraum* in his own lifetime, but the means used to realize these aims were determined by the opportunities available to him at different phases. He was both an ideologue and an opportunist, who utilized the same dual strategy in foreign policy that had proven so effective in the Nazi seizure of power. To pacify and divide his opposition he pursued at times the peaceful resolution of disputes through diplomacy. Yet he took every opportunity to violate treaties, and he did not hesitate to threaten the use of force to intimidate opponents. It was never his intention to launch another world war, but rather to settle accounts with individual enemies through diplomatic maneuvers or through a series of localized wars, if necessary. He understood from the beginning that reaching his objectives would require the use of force and war at some point. Still, he tried to avoid military confrontations unless Germany had the advantage.

When Hitler assumed leadership of Germany, the country had no hope of challenging France or even Poland. The Treaty of Versailles had weakened Germany to such an extent that her 100,000-man army could not provide even an adequate defense of the country's borders. The demilitarized Rhineland left the industrial heartland of Germany open to occupation. The country lacked air and naval power, offensive weapons (including modern artillery and tanks), and the necessary war industries to support military action. It appeared that Germany, even under the control of a nationalistic and bellicose Hitler, was contained by these objective military and economic factors. Indeed, few European statesmen were either aware of or took seriously the fantastic foreign policy objectives of Nazi ideology. Few had read *Mein Kampf*, and those who had found many of the goals stated therein to be so outlandish that they were considered unrealistic and unattainable. It was fairly clear that Hitler would try to rebuild the strength of Germany and alter the Treaty of Versailles, but the ideas of *Lebensraum* and establishing a European empire were difficult to believe. Many tended to dismiss these more extreme goals as mere political rhetoric aimed at acquiring the political support of the nationalists in Germany. Now that Hitler was in power, some statesmen held, the responsibility of governing would force him to be more moderate and realistic. When Hitler compromised on various aspects of the Nazi ideology in domestic policies, it was logical to expect similar compromises in foreign affairs. Many of his early moves appeared to confirm this assumption, but such compromises were always done for the sake of expediency and usually were merely tactics used by the *Führer* to outwit his opponents.

Despite Germany's apparent debility in 1933, the postwar situation in Europe had created certain advantages that a clever politician like Hitler could exploit. Next to Russia, Germany remained the most populous country in Europe; it also retained the industrial potential to become the dominant economic and military power on the Continent. Moreover, the postwar settlements had left Eastern Europe fragmented into various small nation-states. The absence of any great power on Germany's eastern frontier meant that containment of Germany in the East would rest upon the military and political cooperation of several of these small states. Such cooperation was difficult to maintain, often granting Hitler an opportunity to divide and conquer. A similar advantage was offered by the mistrust and suspicion that existed between Communist Russia and the capitalist West. Conflicting interests and disagreements over how to handle the German problem also prevented the French and British from developing a consistent policy for containing Hitler. The British recognized that many of the provisions of Versailles were unjust, and they favored a policy of peaceful compromise to accommodate legitimate German demands for revision. The French urged a harder line of resistance backed up by force.

Perhaps one of Hitler's greatest advantages was the legacy of World War I. Most people were repulsed by the slaughter and destruction of these four years that had left over 8 million dead. Antiwar and pacifist sentiments were strong in all countries, creating an aversion to armaments and military alliances, since it was believed that these had caused the Great War. With modern technological advances, including air power that opened up civilian centers to devastating bombing attacks, a second European war promised to be significantly more destructive than the first had been. Thus it was quite difficult for the leaders in the democratic states to win popular support for armaments or military action. While most Germans shared this aversion to war, Nazi totalitarian control meant that German public opinion could not serve as an effective restraint on Hitler's plans for rearmament or his saber rattling. Here he had a distinct advantage over many Western statesmen. The horrors of the First World War had created an atmosphere in which most people wanted all peaceful avenues of compromise to be tried before resorting to force, and Hitler proved most adroit at manipulating hopes for maintaining peace.

At first Hitler stressed Germany's desire for peace and its legitimate demands for treaty revisions on the basis of "equal rights" among nations. Shortly after becoming chancellor, he made a long speech before the Reichstag on May 17, 1933, dealing with the question of peace, noting Germany's willingness to renounce force (because the sacrifices of war would be greater than any gains) and emphasizing his desire to seek the peaceful resolution of differences. Throughout the thirties he repeated this call for peace but also warned of the potential for conflict if Germany's legitimate demands were not recognized. His statements about the need for change were often bellicose in tone and content; he frequently reverted to threats. By combining calls for peace and negotiation with threats of force, Hitler created confusion about his actual intentions.

During these early years, Germany was so weak and unprepared for any kind of military action that Hitler's threats were not backed up by power. Therefore, he proceeded cautiously and slowly. He would gain what he could through diplomacy, threats, and calculated risks in violating parts of the Versailles Treaty. At this time, other powers knew that Germany could be defeated in a war. The problem was trying to determine whether enforcement of the treaty against specific violations was worth a conflict, particularly when there appeared to be some validity to German demands. Since Hitler did not want to risk forcing his opponents to take action against him while his country was unprepared, he never provided them with any single action or demand they would consider worth another war. With each change in the treaty and the military balance in Europe, however, Germany became stronger. The cost of enforcing the treaty against future violations rose accordingly, and this in itself served as a further deterrent to future military action.

Hitler cleverly exploited the divisions among other nations in order to hinder the formation of any united front against Germany. This tactic was most effective when he played upon the real interests and security needs of particular states. Sometimes he did this by making concessions to one power, giving the impression that one could successfully negotiate with him and thereby enhance one's national security. This not only split his opponents, creating further suspicions among them, but also tended to reinforce the illusion that Hitler's intentions were peaceful.

During his first years in office, Hitler did not accomplish a great deal in foreign affairs. He was preoccupied with consolidation and expansion of his power at home, and Germany's weakness and the international situation did not allow him much flexibility. Initially emphasizing peace and negotiation, Hitler continued German participation in the European disarmament conference for most of 1933. When these negotiations failed to yield concessions from the other powers for expansion of the German army, Hitler withdrew Germany from these talks and the League of Nations. Although to the German people Hitler appeared to be exerting strong leadership in their national interest, these moves neither enhanced Germany's position nor involved much risk. Withdrawal from the disarmament conference and the League violated no treaties and did not change the European balance of power that kept Germany in check.

Early in 1934, Hitler scored a diplomatic victory in his negotiations with Poland, but thereafter Germany's position deteriorated. The ten-year nonaggression pact signed by Germany and Poland on January 26, 1934, served a twofold purpose. It gave some credibility to Hitler's public claims that he wanted to maintain the peace, while at the same time it created suspicion between France and Poland, two powers allied in containing Germany. This did not alter the Franco-Polish alliance, and the Soviet Union's entry into the League of Nations in 1934, leading to a Franco-Soviet alliance the following year, indicated that Hitler still confronted formidable opposition on most fronts.

Germany's weakness was clearly pointed out when Hitler had to back down on the Austrian question in the summer of 1934. Since German annexation of Austria had been one of Hitler's major goals, he supported the Austrian Nazi movement financially and politically on the assumption that it would eventually acquire power legally, as he had done, and set the stage for the peaceful unification of Austria with the Reich. To prevent such a Nazi takeover, the Austrian chancellor, Engelbert Dollfuss, banned the Austrian Nazi party in the summer of 1934. After significant economic and political pressure on Austria by Hitler failed to change Dollfuss's policy, the Austrian Nazis attempted a coup. Although they managed to murder Dollfuss, the Austrian Nazis failed to seize power. Their party was suppressed, and the leaders of the coup were executed by the Austrian state. Hitler had not planned the coup, but he had hoped it would succeed. He could offer no assistance to his fellow Nazis, because Italy supported the Austrian government and had mobilized troops on the Austrian frontier to preclude any German intervention. These events showed that Nazi Germany was not even strong enough to challenge Italy, and Hitler suffered a major diplomatic defeat.

Although the tide began to shift in Hitler's favor the following year, he still had to pursue a slow, cautious course. Changes on the international scene presented more opportunities and made it easier for him to implement his strategy of dividing his opposition, but he continued to work from a disadvantageous position. Hitler's first diplomatic success of 1935 was achieved through cooperation with the League of Nations rather than in opposition to it. The Treaty of Versailles had placed the Saar region of Germany under the control of the League for a period of fifteen years, the future of this territory to be determined by a plebiscite held in 1935. Realizing that the overwhelming majority of people in this area would vote for a return to Germany, Hitler supported the plebiscite and turned it into a national issue. When 90 percent voted for reunification with Germany, Hitler took personal credit for the elimination of this part of the oppressive Versailles *Diktat*.

As time passed, Hitler became more confident that he could pressure the major powers into making concessions to Germany. Calculating that these countries would not take military action against certain breaches of the Versailles Treaty, he began to violate the provisions of this agreement more openly. Although the rearmament program Hitler had started earlier was a clear violation of the military clauses of Versailles, initially it was neither extensive nor publicly acknowledged by the Germans. But in March of 1935, Hitler blatantly announced that Germany had established an air force and that he was reintroducing conscription so as to expand the army to more than 500,000 men. Thereafter, German rearmament proceeded at a rapid pace, without regard for the other military restraints Versailles had imposed. German rearmament included the development of offensive weapons, a tank corps for mechanized warfare, and expansion of the navy. As Hitler had suspected, the other powers protested but could not agree on action against Germany.

Along with these moves, Hitler attempted to realize one of his major foreign policy objectives—an alliance with Britain. He hoped to accomplish this by using Germany's increased strength and his own willingness to negotiate to convince the British that such cooperation was in their national interest. Though an alliance did not materialize, Hitler did manage to negotiate a naval agreement with Britain by June 1935. Since this treaty restricted German naval strength to 35 percent of that of Britain, the British interpreted the agreement as evidence that one could negotiate with Hitler and thereby keep German rearmament limited. In reality, this was Hitler's first decisive diplomatic triumph, for the British had, in effect, acknowledged Germany's right to rearm, making the military clauses of Versailles meaningless. Hitler never allowed himself to be restrained by his treaty with Britain; his primary concern, in any event, was with land power and not the navy. Equally significant, this treaty drove a wedge of suspicion between the British and French, hindering their future cooperation in containing Hitler.

In 1936 Hitler was again able to exploit the international situation to improve Germany's strategic position. Mussolini's invasion of Ethiopia in October 1935 made it possible for Hitler to eliminate another important provision of Versailles, as well as to move Italy to cooperation with Germany. The invasion of Ethiopia placed Britain and France in a dilemma. They opposed the Italian aggression but did not want to go to war to defend the charter of the League of Nations; they also feared that military intervention against Italy would drive Mussolini closer to Hitler. Their solution was to institute economic sanctions against Italy and reject a policy of military action. The effect of this policy, however, was the alienation of Italy; it also convinced Hitler that the Western democracies were not willing to fight to defend the League or the Versailles Treaty.

Intuiting that the time was ripe for action, Hitler ordered German troops to move into the Rhineland on March 7, 1936. Although the Rhineland was a part of the German Reich, it had been demilitarized under the Treaty of Versailles. The demilitarized status of this region had significantly enhanced French security while weakening that of Germany, since the industrial heartland of Germany was defenseless against invasion. By remilitarizing the Rhineland, Hitler altered the balance of power in Germany's favor. He did so at tremendous risk and against the advice of his own military command. Both Hitler and his generals knew that the German army was unprepared for any military confrontation and that, given the overwhelming superiority of French forces, German troops would have to retreat or suffer a devastating defeat in the event of a French invasion. Nonetheless, Hitler correctly estimated the reaction of the other powers; his bluff and rash action paid off immensely.

Preoccupied with Italy's aggression in Ethiopia, Britain and France were taken by surprise and were unprepared to resist. The French government was unstable and indecisive, and the French military, though strong, had no plans for an invasion of Germany. Neither the military nor the civilian leadership wanted to take responsibility for a war. France was unwilling to use force without British support, but in keeping with a policy of appeasement toward

Hitler, the British urged caution. Once again Hitler met only with protests rather than overt resistance.

Hitler succeeded because of his keen sense of timing and his ability to calculate fairly accurately the response of Western leaders. As had been the case with so many of his diplomatic maneuvers, he justified his actions with legal claims and created confusion about his future intentions. Hitler argued that Germany was merely asserting its right of sovereignty over part of its own territory and upholding the principle of self-determination. Trying to prove that his actions were purely defensive and peaceful, Hitler offered to negotiate a twenty-five-year nonaggression pact with France and Belgium. To legitimize his actions further, he held a national plebiscite on March 29. The results showed that 99 percent of those Germans who voted supported Hitler's assertion of complete German sovereignty in the Rhineland.

The crises over Ethiopia and the Rhineland allowed Hitler to cause a split between Italy and the Western democracies. Angered by sanctions against Italy and convinced that the democracies were unwilling to take strong measures to contain Hitler, Mussolini reoriented his policy away from the West and in favor of Germany. Germany's support of Italy in Ethiopia, and subsequently of Italian intervention in the Spanish Civil War, brought the two nations closer together. This realignment culminated in a German-Italian treaty of cooperation signed on October 23, 1936. Thereafter, this new relationship was referred to as the Rome-Berlin Axis. Italy no longer served as a counterweight to Germany in Central Europe, and less than two years later, Hitler and Mussolini formed a military alliance.

Throughout 1937 Hitler did not take additional risks and seemed content to consolidate his gains. He had not abandoned the quest for *Lebensraum* but realized that he needed greater power and the right opportunities before he could take another major step toward its acquisition. While he waited for opportunities to emerge, he continued to build up Germany's military strength so that the new *Wehrmacht* could be a more effective tool in foreign policy.

Hitler's intentions were revealed at a secret meeting with his top military leaders held on November 5, 1937. The goal of German foreign policy, he informed them, was the preservation of the racial community through the acquisition of *Lebensraum*. He expected that eventually Britain and France would oppose Germany's attempt to dominate the Continent, and Germany would ultimately have to resort to force. Therefore, Germany must be prepared for war by 1943–1944 at the latest, since after this time the military balance would no longer be in its favor. It would also be advantageous to Germany to annex Austria and Czechoslovakia before engaging in a conflict with the Western powers, because this would remove the threat to Germany's flank, as well as greatly increase its military and economic power. Hitler believed that these annexations could be achieved without war, and he left open the possibility for action at an earlier date if the right opportunities presented themselves.

The *Führer*'s talk alarmed Germany's military leadership. They feared that his plans were unrealistic and would lead Germany into a war for which the country was militarily and economically unprepared; the result would surely be disastrous. Those who expressed reservations about Hitler's views found themselves removed from their official positions within a matter of months. The *Führer* was determined to acquire the necessary living space for the *Volk* during his lifetime and would not alter his foreign policy course.

The next opportunity came much sooner than Hitler had expected. After the 1934 fiasco in Austria, Hitler had followed an evolutionary policy toward bringing this country into the Reich, but events in 1938 led him to take more immediate and radical action. By this time, Hitler felt he had acquired tacit approval of the Western powers for a gradual and peaceful resolution of the Austrian question. Even Mussolini was no longer in a position to block German moves in this direction. Hitler had intended that German pressure from outside, combined with increasing influence by the Austrian Nazis from within, would eventually turn Austria into a German satellite, followed by an *Anschluss*, or unification, of the two countries. Early in 1938, Hitler's threats and pressure forced the Austrian chancellor, Kurt von Schuschnigg, to accept closer military and economic ties, as well as to appoint an Austrian Nazi leader, Arthur Seyss-Inquart, minister of the interior.

When Schuschnigg realized that Hitler's policies and the Nazi presence in his government were subverting Austria's sovereignty in preparation for an *Anschluss*, he scheduled a plebiscite to show that Austrians wanted to remain independent. Caught completely by surprise, Hitler moved swiftly to prevent the plebiscite he knew would go against an *Anschluss* and thereby destroy his legal pretext for annexing Austria. Abandoning his evolutionary policy, Hitler encouraged Austrian Nazis to take more radical action, while he privately threatened Schuschnigg with an invasion if the plebiscite was not cancelled. Not wanting to lose this opportunity, Hitler invaded Austria on March 12, even though the plebiscite had been called off. Once again, Hitler was able to cloak his actions in the mantle of legality, because Seyss-Inquart had become the new chancellor of Austria shortly before the invasion and invited the German troops into his country for the purpose of establishing domestic security.

Although Hitler had, at first, planned to turn Austria into a satellite, he changed his mind after the invading troops were welcomed by large crowds rather than confronted with resistance. Hitler annexed Austria on March 13, and a plebiscite held throughout the Reich on April 10 again resulted in 99 percent of the vote in favor of the *Anschluss*.

At this point, the *Führer's* confidence soared, while his respect for the courage of Western leaders diminished appreciably. Less willing to wait, he was now more inclined to force events and take greater risks than ever before. On April 21, 1938, Hitler secretly ordered the *Wehrmacht* to prepare for the destruction of Czechoslovakia in the near future through military force. The generals warned that such plans were exceptionally dangerous. Czechoslovakia had a well-trained modern army of 800,000 men entrenched behind strong fortifications and supported by a sophisticated armaments industry. In addition, the Czechs had defensive alliances with France and Russia. The size of the German army could barely match that of Czechoslovakia alone; it was greatly inferior to the combined strength of the Czechs, French, and Russians. A full-scale attack on Czechoslovakia would also leave Germany's western border virtually defenseless against a French invasion. Finally, the German army was not ready for war, and the German economy was not yet geared for such a massive effort. Just a month earlier, the majority of German tanks and trucks had broken down during the invasion of Austria. It was at this time that some German military leaders were so alarmed that they plotted the arrest of Hitler.

Hitler did not expect to become involved in a general European war. His strategy was not to wage total war, but to win a series of quick victories against individual opponents. Victory would be realized through a *Blitzkrieg* (lightning warfare) that defeated an enemy before it could totally mobilize and other countries could come to its assistance. Using surprise and a tremendous concentration of all their forces at the very beginning, the Germans would overrun their enemy within weeks. The *Blitzkrieg* required massive air power, tanks, and a daring offensive strategy of quickly annihilating enemy forces; exploitation of this breakthrough would force a surrender. The *Blitzkrieg* strategy did not demand the total mobilization of an economy for a long, exhaustive war or the maintenance of large reserves of men and materiel.

Hitler had so much confidence in the *Blitzkrieg* that he acted against the advice of his military advisers. This strategy initially proved so successful that Hitler did not mobilize the German economy for total war until 1942. Of course, Hitler's immediate plans also were based on the assumption that the Western powers would not fight to defend Czechoslovakia. He had stated privately as early as 1937 that the West had already "written off the Czechs." The possibility still existed that he could annex Czechoslovakia without going to war.

Hitler's public justification for the dismemberment of the Czech state through either war or diplomacy was the plight of the 3.5 million ethnic Germans the Treaty of Versailles had left inside Czechoslovakia. Most of the German minority lived in the Sudetenland, an economically valuable and strategically important area along the Czech border with Germany and Austria. The grievances of the Sudeten Germans against the Czech state had led to the rise of a strong German nationalist movement in the Sudetenland. By the mid-1930s, this movement had the support of almost 70 percent of the Sudeten German population. Their leader, the pro-Nazi Konrad Henlein, began demanding autonomy for this region. Both the real and contrived problems of the Sudeten Germans added credibility to Hitler's charge that they were denied the right of self-determination and lived as an oppressed minority, which he was obligated to defend. In the spring of 1938, Henlein was directed by Hitler to make demands that the Czechs could not accept, thereby giving Germany a reason to intervene. The Czech situation soon turned into an international crisis that dominated the European scene for the rest of the year.

Wanting to avoid war, Britain and France in August 1938 forced the Czechs to accept autonomy for the Sudeten Germans. Since this concession undermined his justification for further action against Czechoslovakia, Hitler demanded, in September, the direct annexation of the Sudetenland by the Reich, hinting that, if necessary, he would resort to war. Again, the British and French attempted to appease Hitler by pressuring the Czechs into granting the Sudetenland to Germany. Hitler remained unsatisfied and raised the stakes by demanding immediate occupation of this area. Hitler's threats and British resistance to this sudden new demand intensified the crisis and created a war scare. Britain, France, and Germany each followed the earlier example of Czechoslovakia by beginning mobilization of their armies. The crisis was defused only by the famous Munich Conference of September 29–30, 1938, where Britain, France, and Italy conceded the Sudetenland to Germany with occupation to take place in October. Although never consulted on this agreement, the Czechs had to accept it as a *fait accompli* or face Germany alone. The Czechs conceded.

This final act of appeasement was generally viewed as a triumph for negotiation and diplomacy. The British prime minister, Neville Chamberlain, was enthusiastically received at home for having preserved the peace and getting Hitler to acknowledge that this was his "last demand." For Hitler, too, it was a triumph. In the last several years he had proven to be a master statesman, if of a unique variety. Starting from a greatly inferior position, he had managed to expand German military, economic, and political power significantly through the destruction of the Versailles system and the alliances designed to contain Germany, while at the same time he annexed important territory. His recent success, in particular, had greatly improved Germany's strategic position because Czechoslovakia was left almost defenseless once the Germans took control of that nation's fortifications in the Sudetenland.

No doubt Hitler's accomplishments in foreign affairs enhanced his standing in the eyes of many Germans. But the series of crises, especially the recent war scare, also created an atmosphere of anxiety among the German people, most of whom dreaded another war. Perhaps they could sense that Hitler's real ambition was not to become a great statesman, but to win a place in history as a warrior.

CHAPTER 12

The *Führer* as Warrior:
Victory and Conquest

hile the West viewed Munich as a conclusion to a tense period of confrontation, Hitler regarded it merely as another preliminary stage in his quest for *Lebensraum*. In a certain sense, Hitler felt cheated by the Munich agreement, because it took away his pretext (self-determination for the Sudeten Germans) before he could exploit it to acquire all of Czechoslovakia. Thus, even before the ink was dry on the Munich Treaty, he began to plan for the total destruction of the Czech state. To achieve this objective, he would follow the now familiar Hitlerian pattern in foreign affairs of combining force and legality. There was, however, a marked change in Hitler's attitude in the coming months, as he seemed more willing, at times determined, to use force.

As it turned out, the Munich agreement had not actually laid to rest the Czech question. The Hungarians and Poles were making demands on parts of Czech territory to which they felt a historic or ethnic claim, while the large Slovak and Ukrainian minorities in Czechoslovakia were agitating for regional autonomy. Weakened further by domestic political divisions, the Czech state had great difficulty coping with these challenges. In this respect, the next stage in the Czech crisis was not created by Hitler, though he quickly exploited circumstances, aggravated the crisis, and forced a showdown. He tempted the Hungarians with support for their territorial claims, while encouraging, and later pressuring, the Slovaks to seek independence. In the meantime, Hitler prepared the *Wehrmacht* for military action against the Czechs and for the occupation of their country.

When the Slovaks declared their independence on March 13, 1939, Hitler sent German soldiers into part of the new Slovak state to protect it against the Czechs. Expecting no help from the West and recognizing his country's precarious military situation, the Czech president, Emil Hácha, traveled to Berlin to try to negotiate with Hitler. Elderly, physically weak, and inexperienced in politics or diplomacy, Hácha was no match for the *Führer*'s skill and brutality. Hitler and his associates intimidated Hácha with hours of verbal abuse and threats of a bloody invasion of the remaining part of Czechoslovakia, including devastating bombing raids on Prague, until the Czech president collapsed. After he revived, Hácha granted Hitler a pseudolegal cover for the destruction of his country. The agreement that Hácha signed on March 15 established a German protectorate over Bohemia and Moravia, the last remnants of the original Czech state, and gave the German army the right to occupy the country. Within hours, the *Wehrmacht* moved into these areas, and Czechoslovakia ceased to exist.

It was only a matter of weeks before Hitler turned his attention to Poland. Using the now worn-out principle of self-determination as justification, Hitler demanded the return of the city of Danzig and a corridor through Polish territory to connect East Prussia with the Reich. He had discovered the plight of the German minority in Poland. As he had done so often in the past, Hitler offered promises of guaranteeing the territorial integrity of the rest of Poland. With the Czech experiences fresh in their minds, the Poles resisted. This time the potential victim of Hitler's aggression did not stand alone. Hitler's violation of the Munich accord finally convinced the Western democracies that his goals were not limited and that he could be stopped only by force.

Hitler's occupation of Czechoslovakia had produced a drastic change of attitude in the West. Appeasement was quickly abandoned by the leaders of Britain and France in favor of a policy of resistance to further Nazi aggression. Britain and France publicly promised to assist Poland in defending its independence and increased their armaments production. To convince Hitler of its determination, Britain introduced its first peacetime draft in history; negotiations also were started concerning a possible anti-Nazi military alliance between the Soviet Union and the West.

Although this response surprised Hitler, it did not dissuade him from his course, as he seriously doubted that the West would honor its commitment to Poland. In any event, he intended to destroy Poland before the West could intervene. He also felt that Poland would have to be eliminated in the near future so that he could launch his attack on the West before Britain and France rearmed. The advances in armaments and military expansion that Germany had made in recent years reinforced his conviction that the Reich would have a temporary military advantage if it employed the *Blitzkrieg* strategy.

While the Polish question kept Europe on the brink of war throughout the spring and summer of 1939, Hitler strengthened his hand. On May 28 Italy and Germany formed the Pact of Steel, an offensive military alliance. Hitler also started negotiating with the Soviet Union in an effort to isolate it from the West. There are few better examples of Hitler's shrewd opportunism or his devious character than his willingness to cooperate temporarily with Bolshevik Russia, whose complete destruction was the ultimate objective of his foreign policy. Still doubting the West's resolve to stand up to Hitler and fearing that the West might try to direct Hitler's aggression against the Soviet Union, Stalin signed a nonaggression pact with Nazi Germany on August 23. The Nazi-Soviet pact virtually removed the possibility of direct military assistance to Poland from other countries. A secret treaty provision allowing the Russians to occupy part of Poland made the task of conquering that country easier, since the Poles would face two powerful enemies at once.

On September 1, 1939, Hitler unleashed the *Blitzkrieg* against Poland. The declaration of war on Germany by Britain and France two days later meant the beginning of the general European war that Hitler had wanted to avoid. But Hitler's plans were not undermined by this development, for at this stage, one could speak of a general European war only in a diplomatic sense. Militarily, the fighting was restricted to Poland, where Hitler had his localized war. Once again Hitler had correctly calculated that the West would not try to intervene militarily by invading Germany. Although the current military strength of Britain, France, and Poland, in fact, easily matched that of Germany, France and Britain's strategy was formulated on the assumption that they held the long-run advantage. Combined populations and economic resources gave them a tremendous potential superiority over the Germans, and they expected to grow stronger while the German armies were tied down in Poland. But Hitler intended to defeat Poland and then France and Britain before they could develop this potential. The failure of the Western powers to follow up their declaration of war with an invasion of Germany allowed Hitler's strategy to succeed.

Attacked by superior numbers on three sides by the Germans and soon from the rear by the Russians, the Poles could not hold out for long. The German invasion was a model of *Blitzkrieg* strategy. The *Luftwaffe* (German air force) struck swiftly against Polish airfields early on the first morning of the attack, destroying Poland's air power within a few days. Simultaneously, German armies consisting of approximately 1.5 million men (more than double that of the Poles) advanced rapidly on all fronts. These attacks were spearheaded by four armored divisions supported by the *Luftwaffe*, which soon won complete mastery of the skies. Poland's mobilization, supplies, communications, and headquarters also were seriously disrupted by constant bombings. Inferior in numbers, with only a few obsolete tanks, the Polish armies were forced to retreat, only to be cut off by the swift advance of the German panzer divisions. Within only two weeks Polish armies were surrendering, while Warsaw itself was surrounded and subjected to massive bombings before capitulating on September 27. On October 5 Hitler was in Warsaw for a victory parade, and Poland already had been divided up between Germany and Russia.

The conquest of Poland in four weeks gave Hitler his first military victory, another major triumph for the *Führer's* personal leadership. The world was shocked not only by the speed of the German advance but also by the overwhelming German power. With less than fifteen thousand of their soldiers killed, the Germans had conquered a nation, annihilated its armies, and captured an estimated 700,000 prisoners.

Although Hitler suffered doubt and anxiety in the months preceding the invasion of Poland, his confidence was rejuvenated by this success. While most of the *Wehrmacht* was still in the East recovering from the Polish war that had exhausted most of its supplies, Hitler ordered his generals to prepare for an almost immediate attack in the West, with mid-November 1939 scheduled as the time for the invasion. Considering the *Führer's* plan sheer lunacy, the German generals protested. They knew that the army would not have numerical superiority or the element of surprise in the West. They believed that such an assault would require much preparation and that it would take a long time to shift the armies from the East. Moreover, the *Blitzkrieg* would not be as effective in winter. General Heinz Guderian, panzer warfare strategist, warned that armored divisions could easily become bogged down; even Göring supported the reservations of the *Luftwaffe* commanders about the use of air power in winter weather. Such protests and advice infuriated Hitler; they did not change his mind. Only bad weather forced the temporary cancellation of the invasion, though Hitler still hoped to begin it during the winter of 1939–1940.

The fears and protests of the generals led the key figures in the anti-Nazi resistance to conclude that the time for a coup had arrived. Beck, Goerdeler, and von Hassell conspired to have the army overthrow Hitler, and several important generals agreed to go along. When Hitler postponed the invasion, the generals did not carry out the coup. Subsequently, it became more difficult to organize another coup, because of the intensified vigilance of the SS and Gestapo following an attempted assassination of Hitler on November 8. A bomb, apparently planted by someone unrelated to the army resistance, exploded shortly after Hitler left a celebration in a Munich hall. In the end, continued bad weather prevented Hitler from attacking the West before spring; this and further hesitation on the part of the generals relegated another conspiracy to failure.

The lull between the defeat of Poland and the spring offensive became known as the "phony war," as the *Blitzkrieg* in the East gave way to the

Sitzkrieg in the West. The Germans were unable to attack and the French remained entrenched behind the Maginot Line of fortifications. With the coming of spring, this proved to be no "phony war," as the German armies invaded Denmark and Norway. Although Hitler had not planned to move into Scandinavia, he did so when the British threatened to extend their control into this area. Norway would have provided the British with a major strategic advantage, as well as allowed them to cut off German ore imports from neutral Sweden. Since Germany received approximately half of its iron ore from Sweden, the defense of this area was crucial to Hitler's war effort. By the middle of February 1940, it was evident that both Hitler and the British considered a Scandinavian offensive strategically necessary. Hitler had his generals improvise an invasion plan.

Beginning on April 9, 1940, German naval, airborne, and army forces captured strategic positions in Norway. The Norwegian army of fifteen thousand men tried to hold out until British troops could arrive, but the Germans quickly established a strong foothold in most parts of the country. The British landed a force of some forty-five thousand soldiers, but they were eventually forced out by the Germans. Meanwhile, the Germans occupied Denmark after encountering only minor, sporadic resistance. The Danes surrendered almost immediately, and the Norwegians did so on June 9. The German army had again proven its effectiveness, and Hitler was credited with having achieved yet another success at relatively little cost.

The German generals remained worried about the impending major Western offensive because they knew Britain and France were not easy prey like Poland and Norway. By 1940 the combined Allied strength of 4 million men greatly outnumbered the *Wehrmacht's* 2 million; there existed rough equivalence in armor; the Germans were superior in the air with about eight hundred more aircraft than the Allies. As had happened so frequently, it was Hitler's daring attitude and gambler's temperament that proved decisive in winning a swift victory, despite the relative balance of forces.

While the original invasion plans were under revision, Hitler became captivated by the bold, though highly risky strategy devised by General Erich von Manstein. His plan defied the military calculations of both sides, and most German generals rejected it. According to strategists, the Maginot Line eliminated a direct assault on France, and an invasion would have to come through Belgium. This was the original German plan, and the French had positioned a substantial part of their strength in the north to meet this threat. Manstein, however, proposed to send the major German force, including several armored divisions, through Luxembourg and into the Ardennes. This tactic would allow the Germans to split the French forces and trap their northern armies. Since most strategists believed that the terrain in this region made it impossible to launch such a massive attack, the French forces and fortifications on the border area of the Ardennes were quite weak. Although Hitler and his panzer generals were confident that they could move a large force quickly through this region, the plan still involved a major risk. The German lines would be stretched very thin across France, and counterattacks could destroy the German armies. Many German generals remained cautious and skeptical, but Hitler took another risk and grasped onto Manstein's daring plan as if it had been his own.

On May 10, 1940, the Germans unleashed their *Blitzkrieg* on several fronts. At first it appeared that the major offensive was through Belgium, which the Germans invaded along with Holland. Holland surrendered in four days; Belgium held out until the end of the month, even though most of the country was quickly overrun by German troops. German panzer divisions passed through Luxembourg, and in the first four days of the offensive cut a wide gap in the French defensive line. As more and more German troops poured into France, the panzer divisions of Guderian and Rommel drove to the sea and trapped the Allied armies in the north. The British and French forces suffered defeat after defeat; they were continually pushed back toward a small pocket along the coast. Hundreds of thousands of French and British troops were saved only by the now famous naval evacuation at Dunkirk, which took place at the end of May. Within a matter of days, the German armies began their move across western, eastern, and central France. A series of decisive German victories and rapid advances forced the French to surrender by June 22. After having waited for a clear indication that a German victory was inevitable, Mussolini finally joined the war on June 10. But his attempted invasion of southern France was repulsed, and his assistance to Germany's war effort was negligible.

Again the world was shocked. The German army appeared invincible, and Hitler seemed to have established himself as a brilliant military leader. Two of the world's great powers had been decisively defeated; in fact, their huge armies had been routed, almost totally annihilated, by the *Wehrmacht* within a matter of weeks. The French lost 125,000 men and another 200,000 were wounded; the British losses amounted to close to 70,000, and all the supplies of the British expeditionary force had been captured or destroyed. With only 27,000 of their own soldiers killed, the Germans had also captured well over a million French prisoners of war. The terms of the armistice left the German army in occupation of most of France, including Paris and the entire northern and western seacoasts. It was indeed one of the most impressive and spectacular victories in military history.

For Hitler, this was truly a historic and dramatic event. It had been the German defeat by the West in 1918 that had prompted him to enter politics. Now he had avenged that humiliation. To emphasize this point, he made the French sign the armistice in the same railroad car where the Germans had surrendered in 1918. At that moment, Hitler's leadership, policies, and strategy appeared clearly vindicated. What others had viewed as unrealistic and unattainable, he had brought to fruition. He had triumphed over the power of his foreign enemies as well as the skepticism of his own generals. He now held mastery over Central and Western Europe, and no major power was in a position to threaten this control. The victory in the West also was received with sincere nationalistic enthusiasm in Germany. At no other point in his political life would Hitler enjoy more popular support, but the greatest impact of the conquest of France was on Hitler himself. Convinced that destiny had brought him to this point, he was guided thereafter mostly by his sense of historic mission. In pursuing this mission, he was now much less likely to be restrained by the skepticism of advisers or the realities that confronted him.

Hitler wanted to turn east as soon as possible in order to fulfill the fundamental aim of all his foreign policy—conquering European Russia, but he hesitated to launch this final strike in the quest for *Lebensraum* so long as Britain remained as a hostile force at his back. Initially, Hitler expected that demoralization would lead the British to see that their national interest could best be served by coming to an accommodation with Nazi Germany. Hitler considered Britain to be a Nordic nation, and he respected its accomplishments and world empire. Hitler did not want to fight the British. If Britain would acknowledge German hegemony on the Continent, Hitler was willing to allow it to retain its supremacy of the seas and its world empire. When it became clear, however, that the British would continue to resist, Hitler began serious and extensive preparations for Operation Sea Lion, the plan for invading England.

Such an invasion was exceptionally difficult. The English Channel prevented the use of the *Blitzkrieg*, and an attack would be conducted against superior British naval power. The troops, supplies, and transports necessary would be immense. Most important of all, Operation Sea Lion would have no chance of success without German control of the air. Nonetheless, August and then September 1940 were scheduled as the original dates for the cross-channel invasion. The entire German war economy was immediately redirected for this effort, causing massive problems for the German economy as a whole.

Starting in August, the *Luftwaffe* under Göring's command tried to soften up Britain for the invasion and attempted to destroy British air power completely. Harbors, ships, air defenses, factories, and other strategic targets were bombed. Because Göring frequently changed targets, sufficient effort was not given to the total destruction of British air bases; consequently, the Royal Air Force survived, though with heavy losses. When, at the end of August, the British bombed Berlin, Germany was shocked, and the *Führer* became enraged. In retaliation, the major *Luftwaffe* force was shifted to massive bombings of London and other British cities. This change saved British air power, while wasting a good part of the *Luftwaffe*, which incurred substantial losses. During the Battle of Britain and the London Blitz, the *Luftwaffe* lost more than one thousand planes. These setbacks and the onset of winter weather essentially ended the air war over Britain, and Operation Sea Lion had to be scuttled.

Hitler then decided to invade the Soviet Union during the spring of 1941, even though he had not secured his position relative to the British. Under Hitler's orders, the *Wehrmacht* had been planning for the Eastern offensive since the fall of France. Some of the outward manifestations of Operation Sea Lion were continued as a blind, but in early 1941, the war economy underwent another massive readjustment for the Russian campaign. However, implementation of the new plan did not take place as scheduled, because events forced the temporary diversion of Germany's military power into other areas, delaying the invasion of Russia and wasting valuable time.

These new problems were initially created by Hitler's ally, Mussolini, in his own quest for glory and territory. The Italian dictator's invasion of Greece in October 1940 had been repulsed, and it led to the intervention of British troops in Greece. Later, a British counterattack in North Africa routed Mussolini's forces in Libya with more than 100,000 Italian soldiers taken prisoner. In response, Hitler dispatched General Rommel, a hero of the French campaign, to Africa with one of his panzer divisions. Rommel succeeded in pushing the British back into Egypt by April of 1941.

Whereas the African campaign involved the diversion of only minor forces, the Balkan situation required a major effort. The Balkans were also more essential than Africa, as Hitler could not move into Russia so long as the British presence there threatened his flank and Romanian oil fields. By this time, Hitler had strengthened his position in southeastern Europe through military alliances with Bulgaria, Hungary, Slovakia, and Romania. On April 6, 1941, Hitler opened an impressive *Blitzkrieg* against Yugoslavia and Greece. The Germans drove the British out of the Balkans in less than six weeks and captured Crete. These new victories seemed to prove once again the invincibility of the *Wehrmacht* and also added significant territory to Hitler's empire.

The *Führer* finally could turn east. Operation Barbarossa, the code name for the invasion of Russia, called for the most massive *Blitzkrieg* to date, but it was based on certain military, economic, and ideological assumptions that proved to be unfounded. Hitler believed that the Soviet Union could be defeated within two to three months. Viewing the Russians as *Untermenschen* (subhumans), Hitler expected their war effort to collapse in the face of his own Nordic warriors and their sophisticated war machine. He believed that the Russian army was weak and poorly led; it also was assumed that communism was so unpopular that the Soviet political system would collapse after the first devastating military defeats. With their armies destroyed and a good deal of their resources and industrial capacity falling under German control, the Russians would be incapable of fighting a prolonged war.

According to Operation Barbarossa, the *Wehrmacht* intended to attack, surround, and annihilate Russia's major armies in the initial phase, while pushing forward to capture the industrial and agricultural heartland of the Soviet Union. Hitler overruled his generals, who saw the capture of Moscow as the quickest way to force a surrender. He demanded that the major thrust be toward areas of economic importance. Therefore, the German armies set out to capture Leningrad in the north, Smolensk in the center, and Kiev in the Ukraine.

The forces that were massed on both sides were truly enormous. The armies Germany and its allies employed in the invasion approximated 4 million men, supported by 4,000 aircraft and 3,300 tanks. In the European theater, Russia stationed perhaps as many as 4 million troops and 10,000 to 20,000 tanks. The Soviets also had the largest air force in the world, with six thousand planes, but these were clearly inferior to the faster, more modern *Luftwaffe* aircraft.

Although he had never trusted Hitler, Stalin was still caught by surprise when the German offensive opened on June 22, 1941. As the *Luftwaffe* blitzed Soviet airfields, destroying some two thousand planes on the ground during the first two days, the *Wehrmacht* rolled across Russia, sweeping Soviet armies aside. Thrown into disarray, entire Soviet armies were annihilated or forced to retreat only to be surrounded by the speedy advances of German panzer divisions. It took the Germans only two weeks to capture Smolensk, along with over a million Russian prisoners of war, and when Kiev capitulated in September, over a half million more prisoners fell into German hands. Meanwhile, Hitler's forces continued their relentless drive toward Leningrad, eventually surrounding most of that city by October.

After these early successes, Hitler finally agreed with his generals that the capture of Moscow would end the Russian war; consequently, he redirected several important divisions toward a drive for the capital. During the Moscow offensive, the Germans captured over half a million additional Russian soldiers. By the middle of November, it appeared that the fall of Moscow was imminent, as German panzers moved to within twenty-five miles of the capital. In casualties and prisoners of war, the Soviet army had sustained losses of well over 2 million; its air force had been virtually destroyed, and only several hundred tanks remained under its control. Vital agricultural and industrial sectors of Russia, along with approximately 35 million of its citizens, fell within the German occupation zone. And the Germans were moving along a two-thousand-mile front from the Black Sea to Finland.

A Russian collapse seemed inevitable indeed. Not since the fall of France had Hitler experienced such exhilaration. His estimates of the Russian people and army, as well as of the Soviet state, seemed to have been vindicated, and he appeared to be on the verge of realizing his dream of *Lebensraum* and a great *völkisch* empire.

Yet Russia had not been defeated. Not only did the onset of an early winter bring the German war machine to a standstill for the first time since 1939, but there were ominous signs that Hitler's assumptions about Russia were incorrect. The war had already lasted twice as long as Hitler had predicted, and the Soviet state was nowhere near collapse. Despite unprecedented losses, Soviet armies still existed, and Russia's war-making capacity was still evident. Winter weather was only part of the problem Germany now faced in the East. Equally significant was the depletion of the *Wehrmacht's* power; its armies had been reduced to under three-fourths of their original strength and had less than half of their panzer force operational. Since the *Blitzkrieg* strategy required the deployment of all forces at the beginning of an offensive, Germany had few reserves in either men or supplies. The German war economy had not been geared for a long war of attrition. The *Wehrmacht* troops were simply unprepared to spend a long winter in the icy cold and snow of Russia.

For Hitler, the jubilation of November turned into the anxiety and pessimism of December. By this time Rommel's victory in North Africa had been reversed, as a British counteroffensive forced the Afrika Korps to retreat into Libya. The greatest surprise, however, was the Russian counteroffensive launched on December 6, 1941. Reinforced by new divisions from Siberia, the Russians not only prevented an attack on Moscow but pushed the Germans back along the entire central front; in some cases the Russians advanced almost two hundred miles. Against the advice of his generals, Hitler refused to allow the German armies to retreat. He removed several of his top generals, including Chief of Staff Brauchitsch and the panzer hero, Guderian, taking direct command of military operations himself. The Russian advance was stopped and the situation temporarily stabilized. For the first time, the Germans were on the defensive, as both sides dug in for the remainder of the winter.

December also brought Nazi Germany into a world war. Hitler had anticipated American entry into the war at some point and had hoped to use the Japanese to tie down the Americans in the Far East when the Japanese bombed Pearl Harbor on December 7, 1941. Hitler's objective was to delay direct American military intervention in Europe until Russia was defeated. To encourage the Japanese to conduct an extensive war against the Americans in the Far East, thereby hindering America's European war effort, Hitler declared war on the United States on December 11. He gambled that America, preoccupied with the Japanese threat, would not be able to send major armies to Europe before the new German offensive in Russia, scheduled for the spring of 1942, knocked the Soviet Union out of the war. Hitler never underestimated the economic and military potential of the United States; he knew that the outcome of the war now rested on a quick victory in Russia.

Time had turned against Hitler; his enemies grew stronger with each month and would soon be in a position to strike back. The first sign of this potential on the part of the Allies became evident in March of 1942, when the British conducted bombing raids on the city of Lübeck, followed in May by a massive bombing of Cologne. By July the Allies began regular bombings of the Ruhr, striking directly at the industrial heart of Germany, the core of the Reich's war economy.

At first the crucial 1942 offensive against Russia seemed to be a repeat of 1941. This offensive had to be postponed, but when it was launched late in June, it initially proved quite successful. Against the advice of his generals, Hitler again directed his main assault on economically strategic areas. His armies pushed to the southeast into the Caucasus, with the goal of capturing Russian oil fields and crippling the Soviet war effort completely. While the Crimea was being overrun, other German armies drove forward to the east, reaching part of the Caucasian oil fields in early August. By September the Germans were nearing Stalingrad and had moved almost as far as the Caspian Sea to the southeast. Hitler's optimism began to return. It was a confidence bolstered by the news of yet another change of fortune in the North African war. Rommel's spring offensive had routed the British, driving them back into Egypt by June 1942; even the strategically important Suez Canal seemed within reach.

These were the last high moments Hitler would know as a military leader. His new Russian offensive was about to stall even before the arrival of another

MAP 12.1
Peak of Nazi and Axis Domination, 1942

winter. Although the Germans had made major advances, quickly capturing hundreds of miles of additional territory and hundreds of thousands more prisoners, they met with fierce resistance, and unlike the year before, major Russian armies were able to escape before being annihilated. Just as the *Wehrmacht* approached its strategic objectives, it was stopped. The major Caucasian oil fields were not captured, and the Germans became entangled in a decisive battle at Stalingrad. These setbacks led Hitler to demand the impossible. He insisted that both objectives, Stalingrad and the Caucasus, be pursued simultaneously, even though his generals protested that the *Wehrmacht*'s resources were not sufficient for such a task.

In the past, Hitler took credit for Germany's victories, but he would not accept blame for its defeats. He seemed convinced, in fact, that Germany did not have to suffer defeats if it displayed the proper will and determination. He argued more frequently with his generals, holding them responsible for the deteriorating military situation. In September he relieved General Franz von Halder as chief of staff and demanded that Stalingrad be taken. As a result, the *Wehrmacht*, short of manpower and supplies, with tremendous logistical problems, and fighting on fronts hundreds of miles wide, was forced to continue two major battles into the winter. The German armies became bogged down in another Russian winter, and when the position of General Paulus's army at Stalingrad became quite desperate, Hitler refused to allow a retreat. Thus the crucial military decisions that would cause Germany's defeat were made by Hitler himself. Hitler had led the Reich to victory after victory; now he would bring it to ruin.

CHAPTER 13

From Domination to Retreat

Before the military reversals in Russia made it evident that the war had turned against Germany, the Nazis believed that they were on the verge of establishing their thousand-year Reich in Europe. Germany's victories between 1939 and 1942 had given the Nazis domination over a vast area stretching from the Don River in Russia to the Atlantic. Germany's hegemony had expanded five hundred miles beyond its western border and more than one thousand miles farther than its 1939 eastern boundary. The Nazis controlled the industrial might of Western Europe, the labor of tens of millions of people, a substantial part of the most valuable natural resources on the Continent, and the most productive agricultural land of Eastern Europe and Russia. Nazi acquisitions had gone far beyond the fondest expectations of earlier German geopolitical theorists and advocates of *Mitteleuropa*.

The consolidation of this control over the long run, along with the rational utilization of these resources, could have made the Third Reich a formidable world power. However, ideology and the character of the Nazi party itself prevented the efficient development of this potential. In fact, the Nazis never formulated a general plan or even consistent policies for administering this vast empire. Nazi rule varied from area to area and year to year, depending upon the changing fortunes of war and the internal struggles for power and influence within the NSDAP itself.

Since Nazi ideology had always been rather vague about the future of Western Europe, ideology played a less significant role in determining Nazi policies in this area. For the most part, the national boundaries of Western European countries remained unchanged. But now the Germans exercised political control over these nations, using differing methods of administration from place to place. Occupied France and Belgium were governed by the German military forces in those regions, whereas Norway was controlled by a German civilian administration. The Nazis allowed Vichy France to maintain an autonomous government, but only so long as it collaborated with the Reich.

Although the Nazis permitted the economic systems of these countries to remain essentially intact, they exploited the productive capacity of these economies for the benefit of Germany. Not only were these countries forced to pay an exorbitant sum to cover the cost of German occupation and administration, but the Nazis acted almost without restraint in extracting technology, hardware, manufactured goods, natural resources, and eventually labor for shipment to the Reich. Though the German civilian and war economies benefited greatly in the short run, such exploitive policies were counterproductive. They further alienated the conquered peoples and prevented the Germans from raising the output of these foreign economies to the highest level possible.

To maintain their empire in southeastern Europe, the Nazis depended upon both allies and direct occupation. Control in Yugoslavia and Greece was divided between the Germans and Italians, with certain areas administered by local authoritarian leaders who collaborated with the Nazis or Italian Fascists. Hitler's allies in this region (Bulgaria, Hungary, Romania, and Slovakia) were reduced to the status of German satellites. They were forced to follow Germany's lead in foreign policy and were often pressured by Nazi attempts at interference in their internal affairs. Although Bulgaria's military contribution remained quite limited, the other satellites had to provide significant numbers of troops and participate in the war against the Soviet Union. These countries also had to enter into trade agreements highly favorable to Germany and, in many respects, gear their production toward Germany's wartime needs. For example, by 1942 the entire Nazi war effort depended upon Romanian oil; the Romanians had to resist German pressure to extract so much oil that the nation's reserves would become depleted.

The diversity in Nazi methods of control in Western and southeastern Europe created other problems. Occupation and administration of conquered territories, like maintenance of the necessary cooperation with satellite countries, required a number of large bureaucracies. Nazi government in Germany was characterized by a medley of inefficient, overlapping, competing, and more often than not self-interested party and state bureaucracies. Not only were many of these bureaucracies expanded to cover the conquered territories, but countless new agencies were established during the war and superimposed on the existing bureaucratic maze. The aims and policies of these rival bureaucracies frequently were contradictory.

In theory, Göring retained authority over economic developments through the Four Year Plan, which had been extended during the war years. However, in most areas he was challenged by new institutions, such as Fritz Todt's Ministry for Armaments and Munitions, and later Fritz Sauckel's organization in charge of forced labor brought from throughout the empire. These leaders competed with each other for influence, while their agencies fought over resources and pursued differing policies toward the conquered peoples. There were even bureaucratic conflicts and party interference in military zones where the army supposedly exercised administrative control. Todt's management of construction gave him the right to intervene in military zones, as did Himmler's capacity as security chief. From the beginning, the army tried to follow a rational, relatively unoppressive occupation policy toward the defeated nations in an effort to ensure their acquiescence and perhaps win the collaboration of some national groups. The widespread police terror against alleged political enemies and the racial policies of the SS, including the deportation of Jews and the seizure of their property, created conflicts between the SS and the army. Attitudes and policies of the SS also alienated most indigenous groups and caused friction with allied states.

The worst examples of how the war effort and the efficient utilization of resources were significantly hindered by the Nazis themselves were in the East. Nazi occupation policies in Poland and Russia were determined by ideology and bureaucratic infighting among rival Nazi leaders. Immediately after conquering Poland, the Nazis proceeded to institute their racial plan of clearing out the East to make room for German colonization. Part of Poland was annexed by the Reich, and the rest was organized as the "General Government," under the authority of the Nazi leader Hans Frank. The task of Germanizing the East belonged to Himmler, who now directed the Reich Commission for the Consolidation of the German People. Barbarous methods were used by the SS to Germanize the annexed areas of Poland. The entire political and social leadership of the country was eliminated, as thousands of Jews, politicians, public figures, and businessmen were removed from their positions, arrested, or in many cases, murdered. Polish cultural and religious life was wiped out. More than 300,000 Poles, with many more to follow in subsequent years, were deported to the General Government; those who were left in the annexed territories existed only as workers for the Reich. Germanization also included the institution of German laws and language, as well as the resettlement in the annexed area of several hundred thousand ethnic Germans from other occupied territories.

The Poles in the General Government were to be dealt with later. Meanwhile, this area became a dumping ground for those, especially Jews, that the Nazis found undesirable. But even here, the attempt at destroying Polish culture continued, though at a slower pace. Polish elites continued to be eliminated, and children were allowed only a few years of primary education. Although at first Frank tried to follow a more moderate and lenient policy toward the Poles, so as to prevent the rise of opposition and to raise their level of production, his efforts were thwarted by the increasing influence of

Himmler, who was determined to institute his fanatical racial policies. The SS treated the Poles as *Untermenschen*, who would temporarily be regarded as slaves and would eventually disappear as a people.

The decisive element in Nazi policies toward Russia was the racial ideology, which was followed with a kind of ruthless inhumanity not seen since the days of Genghis Khan. Nazi rule in Russia was also characterized by counterproductive bureaucratic struggles. Lines of authority, priorities, and specific bureaucratic jurisdictions were never clearly delineated. The military supposedly maintained authority in the war zone, but had to relinquish control to the Nazi party administration in pacified areas. However, quickly changing fronts and partisan warfare behind the lines often made it difficult to determine the difference between military and civilian zones. Because the SS also operated at times within strictly military zones, there was conflict between Himmler and the army command. In theory, civilian administration of Russia was centralized under Alfred Rosenberg, whom Hitler had appointed Reich minister for the occupied eastern territories in 1941. Yet Rosenberg exercised the least power in these areas, finding his authority and policies ignored by other party organizations. Himmler, Göring, Todt, and Sauckel vied for control with Rosenberg, as well as with each other.

It soon became clear that Himmler was emerging as the dominant force, since he shared the identical ideological views and prejudices of Hitler himself. Both believed that *Lebensraum* required the decimation of the Slavic masses, who were to be replaced by German colonizers. Like Poland, occupied Russia was to be denied its political leadership and all institutional manifestations of its former society and culture. Tens of millions of Russians were to be driven eastward beyond the Ural Mountains, which were designated as the future German frontier; the millions who remained would be cast into slavery until, in the long run, they died out.

These future plans for Russia were established even before the eastern invasion began. The "Commissar Decree" of May 1941 and subsequent directives of a similar nature instructed the SS to liquidate Russia's political leadership by killing high-ranking party and state officials, Jewish Communists, and anyone else considered a political or ideological threat, including prisoners of war if necessary. These bloody directives were implemented by SS *Einsatzgruppen* (special action squads) that followed the German army across Russia. It is estimated that tens of thousands of Russians were executed by these *Einsatzgruppen* in the initial phase of the war. Where civilian resistance was suspected, entire villages were destroyed and all males murdered. Russian prisoners of war were treated as *Untermenschen*, often deprived of the basic necessities of life. Although figures vary, it is generally accepted that 2 million Russian prisoners of war died, with the fate of another million simply unknown, out of the 5 million Soviet soldiers who fell into German hands.

Himmler proceeded with his program of Germanization throughout Europe. Attempts were made to relocate groups of ethnic Germans from Russia to the Reich. Until almost the end of the war, the SS continued to resettle hundreds of thousands of these so-called *Volksdeutsche*. Efforts were also made to identify individual Nordics living within Slavic populations, so that these biologically superior types could be reintegrated with their German brothers. Those who passed the biological screening process established by the SS were scheduled for resettlement in German areas. Countless thousands were identified for re-Germanization, including tens of thousands of children with the "proper" Nordic traits, who were taken from their parents in various parts of Europe and placed with families in the Reich to be raised as true Germans.

Unquestionably, these racial policies hurt the German war effort during its most desperate phase. The treatment of the Russian people and Soviet prisoners of war stiffened Russian military and civilian resistance. Productivity of the conquered peoples fell far short of what it could have been, and an important source of labor was murdered or alienated. Such policies also required a tremendous effort on the part of the Germans. While soldiers were badly needed at the front, the SS was growing in size and utilizing much of its manpower in liquidation, terror, and resettlement. Supplies and transports were diverted from military use and into these SS operations.

Rosenberg wanted to pursue a more lenient policy toward the conquered Russians in order to acquire their collaboration in the war against communism, and the military wanted to organize anti-Communist Russians into an armed force to assist the *Wehrmacht*. But Himmler and Hitler, motivated by racial fanaticism and hatred, prevented the use of these potential resources for several years. Only toward the end of the war was the army allowed to use Russians as soldiers fighting for the German cause. By that time, it was too late.

Hitler displayed little concern for the economic or military impact of these racial policies for another reason. Originally expecting a quick end to the war in the East, he saw no need for such manpower to be mobilized economically or militarily for war. Such labor was to be utilized after victory for constructing his eastern empire. A similar confidence in victory led Hitler to neglect general economic planning for a prolonged war. The German economy had been geared toward the needs of the *Blitzkrieg* strategy, which required the production of weapons and supplies for immediate use. Consequently, Hitler allowed the German economy to be mobilized for total war only after the Russian campaign showed that Germany was in for a long and desperate struggle.

Since the *Wehrmacht* had exhausted so much of its materiel in the initial Russian invasion, the offensive scheduled for 1942 demanded a tremendous increase in output from the war economy. The figure in charge of meeting these enormous demands was Albert Speer, Hitler's architect, who took over the Ministry of Armaments and Munitions with greatly expanded authority after the accidental death of Todt in early 1942. Speer soon proved to be the most competent and effective administrator of the Third Reich, succeeding against major obstacles created by shortages, bombing raids, and the machinations of Nazi competitors. In determining the most efficient types of armaments and acquiring the necessary resources to produce them, he had to engage in a constant battle with the military and administrators of the Göring Four Year Plan. Nonetheless, Speer did prevail in most cases, and output in armaments production expanded at an unprecedented rate. Still, Germany did not reach the stage of a totally mobilized war economy until the struggle was nearing its end in 1944.

The demands of increased production at a time when so much of Germany's manpower was being absorbed by its multi-million-man army and dying by the tens of thousands created an acute labor shortage. Even before Speer took over, the Reich found it necessary to employ hundreds of thousands of foreign workers in German industry and agriculture. Total mobilization required millions more. For this reason, Fritz Sauckel had been charged in 1942 with drafting forced labor from across Europe. Most of the new workers came from Eastern Europe and Russia. Before Sauckel was through, 7 million foreign laborers were shipped to the Reich, and perhaps an equal number were forced to work for the Germans in the occupied countries.

Even in this crucial area of manpower, ideology and bureaucratic conflicts caused major problems. Speer wanted to utilize all available manpower and do so in the most efficient way, but the SS was destroying necessary manpower by murder and dehumanizing policies of containment and work, diverting other essential resources in the process. Sauckel posed another problem by insisting that foreign workers be deported to the Reich, where he could control them under his own bureaucratic empire, whereas Speer knew that they could be more productive if employed in their native areas and treated as human beings rather than as animals or expendable units of production. For the most part, Speer lost the bureaucratic wars over these issues to Himmler and Sauckel. In some cases, Speer did improve the living and working conditions of foreign laborers.

The treatment of foreign workers in Germany was a microcosm of the grand Nazi racial vision for the future existence of the conquered peoples of Europe. It was to be a master-slave society reminiscent of the premodern world.

While all foreign workers endured harsh conditions, Slavs faced particular ter-ror. The conditions of Frenchmen and other westerners varied. Several hundred thousand Baltic workers (as Aryan racial kin) were even recruited as employees; many later applied for German citizenship. In contrast, Slavs, as inferior *Unter-menschen,* were considered economically necessary but problematic racial aliens within the heart of the Reich at the very time when that regime was engaged in Germany's systematic internal racial purification through sterilization, eu-thanasia, and deportation of Jews to the East. Without any legal protection or recourse, they were totally subject to economic exploitation, strict discipline, denunciations, and the whims of their employers or communities, as well as to Nazi racial control. Overt resistance or violation of strict Nazi racial regulations against sexual relations with Aryan women meant execution. Yet, here too, the duality between Nazi racial policy and traditional culture and individual choice clashed. German women and men (including certain Nazi officials) had sexual relations with foreign workers. German Catholics opposed executions, and in-stead of demeaning Poles as racial inferiors, German priests often sympathized with them as fellow Catholics.

The transformation of the conflict from Hitler's *Blitzkrieg* struggle into a total war in 1942 brought the cruel reality of war to the home front. Some of these effects were still offset by Hitler's demand that civilian consumption not be drastically reduced. Believing that Germany lost World War I because of a breakdown on the home front, he saw civilian morale as an essential compo-nent of the war effort. Economic hardships and shortages gradually increased, but the Germans never had to endure the starvation and other deprivations that they had experienced between 1914 and 1918. Planning, early ration-ing, and the exploitation of labor, food, and other resources from occupied Europe shielded the Germans from the worst economic effects of total war until the very end. The burdens that did exist, though, fell disproportionately on the lower classes in the cities. Farmers and peasants protected their own resources, while those with money could buy on the vast black market in a system that became progressively more corrupt.

A combination of ideology and concern for home front stability also prevented the full mobilization of German women for war production. Al-though World War I had established the centrality of female labor for waging total war, Hitler refused to allow compulsory war work for most women even when his own military and civilian administrators saw this as an absolute ne-cessity. Only in the desperate military and war production situation of 1943 did the Nazis require women to even register for possible mobilization. Still, many middle-class women legally or otherwise evaded work, as did some from the working and lower-middle classes. In the end, only about half a million more German women were working by the end of the war than had been employed in 1939. The 6 million women without children remained a crucial untapped labor reservoir. The Third Reich used propaganda appeals to patriotic duty to urge women to voluntarily join the work force, but apprehension over domestic stability prevented compelling them to do so.

Those working- and lower-middle-class women who did work had to bear a dual burden of employment and sustaining households without fathers at a time when rationing and shortages put a major drain on their time and energy. Many of these women were also transferred to jobs previously held by men without receiving the same level of pay. In general, working women earned approximately one-third less than male workers in the same industries. By late in the war, working hours increased to fifty-six per week in factories; women on farms worked as much as fifteen hours a day. Complaints and Nazi token efforts to protect these women from the detrimental effects of such burdens were ineffectual; health, children, and family life suffered dramatically from these wartime conditions.

On the other hand, the war opened up new opportunities for German women in public life. Whereas earlier the Nazis had either purged women from civil service positions or criticized their presence in the professions, the party now encouraged their entry into these fields to fill the serious gap left when millions of men went to the front. More women attended the universities than ever before and began to assume professional roles for which Nazi ideology had deemed them naturally unsuited or incapable. Their presence in Nazi organizations and in volunteer work allowed hundreds of thousands of women to demonstrate responsibility, exercise authority, and acquire recognition for their performance.

It was also under wartime conditions that the regime experienced its greatest disappointment with German youth, the societal segment on which it had placed its hopes for the future of National Socialism. Instead of standing as models of Nazi character building, even members of the poorly led and instructed Hitler Youth engaged in small-time criminal activity, vandalism, corruption, and sexual deviance. Instead of a new morality, sexual promiscuity, disease, and exploitation of girls by the Hitler Youth increased. The problem became particularly acute as older adolescent leaders went off to war and immature, often incompetent younger teens abused their authority. Outside the Hitler Youth, opposition among the young grew to its authority and idealistic goals as well as to such abuses. Although few such youthful nonconformists were politically or ideologically motivated, their very existence constituted a public rejection of Nazi social ideals or behavioral expectations. Various working-class youth gangs such as the *Edelweisspiraten* not only engaged in juvenile delinquency and crime but attacked Hitler Youth members directly. Middle- and upper-middle-class youth of the Swing Groups meanwhile defied Nazi *völkisch* expectations and indoctrination by openly flaunting their preference for Anglo-Saxon hair and dress styles. More embarrassing to the regime was the attraction of Swing Groups to the modernist culture condemned by the Nazis, especially the very jazz music party ideologues had chastised as racially decadent and morally destructive to youth. While the regime cracked down hard on proletarian youth deviants, it had difficulty acting against the Swing Groups because their cultural deviance was not always proscribed by law and they belonged to privileged and well-connected families.

Although the German civilian population avoided the economic suffering and deprivation of World War I, the Nazi state could not protect them from the devastating effects of wartime bombing. Spectacular technological developments in air power had now made major cities and their civilian populations far from the front vulnerable to terrorizing and highly destructive air raids. What had originally begun as British retaliation for German bombings of London escalated into a major aspect of the Allied war plan for the defeat of Nazi Germany. The dual objective was to reduce Nazi war production and damage German morale. By 1943 the Strategic Bombing Campaign of the British and Americans subjected various German cities in the Ruhr industrial area to relentless bombings day and night. Some cities found themselves attacked more than a hundred different times throughout the war. In the last year and a half of the war, more than a million tons of bombs were dropped on German cities.

The most catastrophic bombings were the "firebomb" raids on Hamburg and Dresden. For several nights in July 1943, incendiary bombs and other explosives caused enormous firestorms throughout Hamburg, not only destroying buildings through explosions and raging whirlwinds of fire reaching 1500 degrees Fahrenheit but also suffocating those in air raid shelters. Eighty percent of Hamburg's structures were destroyed and at least thirty thousand civilians killed. Similar firebomb raids killed thousands in other cities. The last major firebomb raid was launched while Germany was almost totally defeated; in February 1945 hundreds of bombers attacked Dresden, a densely populated city with no military or industrial significance. As in Hamburg, the firestorms gutted the city and left about thirty thousand civilians dead and perhaps an equal number missing.

By the end of the war, the bombings had left millions of Germans homeless and propertyless as most major cities were in ruins. The Allied bombings had killed approximately 600,000 German civilians and seriously wounded another 800,000. Although historians disagree about the effects of the air war on German civilian morale, the population was definitely terrified by it and lived in a constant state of anxiety. However, any effect on morale that resulted still failed to turn the Germans toward resistance or significantly hurt the economic war effort. Despite the massive destruction, as well as significant losses of Allied crews and planes, the Strategic Bombing Campaign had a quite limited impact on the German capacity to wage war, as it reduced industrial production by only 10 to 20 percent at most.

Despite its ability to withstand the Allied air offensive against its industry, transport system, and cities, Germany was losing the economic war to its enemies. The Soviet Union alone was now outproducing the Third Reich in both quality and quantity of weapons and material. The Soviet Union recovered from its unprecedented losses in casualties and captured in the early stages of the Nazi *Blitzkrieg* to achieve numerical superiority in manpower as well. In the last two years of the war, Germany produced an astounding 8,500 tanks, but Soviet production reached twice that level. And Soviet tanks, such as the T-34s and KV-85s, were superior to German models. German tanks also faced extensive and well-equipped Soviet antitank units, while *Wehrmacht* infantry were decimated or panicked by Soviet Katyusha rocket launchers. The Soviets made similar improvements in aircraft, artillery, and automatic weapons. The enormous quantities of food and trucks provided by the American lend-lease program further enhanced Soviet war-making superiority. In 1943 the Soviet army had over 6 million men to Germany's 3 million on the eastern front, and Soviet soldiers were far better equipped for the horrendous conditions of winter warfare in Russia.

Outmanned and outgunned, German soldiers engaged in years of brutal warfare on the eastern front that resembled the costly battles of attrition and trench warfare of World War I. In addition to suffering devastating casualties, German soldiers started to exhibit mental and physical exhaustion, disease, and hunger. Under such conditions, German soldiers became more susceptible to Nazi propaganda that they must continue this vicious struggle for survival in order to protect their country from the hordes of "Asiatic" barbarians and Bolsheviks pouring out of Russia. They also were more vulnerable to Nazi anti-Semitic propaganda that demonized Jews as less than human, on the one hand, and depicted them as powerful forces behind Germany's international enemies on the other. Eventually, this resulted in barbaric acts by German soldiers against Russian civilians and soldiers as well as Jews. While the *Wehrmacht* tolerated such ruthless behavior to relieve the fear and frustration of soldiers, it also had to resort to severe punishment to maintain discipline and the willingness to fight. Hundreds of thousands received harsh sentences, while perhaps as many as fifteen thousand were executed by the *Wehrmacht*. In contrast, throughout the whole war, the British executed about forty of their men.

By 1943 Hitler's forces began to experience an almost constant stream of military defeats. Hitler's refusal to allow General Paulus to retreat left the German armies at Stalingrad surrounded for several brutal winter months. After his army had been decimated by over 200,000 casualties, Paulus surrendered to the Russians on February 2, 1943. This was a turning point in the war. It was quickly followed by a successful Russian offensive that forced the Germans to retreat from the Caucasus; another Soviet attack soon opened up a supply corridor to Leningrad. By spring 1943 the Germans were able to halt the Russian advance at approximately the same place the front had been in early 1942. But now the Russians had the advantage in manpower and material. Beginning with a Soviet offensive in the summer, the Russians won victory after victory, steadily pushing back the Germans during the next year and a half. By the end of 1943 the Russians had recaptured Smolensk and Kiev; they were in Romania in April of 1944 and in Poland by summer of that year.

In the Mediterranean and Western theaters, the German predicament was similar. The spring of 1943 brought an Allied victory in North Africa, opening the way for a successful invasion of Sicily in July. Thereafter, Mussolini was removed by the king of Italy, and an armistice was signed between the Italians and the Allies. Although German troops then took control of Italy, they were soon faced with an invasion of Allied troops, who fought their way up the Italian peninsula during the next two years.

The Normandy invasion of June 1944 opened the major Allied campaign against Nazi Germany in the West. The Western Allies had amassed twelve thousand planes and six thousand vessels in England for landing an invasion force of over a million men in Nazi occupied France. Within a month after the initial assault on the beaches, the Allies had a million troops in France. Allied armor divisions soon broke out of the German containment efforts and spread across France. Rapid Allied advances followed, while the Germans gradually retreated toward the Reich.

The *Wehrmacht* also faced an enemy behind its own lines, as popular resistance movements emerged throughout occupied Europe. Nazi occupation methods, especially their racial and economic policies of brutality, terror, exploitation, plunder, and forced labor, had driven countless thousands into armed resistance. Some resisters spied for the Allies, while others engaged in sabotage, disrupting Nazi communication and transportation networks. Particularly in the East and the Balkans, resistance soon reached the stage of well-organized and extensive partisan warfare. All these movements were motivated mainly by antinazism, but in some cases, the partisans fought for national liberation, while in others they fought for the Communist cause. Brutal and swift German reprisals against civilians, as well as partisans, only hardened the resistance. The heroic efforts of the various resistance movements were a significant contribution to the struggle to end Nazi domination of Europe.

CHAPTER 14

The Holocaust, Resistance,

and Defeat

Of all the conquered peoples, the Jews were singled out for special treatment by the Nazis. Ideology took precedence over most other considerations, because the party racists, Hitler and Himmler in particular, believed that the Germans were engaged in a racial war for survival with the Jews. Before the war it had been Nazi policy to make Germany *judenrein* by forcing the Jews to emigrate, and to a large extent, this approach worked. The conquest of Europe, however, brought several million more Jews under Nazi control in an area that was to become completely Germanized. During the first years of the war, genocide was not planned as the solution to this new problem. As late as 1940, the Nazis were still discussing the possibility of shipping the Jews to the French colonial island of Madagascar, where they would live under Nazi guard. Meanwhile, a substantial portion of Poland's 3 million Jews were being rounded up and concentrated in ghettos in the General Government area.

When neither the Madagascar plan nor ghettoization in Europe appeared to provide a feasible long-term solution to the problem of making Hitler's empire *judenrein*, the Nazis decided on a radical alternative—genocide. The war gave the Nazis both the will and the opportunity to institute the barbarous policy of murdering millions of innocent men, women, and children. Initial military victories tended to reinforce Nazi myths about a master race on the verge of creating a great empire. Nazi ideologues became convinced more than ever before that their historic mission included the destruction of the Jewish race. The war had also placed the majority of Europe's Jews in their hands. While most of the world was preoccupied with the war itself and in an atmosphere of mental and moral numbness created by unprecedented destruction where millions were dying and life itself became cheap, the Nazis saw an opportunity for secretly carrying out their murderous plan without opposition or interference. Thereafter, when the Nazis spoke of the "Final Solution" to the Jewish problem, they meant genocide.

The Nazis had already established a precedent for such systematic mass murder with the Euthanasia Program, which some historians consider the

MAP 14.1
Nazi Extermination Camps

first stage of the genocide to follow shortly thereafter. In late 1939 the Nazis escalated their earlier practice of biological purification of the "unfit" from sterilization to a new deadly level. The first victims were, in fact, those non-Jewish Germans whom Nazi eugenic policies deemed "lives unworthy of life." Though authorized by Hitler and implemented under the guise of allegedly sound and necessary medical and hygienic principles, this program, labeled T-4, began secretly in hospitals and asylums. Tens of thousands of those categorized as incurably sick, mentally ill, deformed, or socially maladjusted were gassed to death in killing centers at medical institutions in Germany. Some seventy thousand to ninety thousand Germans were murdered under T-4 before protests from religious leaders led to its public suspension. But the program continued secretly on a smaller scale throughout the war; concentration camps were also examined for such people, and they met a similar fate. Initiated by party racial ideologues and convinced eugenicists in the medical and scientific community, the Euthanasia Program was, however, carried out by ordinary physicians, medical personnel, and state bureaucrats in public institutions. Many of these ordinary Germans, now experienced in the systematic murder of designated social groups, were subsequently sent to the occupied eastern territories where they lent their expertise to medical experimentation and genocide in concentration camps or in support of SS shooting squads eliminating external racial threats.

After the beginning of the war, the concentration camp system was greatly expanded and its purpose altered. Starting in 1939, more German Socialists, Communists, and various alleged political opponents, along with common criminals or those labeled as social deviants, were sent to camps by the thousands. To these were added political prisoners and captured soldiers from different parts of occupied Europe. The number of camps was increased until there existed some twenty major centers with more than a hundred more satellite camps of smaller size. Eventually, hundreds of thousands of non-Jews were imprisoned in camps at any given time on grounds of race, ideology, political suspicion, religion, or physical and mental condition. Priests and nuns, Jehovah's Witnesses, homosexuals, artists, intellectuals, and major political figures were all thrown together. Most were used as slave labor while subjected to brutal, dehumanizing treatment and confined in conditions of deprivation. Terror, torture, sexual perversion, and medical experimentation were all a part of camp existence. Although the exact figures remain unknown, several hundred thousand, perhaps well over a million, non-Jews perished in the Nazi concentration camps.

While the Nazis greatly expanded the number of non-Jewish prisoners in concentration camps in the early stages of the war, they also began to concentrate Polish Jews into ghettos. By April 1941 most Polish Jews had been transported to these isolated and vastly overcrowded sections of cities such as Warsaw, Cracow, and Lublin. Even before the Nazis had conceived of the policy of genocide, almost seventy thousand Jews died in Warsaw alone due to hunger, disease, or other deprivations. When the Nazis invaded the Soviet Union in June 1941, they established some additional ghettos in certain newly occupied towns and cities (e.g., Lodz, Minsk, Vilna). It was also with the invasion of the USSR that the Nazis began the systematic murder of Jews. Although at this point the genocide of the entire European Jewish population had not as yet been envisioned, the decision to solve the "Jewish Question" at least in part through mass killings had probably been taken by Hitler and Himmler sometime during the winter of 1940–1941. The Commissar Decree of May 1941 instructed SS *Einsatzgruppen* to execute Jewish males as part of the general elimination of enemies in occupied Russia. That same month the SS was ordered to block the emigration of Jews from Belgium and France. And the policy continued to evolve thereafter toward complete extermination.

The three thousand SS men selected for these *Einsatzgruppen* were not the sole perpetrators of these crimes. They were reinforced by Reserve Police Battalions consisting of older or militarily ineligible Germans whose official duty was merely to maintain order in occupied areas. When ordered to participate in the roundup and shooting of Jews, most of these "ordinary Germans" proved just as capable as the SS in carrying out the brutal murder of Jewish men, women, and children at close range. Historians seriously disagree about the motivations that turned average Germans into perpetrators of horrendous war crimes. Some emphasize longstanding anti-Semitism, Nazi racial ideology, and indoctrination through Third Reich propaganda; others attribute it to submission to authority, peer pressure, and wartime circumstances; and still others see a combination of these factors.

However, the phenomenon of ordinary citizens becoming perpetrators, whether willingly or under duress, was by no means restricted to Germans. The eastern areas conquered by the Nazis were regions where anti-Semitism, usually more intense and violent than in the West, had been pervasive for centuries. The Nazi conquerors could exploit this hostility by encouraging indigenous populations to take action against their Jewish neighbors or by recruiting local inhabitants as auxiliary units for their murderous execution squads. Ordinary men in the Baltic States, White Russia, Ukraine, and parts of Russia became integral parts of the SS killing machine. In implementing their systematic murder of Jews, the SS could also rely upon the collaboration of certain governments such as Romania that were allied with Nazi Germany.

It is now also established that the *Wehrmacht* likewise participated in the Holocaust. Not only did the German army in most cases not interfere with the SS roundup and execution of Jews, but certain units of the army and individual soldiers actually took part in the killings or facilitated them through various forms of cooperation. Under the pretext of destroying what the Nazis had designated as the danger of "Jewish-Bolshevism" and of counteracting partisans, the army systematically executed Jews in certain areas of Russia. The orders of certain commanders also encouraged their soldiers to kill Jews by calling for the complete destruction of the "Jewish-Bolshevik" menace. In Serbia, German commanders executed Jewish refugees in retaliation for partisan attacks on their troops. At Babi Yar outside of Kiev in 1941, the German army allowed one of the most ghastly atrocities to occur when the SS shot thirty-three thousand Jewish men, women, and children in large pits.

The *Einsatzgruppen* actions, which ultimately killed between 1 million and 2 million Jews, continued throughout the war, though most of these Jews had been killed by the end of 1942. But by July 1941, the Nazis had determined that a quicker and more efficient mechanism of destruction was needed. By this time Nazi policy had evolved to the point of planning the actual genocide of Europe's 11 million Jews through either slave labor or immediate extermination. These plans were finalized at the highly secret Wannsee Conference in January 1942, after the new process of extermination had already begun. This plan called for the systematic removal of all Jews from Nazi-occupied Europe or allied states, including those already concentrated in ghettos. Jews across Europe were to be rounded up and transported to the East in a cold, ruthless, and methodical manner so that the "Final Solution" to the "Jewish Question" could be implemented.

Newly established or expanded concentration camps in Poland were now transformed into major centers for systematic mass murder. The camps at Chelmno, Belzec, Treblinka, and Sobibor functioned purely as extermination centers where Jews were gassed as soon as they arrived from across Europe. Auschwitz and Majdanek, however, served as both slave labor and extermination camps. In addition to being starved, overworked, and brutalized, some prisoners were used by SS doctors for human medical experiments that tortured, mutilated, or killed them, often through slow, painful methods that would not be used on experimental animals. As the war turned against Germany, the pace of exterminations was accelerated. When the collapsing eastern front forced the destruction of these camps, the surviving prisoners continued to suffer deprivation and death as the SS forced them to march back to the Reich, where they would work as slave labor until liberation.

With the invasion of the Soviet Union, the Nazis had also selected Gypsies for systematic destruction. Historians disagree whether race was the determining factor in singling out the Gypsies as a group to be killed and whether the Nazis ever had a general plan for their extermination. The disagreement emanates from the inconsistent, contradictory, and vacillating attitudes and policies the Nazis displayed toward Gypsies. In some cases, the Nazis applied racial criteria, while in others they classified, persecuted, killed, or exempted from deportation Gypsies on the grounds of social behavior, legal status, or perceived loyalty. The official justification for killing Gypsies in the Soviet Union was that they were Communist spies not a racial enemy. But whether resulting from racial theory, social prejudice, or wartime local circumstances, the outcome was an escalating process toward mass murder. Shootings, deportations, inhumane labor camps, sterilization, and gassing in Auschwitz ultimately became the fate of Gypsies as well as Jews.

In the end, more than 200,000 Gypsies and almost 6 million Jews had been systematically murdered by the *Einsatzgruppen* and the gassings in the camps. This Holocaust was the result of an irrational racial philosophy pushed to its extreme logical conclusion and instituted with the most efficient means of organization and technology the mind could create. It provides the clearest proof of the barbarism and hatred that had always been at the very core of nazism.

Although racial anti-Semitism was the motivation and driving force behind this genocide, other factors were clearly at work in the persecution and ultimately the destruction of European Jewry. While the party justified its actions in terms of the lofty ideological necessity of counteracting the Jewish menace, local Nazi officials and those in the party's upper echelons exploited the suffering of Jews not in the interest of national socialism or Germany but to enrich themselves. Typical of the pervasive corruption of the Third Reich, they engaged in the systematic looting of Jewish property and assets in Germany and across Europe. Their continent-wide plundering included everything from large businesses, banks, investments, and valuable art collections to minor household items, which ended up in the hands of individual Nazis or major organizations such as the SS.

Similarly, the implementation of Jewish persecution and ultimately genocide depended upon the cooperation and initiative of Germans and other Europeans who did not share this Nazi racial worldview or agree with the goal of extermination. Some succumbed to fear, coercion, or obedience to authority, but others did not. As with the persecution of Jews in Germany, the widespread complicity of organizations and individuals, who either assisted the Nazi system of persecution or remained bystanders, was strongly affected by economic or professional self-interest. All levels of bureaucracies and business, German and non-German alike, were involved. This included national, state, and local governments in the occupied territories such as France and Belgium, who willingly participated in "Aryanization" of Jewish property. Though circumstances and motivations varied greatly from place to place, the one common denominator was that the Jews were expendable to advance individual, institutional, or national interests of Germans and other Europeans. Ultimately, the economic destruction of Europe's Jews was one accelerating phase in the path toward their murder.

Throughout the years of oppression, roundups, ghettoization, and murder, Jews did not remain completely passive. But their responses were greatly circumscribed by their own powerlessness and the lack of outside support. Totally under the control of the Nazis, very rarely having any access to arms, and usually unable to count on any assistance from non-Jewish communities, Jewish armed resistance remained limited. The Nazis further hampered armed resistance by invoking a brutal policy of "collective responsibility" that threatened to severely punish or murder an entire Jewish group or community for any individual acts of resistance. Nonetheless, where feasible,

Jewish armed resistance did occur. Heroic armed uprisings took place in the Warsaw ghetto in 1943 and on a smaller scale in other ghettos, though all were ruthlessly crushed. Although overt resistance was most difficult in the tightly controlled concentration camps and extermination centers, some Jews did revolt even under these circumstances. In 1943 several hundred Jews in Sobibor and Treblinka revolted and attempted to escape; almost all of them were killed. The most effective kind of armed resistance came from those Jews, including many escapees from the ghettos, who joined the partisans fighting in the forests across occupied Europe.

Out of necessity, however, most Jewish resistance had to be clandestine and nonviolent. This consisted mainly of resisting efforts at starvation and dehumanization of Jews in ghettos, as well as evading Nazi policies restricting Jewish educational, cultural, and religious practices. To ensure the physical and cultural survival of the Jewish community, Jews smuggled food into the ghettos and established secret political, welfare, and cultural organizations. And under the most horrendous circumstances, Jews kept their religion alive.

Although there was little more that the Jews under Nazi control could have done to avoid their ultimate fate, at least several hundred thousand more could have been saved with the assistance of others. But indifference, anti-Semitism, and self-interest determined that such needed crucial aid would not be forthcoming from non-Jews in Europe and America. While Nazi policies of reprisals against any individual or group that assisted Jews seriously inhibited such aid, at least part of the inaction can be attributed to the traditional anti-Semitism in Eastern Europe or to the economic gains made by indigenous populations by the removal of Jews in their regions. The populations of Western Europe likewise remained generally apathetic toward the plight of Jews. And the record of the Protestant and Catholic churches generally shows a similar reluctance even to condemn Nazi atrocities toward Jews.

Equally important, though, among the populations of Italy and Denmark there existed widespread resistance to Nazi anti-Semitic policies and the deportations of Jews. And elsewhere countless individual government officials, clergy, and average citizens in Eastern and Western Europe risked their own lives to assist or rescue Jews. Motivated by religious belief, basic human decency, or anti-Nazi sentiments, such people rescued perhaps tens of thousands of Jews. Among such people, Jews found food, hiding places, or routes of escape.

The response from Britain and the United States, on the other hand, remained woefully inadequate given the enormity of the atrocities and the possibilities for more forceful action. Although once the exterminations started, the Western democracies could not have prevented the genocide of most European Jewry, they could have done much more earlier and at the time to save large numbers of Jews. But the anti-Semitism and indifference that characterized the basic response in occupied Europe was likewise evident in Britain and the United States. While Britain refused to open Palestine to Jewish immigration, the United States maintained its tight restrictions on immigration. Preoccupied with the war and suffering from their own anti-Semitism, the U.S. State Department and the military made no effort at rescue or bombing the gas chambers at Auschwitz. They also failed to threaten neutral countries and those allied with Nazi Germany not to cooperate in the repression, deportation, or extermination of Jews.

Initially, one key problem for the victims of genocide as well as those who might have assisted them was believing that the Nazis were actually determined to exterminate millions of people to fulfill their extreme racial ideology. The Nazis had been careful to hide this "terrible secret" from all but those directly involved. Still, even after incontrovertible evidence demonstrated the reality of such genocide, the Western democracies did not alter their response. Neither did responses in occupied Europe change significantly once knowledge of the mass shootings and gassings began to leak out. That the war turned against Germany in 1943 appears to be more important in increasing the willingness of individuals or governments to assist Jews or at least be less cooperative with Nazi deportations to the extermination centers.

Like populations elsewhere in Europe, millions of Germans did not know of the "Final Solution." Many of those Germans who did hear of the mass killings in the East found it impossible to believe, but others avoided comprehending what they knew to be true. Even among those informed of the death camps or shootings, the reaction was mostly indifference or helplessness. The response of some Germans was probably due to traditional anti-Semitism reinforced by years of Nazi propaganda. But even among those less susceptible to anti-Semitism, the Jewish problem had for the most part become an abstraction from which they had been isolated for several years. Most German Jews had either emigrated or were in concentration camps in the East. Moreover, most Germans were mainly concerned with the war itself rather than the suffering or even survival of the Jews. The ceaseless, devastating bombing of their cities and the fate of their own close relatives fighting and dying at the front were much more immediate and personal to the average German. The Nazi oppressive dictatorship and enormity of wartime killing and destruction had themselves tended to desensitize people to atrocities and wide-scale death. Many Germans merely integrated the killings of Jews in the East into the general mental picture they had of the entire destructive and deadly wartime situation.

As they had throughout the Third Reich, individual German citizens, clergy members, and even public officials continued to assist those few Jews still in Germany, while other Germans assisted Jews in occupied Europe. It was, in fact, a German industrialist, Eduard Schulte, who risked his own life to first provide credible evidence to the West about Nazi genocide. Although Schulte's efforts held out the hope that a strong response from the Western democracies would either stop or impede the "Final Solution," most individual efforts by average Germans could not halt the killing machine. The heroic efforts of certain Germans could at best save small groups of Jews, while doing nothing to prevent the continuation of mass murder. Only a widespread and well-organized resistance movement would have had any chance of effectively hindering Hitler's plans.

However, such a popular resistance movement never emerged in Germany. The Nazis had destroyed most potential centers of organized resistance in 1933. Thereafter, the terror and efficiency of the Gestapo inhibited the formation of nationwide resistance networks. In 1942–1943 "The White Rose," a handful of heroic students at the University of Munich in collaboration with Kurt Huber, a philosophy professor, distributed anti-Nazi leaflets calling for passive resistance. Captured by the Gestapo, the leaders, brother and sister Hans and Sophie Scholls, were tortured, publicly tried, and executed along with Huber.

In addition, beginning in 1939, resistance was further complicated by special wartime factors. Nationalism and patriotism made it difficult for most Germans to attempt to overthrow the existing government while their country was engaged in a war, especially after the Allies demanded unconditional surrender from Germany. Many of those most likely to serve as leaders and organizers of popular resistance movements had been placed in concentration camps by the early stages of the war. Those who remained active did not receive assistance, or even moral support, from the Allies, who were seeking the total defeat of Germany and not merely an end to the dictatorship.

A small but prestigious group of resisters, however, felt that the total defeat and occupation of Germany by the Allies was both justified and necessary. During the war these men met secretly at Kreisau, the estate of Count Helmut von Moltke, to discuss the fundamental principles for a morally rejuvenated and greatly transformed Germany following national socialism's complete obliteration. This eclectic group of idealistic and romantic men in their thirties and forties consisted of devoted Christian aristocrats, Protestant and Catholic leaders, and Socialist intellectuals. Though vague on details, they envisioned a society based upon Christian moral and socialist economic principles derived from divine and natural law. The dignity and freedom of the individual would be guaranteed, monopoly capitalism replaced by a controlled economy with worker rights, and powerful institutions decentralized in favor of local control. Committed to morally based nonviolence, the Kreisau Circle remained distant from the active resistance and conspiratorial plots. Some members subsequently displayed criticism of assassination attempts and plans to overthrow the regime by those conservatives who did not share their future of a spiritually based and more socially equitable Germany.

Thus the overt German resistance continued to remain limited to members of those conservative and military circles that had planned several aborted coups since the 1930s. Their final attempt came after reversals on the eastern front and the Normandy invasion convinced the conspirators that either Hitler must be eliminated or Germany would end up as a piece of occupied rubble. The new plot, called *Valkyrie*, was conceived at a time when the Gestapo had intensified its security activities, arresting several prominent German resistance leaders and driving a few others into hiding. According to *Valkyrie*, Hitler would be assassinated and immediately thereafter troops loyal to the conspirators were to occupy Berlin, cut communications, and arrest Nazi leaders at strategic points in different parts of Europe. In addition to Beck and Goerdeler, the conspiracy had the support of a few generals, including Rommel and some members of military intelligence.

On July 20, 1944, Count Claus von Stauffenberg left a bomb in a briefcase at Hitler's headquarters in Rastenburg. Though wounded by the explosion that destroyed the entire room, the *Führer* survived and was still able to function reasonably well. The coup then began to collapse. A chance for success remained, but things began to go wrong. Rommel was out of action before the coup was launched because of an accident, and the lack of his presence, along with the reluctance of certain generals to go forward without him, proved fatal to the entire conspiracy. Some attempts were made to carry out the plan, but key figures did not take the action required of them, and the Nazi leadership recovered quickly. Thus the final attempt by the anti-Nazi German resistance failed.

The dictatorship reacted as expected. The following day, the Gestapo began arresting the major conspirators, along with thousands of other participants and suspects. A few leaders of the conspiracy, such as Beck and Rommel, committed suicide. Several thousand others were placed on trial before a people's court. Approximately five thousand of those convicted were executed by shooting or hanging from meat hooks. Both the trial and the ghastly hangings were filmed to be shown as a deterrent to others.

At this point, few military or Nazi leaders could deny that the war was lost. Yet the *Führer* refused to accept the inevitable. He insisted that a victory could be won through will, determination, obedience, and his secret *Wunderwaffen* (miracle weapons). His armies were ordered not to give up any territory or to retreat, while Goebbels's propaganda machine tried to stiffen German morale and willingness to fight by asserting that a final victory was at hand. The Germans had indeed invented *Wunderwaffen*, namely the jet plane, the V-1 flying bomb, and the V-2 rocket, which gave the Nazis a technological advantage over the Allies in a few areas. But these weapons were not sufficient to deter the Allied advances. Although almost ten thousand V-1 and V-2 rockets were launched against England, their damage was limited, and these attacks ended when the rocket bases in Holland were captured by the Allies. The jet planes, on the other hand, were not produced in sufficient numbers, nor was there adequate fuel for them. Germany remained without effective air power during the final months of the war.

None of this, however, convinced Hitler to adopt a more rational strategy. Instead, he launched a surprise counteroffensive with panzer divisions in December of 1944 in the hope of splitting the Allied forces in the West. But this, too, failed, allowing the Allies to proceed toward Germany at a faster pace. The Allies crossed the Rhine on March 7, 1945, as the Russians occupied most of eastern Germany. By mid-April the battle for Berlin had begun with a massive Russian attack on the capital.

The useless slaughter continued because Hitler refused to surrender. Beginning with the defeat at Stalingrad, the *Führer*'s behavior was characterized more and more by irrational outbursts and fantasizing, particularly after the attempted assassination of July 20, 1944. Hidden away in his underground bunker in Berlin, he demanded unrealistic sacrifices from his troops and his people, sometimes maneuvering on a map armies that no longer existed. He recruited boys into the armed forces and had civilians organized into a type of home guard to resist the Russians. The man who wanted to create the greatest civilization in history became determined to reduce Germany to rubble and ashes so as to deny the Allies any material benefits from their victory. Nazi leaders were instructed to destroy everything of military or economic value before the enemy occupied an area.

The great *Führer*, the alleged personification of the spirit of the *Volk*, would accept no blame or responsibility for the defeat. To explain the collapse of his short-lived empire, he reverted to the stabbed-in-the-back myth he had embraced as an explanation for the defeat in 1918. His generals, he said, had failed to follow orders and had engaged in treason against him. To this he added another specious argument, contending that the German people also had failed him. Hitler berated his own people—formerly his master race—as unworthy and incapable of fulfilling the great historic mission for which they had been chosen.

But the failings of the German people were not the ones Hitler claimed. They failed in the areas of moral behavior and the fundamental humane principles on which civilized society rests, though these were of no concern to the *Führer*. What he did value and demand—obedience, a willingness to fight, endure, and sacrifice—the German people provided. They never offered any mass resistance; they followed his orders, perpetrating or acquiescing in some of the worst crimes in human history. They endured the terror of the regime and the Allied bombings that destroyed most of their cities; over 6 million Germans died in the war. During all this, the morale of the German people did not break, and they usually did what the *Führer* ordered and expected, fighting on long after such a struggle was not only fruitless but irrational.

Some of those closest to the *Führer*, however, including some of the most diehard Nazis, did desert him in the end. Speer refused to follow Hitler's scorched-earth order and publicly pleaded with the German people not to destroy what was left of Germany. In late April Göring, Hitler's appointed successor, tried to take over the leadership of Germany even before the *Führer* was dead. Himmler also attempted to assume political control of the government and tried to negotiate with the Western Allies on Germany's behalf. An infuriated Hitler removed Himmler from office and had the SS arrest Göring.

During the last days in Hitler's bunker there existed a bizarre atmosphere of unreality. The Russians were closing in from all parts of the city. Yet a semblance of normality in governmental activity and even social life continued among Hitler's coterie of political associates, staff, and friends beneath the ground. On April 20, 1945, the *Führer's* birthday was celebrated with a small party. Then on April 29, Hitler married his longtime mistress, Eva Braun, in another bunker ceremony. The formalities over, he immediately returned to political affairs, dictating his last will and testament, the nature of which was typically Hitlerian. It included the usual vicious attacks on the alleged power of the international Jewish conspiracy, urging others to carry on the struggle against the Jews. His ruthless personal secretary and chief of the party chancellery, Martin Bormann, was named head of the Nazi party; Goebbels was appointed chancellor; and Admiral Karl Dönitz was designated as the new president and military chief.

The following day, April 30, 1945, Hitler and his new bride committed suicide. She took poison and the *Führer* shot himself. Their bodies were then burned with gasoline, as Hitler had instructed, and their remains quickly buried. After a futile attempt to negotiate with the Russians, Goebbels then followed the example of his beloved *Führer* and committed suicide with his wife by having the SS shoot them. Bormann was killed during a desperate attempt to escape from Berlin. Himmler later committed suicide on May 23, after being captured by the British. On May 1, the Russians reached Hitler's bunker, and on May 7, Admiral Dönitz signed the unconditional surrender of Germany. The Third Reich had finally been destroyed.

Countless volumes have been written describing, as well as attempting to explain, the roots, character, and crimes of the National Socialist movement. Many questions still remain open; historical debates over the causes and responsibility continue, as does the shock that these events had occurred in the modern world and in the very heart of Western civilization. Accordingly, much has been learned and much is still to be understood from this experience. But if one wanted to illustrate the true nature of nazism and the mentality of its leaders with a single example, one of the final acts of Josef Goebbels would suffice. Before arranging his own death, Goebbels had his six children poisoned to death in Hitler's bunker.

PART FIVE

The Struggle for
Justice and Historical Memory

CHAPTER 15

From Nuremberg to
Vergangenheitsbewältigung

Various historians have used the term *Götterdämmerung* (the twilight of the gods) to describe the final days of the Nazi dictatorship. *Götterdämmerung* was the final opera in Richard Wagner's cycle of mythological dramas, *The Ring of the Nibelung*. In many respects, this is indeed an appropriate symbolic representation of the events at the end of the Third Reich. The Nazis did act like gods, creating and destroying almost at will, disposing of the lives of millions of people with aloof detachment in some cases and diabolical vengeance in others. And the final days in the bunker resembled a drama acted out in an unreal and almost mythological setting beneath the ground, with Hitler's suicide as the climax to the epic. Yet a case could be made that the events in the bunker were not the last act of this *Götterdämmerung*. The twilight of these gods did not finally arrive until the Nuremberg trials, where all the crimes of the Nazi regime were recounted in detail before the entire world, while what was left of the top echelons of the Third Reich watched from the witness stand awaiting their final judgment.

Between November 1945 and August 1946, the International Military Tribunal held at Nuremberg tried the major leaders of the Third Reich. Most of the defendants refused to acknowledge the legality of the process or any responsibility for crimes. Those who had directed the most destructive war in history, like those who participated in the extermination of millions of people, either showed indignation toward the prosecution or tried to blame Hitler and other superiors who were already dead. Despite the abundance of evidence and documentation supporting the charges, only a few former Nazi leaders accepted their guilt. Of the twenty-four defendants convicted, twelve were sentenced to death and seven to various prison terms. Although Göring committed suicide shortly before his scheduled execution, the others condemned to death were hanged in October 1946. The trial records and an abundance of other historical documentation provide ample and irrefutable evidence of Nazi intentions and deeds of an oppressive, inhumane, and murderous nature.

Nevertheless, the Allied trials of the major war criminals at Nuremberg were not the end of the efforts to come to grips with the horrors and atrocities of the Nazi experience. The Allies, Nazi victims, and anti-Nazi Germans were determined to eradicate all vestiges of nazism, while bringing to justice those beyond the top leadership who were guilty of crimes. Allied and German courts handled thousands of criminal cases against Nazis, resulting in prison terms for thousands and death sentences for a few hundred. Meanwhile, the purge of Nazi members, institutions, and symbols through the Allied policy of "denazification" led to the internment of tens of thousands of Nazis and prohibited many more Germans considered compromised from employment. Special attention was paid to keeping Nazis out of government office or other areas of public life such as the press and education. When German courts took over jurisdiction of denazification in 1946, they examined almost a million cases. Denazification procedures and prosecution of Nazis reached their high points in 1945–1949.

During the 1950s, several factors soon halted this vigorous confrontation with the Nazi past and its continuing legacy. Among these was the need to reconstruct a devastated country and establish democracy in West Germany, simultaneously with the onset of the Cold War. Memory of nazism, like prosecution of war criminals, was sacrificed for national unity and healing. The newfound Federal Republic accepted responsibility for the Holocaust, paying financial restitution to Jewish survivors and supporting the new state of Israel. But otherwise reconciliation and silence typified the public atmosphere of the 1950s. Under amnesty laws between 1949 and 1954, hundreds of thousands received lightened sentences or were freed; many compromised and suspect individuals also returned to public life. Although some war criminals continued to be prosecuted, other serious perpetrators escaped justice. Thus, while the Holocaust quickly became an integral part of West German postwar memory, coming to grips with nazism more generally was postponed in order for democracy to be nurtured and an anti-Communist front established with the Western powers against the Soviet Union. The divisive subject of the extent of the German people's complicity during the Third Reich was particularly evaded. In the East, the Cold War (and the need to win popular support for communism) also led the German Democratic Republic to abandon its pursuit of the Nazi past. It likewise constructed a Communist ideological narrative of that past in which there was little or no place for the Holocaust. Thereafter, the serious struggle over memory became primarily a West German question. In the face of such a broad West German consensus eschewing or denying "collective guilt," some new German leaders did insist that Germans must at least show "collective shame" for the crimes perpetrated in their country's name. Nonetheless, this first phase of what came to be called *Vergangenheitsbewältigung* (coming to grips with the past) involved more forgetting than remembering.

By the 1960s a heightened political and moral consciousness led many Germans to reject as inadequate the earlier version of *Vergangenheitsbewältigung* with its emphasis upon silence. This reaction was especially intense among the generation engaged in the youth revolt of that era. The outcome was a national soul searching, accompanied by specific legal and political action to admit national guilt and responsibility. The renewed trials of Nazi war criminals once again shocked the nation with irrefutable exposures of the nature of these crimes and the breadth of Germany's complicity. The continued pursuit of war criminals was also facilitated by the eventual elimination of the statute of limitations for murder and genocide. Meanwhile, Social Democratic chancellors such as Willy Brandt and Helmut Schmidt offered public admissions of guilt for Nazi and wartime German atrocities in the East. Such public acts raised the consciousness of German responsibility beyond the Holocaust to the incalculable number of other Nazi victims. The churches, educational institutions, and public intellectuals also contributed significantly to this new moral awareness and reckoning. Moreover, in coming decades historical research would gradually erode the apologetic claims of many Germans that they, too, were helpless victims of an all-powerful totalitarian Nazi dictatorship. Studies disclosed the complicity, sometimes active support, of more and more institutions, from the churches to the legal and medical professions.

This trend toward a more open and candid form of *Vergangenheitsbewältigung* continues to the present. Nonetheless, it has persisted in the midst of continual controversies that periodically ignite into public firestorms in Germany. The *Historikerstreit* (historians' dispute) of the 1980s erupted when certain scholars were accused of trying to equate German suffering to that of the victims of the Hitler dictatorship, as well as of comparing Nazi crimes to those of Communists. A decade later, another public eruption occurred over the traveling exhibit Crimes of the Wehrmacht: Dimensions of a War of Annihilation, 1941–1944. That exhibit vividly documented the participation, or acquiescence, of German soldiers in the atrocities committed against Jews and Russians (soldiers, POWs, and civilians). These and other revelations shattered the "myth of the clean *Wehrmacht*" that had sharply differentiated this highly respected traditional German institution from the barbarities of the SS. That distinction between honorable patriotic soldiers and fanatical SS criminals had been propagated during the 1950s phase of *Vergangenheitsbewältigung*. Indeed, revelations of Nazi affiliations, or wartime activities, can still destroy the careers of public figures, as can a mere misspoken allusion to some aspect of this contested past. These trends, however, were occasionally counterbalanced by the insistence that there were Germans that had not succumbed to national socialism but merely tried to survive it. Likewise, the army conspirators who attempted to assassinate Hitler on July 20, 1944, were cited as resistance heroes. In recent years, there has also been a refocus on German wartime suffering, as works on the devastating and morally questionable Allied bombings of German civilians acquired popularity. This resurgence of German victimization can also be detected in revelations and revitalized debates over Soviet atrocities against German civilians, including the mass rapes of German women and girls.

Differing perspectives on the true nature of this past (and how it should be remembered and dealt with) contest each other in contemporary Germany. To some, the dreadful enormity and historical uniqueness of nazism obligate the Germans never to forget. They argue that, without this inexorable memory, the Germans can neither learn the necessary lessons from the past nor bear the requisite moral accountability. The establishment of institutions for the study of national socialism and anti-Semitism, like continued public education, are clear manifestations of these deeply held sentiments. The 2005 creation in Berlin of the Memorial to the Murdered Jews of Europe stands as an architectural testament to the link between the new Germany and its disquieting history. Other Germans, however, sincerely feel that the oppression and crimes of the past, though horrible and undeniable, should not unduly burden the present and future. In their minds, younger generations of Germans in particular, born decades after the Third Reich, have the right to normalcy without being forced to bear the guilt for the deeds of their ancestors over which they had no control. Clearly, almost a century after the founding of the Nazi party in 1919, the burden of the historical memory of that movement remains an integral part of contemporary German consciousness, identity, and public debate. The continued prevalence of this "Unmasterable Past" in itself attests to the magnitude and repercussions of the very idea of national socialism and the horrendous dictatorship that it spawned.

CHAPTER 16

The Intractable Nazi Legacy in Film:
Propaganda and History

From the early years of the NSDAP to present public controversies, the mass media has remained an essential conduit in the struggle over nazism and its burdensome legacy. Communication technology was a significant instrument in the Nazi rise as a mass political party with an effective nationwide political machine. The radio, loudspeaker, quickly mass-produced propaganda posters, and illustrated publications contributed prominently to the Nazis' meteoric electoral successes. Mass rallies and rapid recruitment of members and voters would have been impossible without these. The Nazis also relied on modern communication techniques to expand and sustain support throughout the triumphal years and decline of the Third Reich. And among the modern media they exploited, film held a distinguished place. From their hosting of film evenings during recruitment drives in rural areas and small towns to their manipulation of the entire cinema industry throughout their years in power, the Nazis insightfully grasped the political and social power of film.

In our contemporary world, where so much communication and learning comes through nonprint new media, film can also be a very useful medium for illuminating and understanding the Nazi historical experience. Certain images or portrayals of this period of history on the silver screen can convey messages and elicit poignant responses far more effectively than the printed word. This is true whether one is viewing documentary footage of celebratory Nazi rallies or of the murderous brutality of their concentration camps. Learning through film can be just as efficacious when viewing the feature films of that era that mass audiences watched, particularly those created by the Nazis as part of their extensive propaganda apparatus.

The films discussed below are intended to introduce the reader to some of the relevant, often most significant, feature and documentary films dealing with Nazi Germany. The selection is directed at the novice and not those well advanced in the field or specializing in film studies. As such, these films do not constitute an exhaustive or exclusive list, but rather are recommendations based upon widely acknowledged significance or proven effectiveness in enhancing historical understanding through classroom use. They have also been selected for their availability through rental, libraries, internet, or purchase. Most are of German origin; all are with English subtitles or dubbed in English. These films can be viewed while reading from the relevant sections of this book, or afterward as a means of continuing to grasp the essence and consequential nature of the Nazi phenomenon. They can be supplemented by the abundant films and documentaries on various history channels. However, since not all those featured on history channels are of equal quality or reliability, caution should be exercised during viewing. The more a viewer learns about Hitler and the Nazis from authoritative historical readings the better prepared he or she will be to discriminate the valuable from the potentially misleading film.

Weimar Republic

The hectic frenzy and modernist features of the big city symbolized to the Nazis much of what was detrimental in Weimar culture and society. These characteristics are vividly captured in the 1927 documentary *Berlin: Symphony of a Great City*. In fact, the entire film industry of post–World War I Germany is especially important for appreciating the modernist trends in art that offended so many traditional-minded Germans. Many conservative middle-class Germans were quite susceptible to the Nazi condemnation of such films as *Kulturbolschevismus* (cultural Bolshevism), by which liberals and the left were subverting the values, morals, and psychological health of Germany. The expressionist 1919 film *The Cabinet of Dr. Caligari* is an excellent starting point, with Fritz Lang's 1931 classic psychological thriller *M* as a counterpart from late Weimar. The Nazis reproached the latter as an example of a society becoming so decadent it sympathized with a psychopathic child killer. In turn, Lang's 1933 *The Testament of Dr. Mabuse*, some argue, foretold the insanity of the criminal regime the Nazis were about to establish. On the controversial Weimar issues of cabarets, prostitution, alluring sexuality, and homosexuality, see *Pandora's Box* (1928), Marlene Dietrich's debut as a sex symbol in *The Blue Angel* (1931), and *Girls in Uniform* (1931). On the plight of the workers and class conflict, similarly exploited by the Nazis, compare Lang's optimistic *Metropolis* (1927) with the revolutionary zeal of the depression-era Communist production *Kuhle Wampe* (1932).

Nazi Germany

Among the documentary overviews of the Third Reich, Joachim Fest's three-hour *Hitler: The Whole Story* remains quite useful. One of the best windows into the Third Reich, however, will always be Leni Riefenstahl's *Triumph of the Will*. Her masterful and innovative documentary of an actual Nazi Nuremberg rally brings the viewer right into the essence of these mass meetings of devoted followers as they experienced it. Yet viewers must be cautious not to fall victim to the very propaganda this film was intended to propagate. Despite its detached documentary appearance, this film is not a disinterested, neutral, objective production. Events and speeches in the film must be considered in the historical context and period in which that September 1934 rally took place (the aftermath of the Röhm purge, Hindenburg's death, and Hitler's assumption of total power). More importantly, the images and overall thrust of the film aim to depict Hitler, the National Socialist movement, and the German people's reception of the Third Reich as the Nazis wanted them to appear. The positive images and popular enthusiasm portrayed are often in stark contrast to the historical reality of that movement as clearly established by historians. A similar recommendation of acclaim and caution can be advised for Riefenstahl's tour de force *Olympia*, a documentary of the 1936 Berlin Olympics.

A good example of the genre of Nazi propaganda film projecting a heroic and idealistic image of themselves is *Hans Westmar* (1933). Based upon the Nazi mythology of the inspiration for their anthem, the "Horst Wessel Song," this film shows their final triumph in the seizure of power after the great sacrifices of their long "Years of Struggle." However, the most popular, and thus most numerous, cinematic productions were not overt propaganda films but those aimed at general entertainment. Yet their content and style was still controlled by Goebbels' cultural and artistic institutions, which often ensured that insidious Nazi themes were concealed within an apparently unrelated moving or captivating story. Typical of what the average moviegoer saw in the Third Reich was *La Habanera* (1937). This adventure-romance (involving Swedes in Puerto Rico) contains distinct, though subtle, ideological messages about race and women. On the kind of art and culture the Nazis promoted, and condemned, see the very informative BBC documentary *Art in the Third Reich* (1990).

Racial Anti-Semitism and the Holocaust

The clever Nazi manipulation of subject matter and German movie audiences' emotions through entertainment films is certainly illustrated in the emotive historical drama *Jud Süss* (1940). Using the most talented and popular actors and actresses of the era, this masterpiece of anti-Semitic cinematography skillfully invoked a captivating story to great effect. It the process, the Nazis were able to interweave every religious, economic, cultural, and racial canard about the alleged despicable nature and threatening power of Jews that has existed throughout Western civilization. Juxtaposing these repulsive images against those of their beautiful and honorable German victims, the Nazis created a powerful, perhaps successful, means of inciting hatred and fear of Jews. The Nazis expressed a similar message in their second cinematic landmark in anti-Semitic propaganda, *The Eternal Jew* (1940). Here the Nazis employed the technique of a documentary to convey the authority of objectivity and the alleged factual truth about Jews to their audience. *The Eternal Jew* is the most comprehensive and succinct Nazi description of every aspect of their racial ideological interpretation of Jews that they ever produced. Since this film deprecates Jews as a dangerous inferior race, and almost begs the question of a solution to the so-called Jewish Question, some scholars believe it served as a conditioning precursor to the Holocaust.

Among all Holocaust films accessible to the English-speaking world, I would recommend the following as must-see. For a heart-rending depiction of Jewish victims, anti-Semites, and bystanders in Nazi occupied Europe, the Czech film *The Shop on Main Street* (1965) has achieved classic status. The barbaric consequences of Nazi anti-Semitic ideology and policies can only be truly felt by witnessing the fanatical cruelty of their war against the Jews in the film footage surviving from the era. The unprecedented inhumanity of the camps and the Holocaust are vividly projected in the horrific documentary footage of the highly acclaimed French documentary *Night and Fog* (1955). Even more disturbing are images of mass suffering and death captured by American and British cameramen upon discovering the camps in 1945. This nauseating evidence of Nazi plans and actions for the systematic murder of millions is made available through a Frontline special under the title *Memory of the Camps* (2005). The 1963 trial of twenty-two SS men in a German court for perpetrating such crimes is powerfully recreated in the 1993 documentary *Verdict at Auschwitz*.

Wartime Germany and Aftermath

Film was an essential component of the Nazi effort to justify Hitler's foreign policy and the disastrous war it unleashed on Europe. Here, too, the Nazis capitalized on documentary depictions of their extraordinary early triumphs to further legitimize their regime, as well as to highlight the mythological greatness of Hitler's leadership and the ideological claims of German superiority. Film later served as an important means of sustaining morale as the war turned against Germany, when death and casualty figures affected every German family and the war came to the home front as allied bombing devastated most German cities. The nature and tone of the Nazi version of the causes, purposes, and nature of their military campaigns in World War II are presented in the collection titled *German Wartime Newsreels, 1941–1945*. Some Nazi films, such as *The Campaign in Poland* (1939), were also directed at foreign audiences with similar self-justifying intent.

Far more accurate and realistic, however, are the footage and still photographs taken by individual German soldiers during the war. The short award-winning documentary *Amateur Photographer* (2004), based upon the photo album of a German soldier on the eastern front, captures the reality of German atrocities against Jews, Russian civilians, and Soviet prisoners of war. Equally poignant for its educational value is *Mein Krieg* (1991), compiled from the footage taken by six German soldiers with their personal movie cameras. Quite revealing are the memories and starkly contrasting perspectives of these former soldiers as they reminisced about their experiences and evaluated their behavior fifty years after the war. Among the German feature films likewise offering realistic portrayals of the war, *Das Boot* (1981) and *Stalingrad* (1993) are highly recommended. The 2004 film *Downfall* depicts the last days of life in Hitler's bunker as his thousand-year Reich crumbles around him when the Russians conquer Berlin.

For brief, though telling, contemporary scenes of the destroyed Germany and demoralized German people, see the British documentary *A Defeated People* (1945). These early postwar years also signaled the beginning of a struggle between East and West Germany to interpret the recent past in light of their respective allegiances to the Western powers or the Soviet Union during the onset of the Cold War. In this respect, two of the first feature films produced in postwar Germany certainly fall within the category of what is now designated as "memory" studies. The West German film *The Murderers Are among Us* (1945) involves a concentration camp survivor and the unbearable wartime memories of a former officer. In conspicuous contrast, the East German film *Our Daily Bread* (1946), in keeping with that regime's later persistent eschewing of the Holocaust, promotes an explicitly anticapitalist, antibourgeois theme with communism as the hope for the revival of the German people and their country. However, the 1955 West German antiwar satire *08/15* (named for an unreliable German machine gun) also fits within the internal struggle over postwar memory. This film's story of young soldiers, basically innocent of Nazi affiliations, forced to fight in a desperate and confused war effort could easily be considered a cinematic version of the myth of the clean *Wehrmacht* being constructed in German memoir and military literature of that era. *08/15* should be balanced by a viewing of the documentary *The Unknown Soldier* (2006) about the Crimes of the Wehrmacht exhibit.

The plight of German civilians enduring Nazi dictatorial rule, Allied bombing, and occupation has been the subject of several excellent German feature films. Very emotionally moving is *Germany—Pale Mother* (1979), tracing the travails of a young couple from the prewar years through the often futile attempts at family reconstruction Germans faced in the Federal Republic. Also well done is *Dresden* (2006), about the terror of the highly controversial Allied firebomb raids of that city in 1945. That this defeat was for many years what Atina Grossman has called a "gendered defeat" is certainly borne out by a recent film based on the 1945 Berlin diary of an anonymous German woman. *A Woman in Berlin* (2008) graphically captures the destitute and powerless predicament of the millions of helpless German women attempting to survive and protect their children in the face of the brutality of vengeful Soviet troops. Such films further facilitate the necessary discussion on the repeated mass rapes of literally hundreds of thousands of German women in the Soviet occupied areas that had been taboo for much of the history of postwar Germany.

CHRONOLOGY

1918	November 9	Weimar Republic established
1919	June 28	Treaty of Versailles signed
	September	Hitler joins the German Workers' Party in Munich (DAP)
1920	February 24	National Socialist German Workers Party (NSDAP) program introduced
1923	Summer–Fall	Great Inflation
	November 8–9	Beer Hall *Putsch* in Munich
1924	April–December	Hitler imprisoned at Landesberg
1925	April 27	Paul von Hindenburg elected president
1928	May 20	Major Nazi defeat in Reichstag elections
1929	June–October	Campaign against the Young Plan
	October	Start of Great Depression
1930	March 30	Heinrich Brüning becomes chancellor
	September 14	First Nazi success in Reichstag elections
1932	April 10	Hindenburg reelected president
	May 30	Franz von Papen becomes chancellor
	July 31	Electoral victory makes Nazis largest party in Reichstag
	November 6	Nazis lose 2 million votes in Reichstag election
	December 2	Kurt von Schleicher appointed chancellor
1933	January 30	Hitler appointed chancellor
	February 28	Reichstag fire
	March 5	Reichstag election yields Nazi-Conservative majority
	March 23	Enabling Act passed
	April 1	Nazi boycott of Jewish businesses
	May 2	Labor unions eliminated; German Labor Front (DAF) created
	July 14	Political parties eliminated
	July 20	Concordat with Catholic Church
	November 12	Reichstag elections with NSDAP as only legal party
1934	June 30–July 2	Röhm Purge
	August 2	Death of Hindenburg; Hitler unites presidency and chancellorship
1935	March 16	German rearmament proclaimed
	September 15	Nuremberg Laws
1936	March 7	Remilitarization of Rhineland
	August	Olympic Games in Berlin

1938	March 12–13	*Anschluss* with Austria
	September 29–30	Munich Conference
	November 8–9	*Kristallnacht* pogrom
1939	March 14	German occupation of Czechoslovakia
	August 23	Nazi-Soviet Non-Aggression Pact
	September 1	German invasion of Poland
1940	May 10	Invasion of France
	August	Battle of Britain
1941	June 22	German invasion of Soviet Union
	December 11	Hitler declares war on United States
1942	January 20	Wannsee Conference on "Final Solution" to the Jewish Question
	June	Second Nazi offensive against Soviet Union
1943	January 31	German army surrenders at Stalingrad
	April	Warsaw Ghetto uprising
1944	June 6	Normandy invasion
	July 20	Attempted assassination of Hitler
1945	April 30	Hitler commits suicide
	May 7	Germany surrenders

SUBJECTS RECOMMENDED FOR READING AND RESEARCH

Weimar Republic

The problems of the Weimar Republic and the reasons for its collapse are among the most important questions relating to the rise and success of nazism. An older, classic interpretation is found in Erich Eyck, *A History of the Weimar Republic* (Cambridge, Mass.: Harvard University Press, 1967). For varying recent general interpretations, see Eric D. Weitz, *Weimar Germany: Promise and Tragedy* (Princeton, N.J.: Princeton University Press, 2007); Detlev Peukert, *The Weimar Republic: The Crisis of Classical Modernity* (New York: Hill & Wang, 1989); Eberhard Kolb, *The Weimar Republic* (London: Unwin Hyman, 1988); and Hans Mommsen, *The Rise and Fall of Weimar Democracy* (Chapel Hill: University of North Carolina Press, 1996). An extremely valuable resource for Weimar research in English is the very extensive group of key documents translated in Anton Kaes, Martin Jay, and Edward Dimendberg, eds., *The Weimar Republic Source Book* (Berkeley: University of California Press, 1994).

An important subject for research is the nature, goals, and responsibility of political leaders and parties for the crisis of democracy. On prominent political figures in the Weimar Republic, see Peter Stachura, *Political Leaders in Weimar Germany: A Biographical Study* (New York: Harvester Wheatsheaf, 1993); William A. Patch, *Heinrich Brüning and the Dissolution of the Weimar Republic* (Cambridge, Mass.: Cambridge University Press, 1998); Andreas Dorpalen, *Hindenburg and the Weimar Republic* (Princeton, N.J.: Princeton University Press, 1964); Klaus Epstein, *Matthias Erzberger and the Dilemma of German Democracy* (Princeton, N.J.: Princeton University Press, 1959); John Leopold, *Alfred Hugenberg: The Radical Nationalist Campaign against the Weimar Republic* (New Haven, Conn.: Yale University Press, 1977); and Henry A. Turner, *Gustav Stresemann and the Politics of the Weimar Republic* (Princeton, N.J.: Princeton University Press, 1963). On other political parties, see Larry E. Jones, *German Liberalism and the Dissolution of the Weimar Party System* (Chapel Hill: University of North Carolina Press, 1988); Werner Angress, *Stillborn Revolution: The Communist Bid for Power in Germany, 1921–1933* (Princeton, N.J.: Princeton University Press, 1963); Richard N. Hunt, *German Social Democracy, 1918–1933* (New York: Quadrangle Books, 1970); and Richard Breitman, *German Socialism and Weimar Democracy* (Chapel Hill: University of North Carolina Press, 1981).

How the crisis of democracy was aggravated further by the political activities of paramilitary groups and the German army is another area of fruitful research. This question generally, and regarding the emergence of the Nazi party and its own paramilitary group (the SA), can be investigated in Harold Gordon, *The Reichswehr and the German Republic, 1919–1926* (Princeton, N.J.: Princeton University Press, 1957); Francis Carstens, *Reichswehr and Politics, 1918–1933* (New York: Oxford University Press, 1966); James Diehl, *Paramilitary Politics in Weimar Germany* (Bloomington: Indiana University Press, 1977); and Robert Waite, *Vanguard of Nazism: The Free Corps Movement in Postwar Germany, 1918–1933* (Cambridge, Mass.: Harvard University Press, 1952).

Weimar cultural life and the role played by intellectuals in the failure of democracy are two of the most important and intensely debated aspects of this period. For the overall problem, see Walter Laqueur, *Weimar: A Cultural History* (New York: Capricorn Books, 1974); Peter Gay, *Weimar Culture: The Outsider as Insider* (New York: Harper & Row, 1968); Otto Friedrich, *Before the Deluge: A Portrait of Berlin in the 1920s* (New York: Harper & Row, 1972); and Peter Jelavich, *Berlin Cabaret* (Cambridge, Mass.: Harvard University Press, 1993). Differing perspectives on the relationship of leftist and conservative intellectuals to democracy, nazism, and the republic can be found in Joseph W. Bendersky, *Carl Schmitt: Theorist for the Reich* (Princeton, N.J.: Princeton University Press, 1983); Istvan Deak, *Weimar's Left-Wing Intellectuals: A Political History of the Weltbühne and Its Circle* (Berkeley: University of California Press, 1968); Jeffrey Herf, *Reactionary Modernism: Technology, Culture, and Politics in Weimar and the Third Reich* (New York: Cambridge University Press, 1984); Martin Jay, *The Dialectical Imagination: A History of the Frankfurt School and the Institute of Social Research, 1923–1950* (Boston:

Little Brown, 1973); Klemens von Klemperer, *Germany's New Conservatism: Its History and Dilemma in the Twentieth Century* (Princeton, N.J.: Princeton University Press, 1957); Jerry Muller, *The Other God That Failed: Hans Freyer and the Deradicalization of German Conservatism* (Princeton, N.J.: Princeton University Press, 1987); and Walter Struve, *Elites against Democracy: Leadership Ideals in Bourgeois Political Thought in Germany, 1890–1933* (Princeton, N.J.: Princeton University Press, 1973).

Economic factors clearly ranked among the most debilitating burdens for the Weimar Republic. The best source for studying the impact of economics on German society is Gerald D. Feldman, *The Great Disorder: Politics, Economics, and Society in the German Inflation, 1914–1924* (New York: Oxford University Press, 1997). See also Gerald D. Feldman, *Iron and Steel in the Great Inflation, 1916–1923* (Princeton, N.J.: Princeton University Press, 1977); Richard Evans and Dick Geary, eds., *The German Unemployed: Experiences and Consequences of Mass Unemployment from the Weimar Republic to the Third Reich* (New York: St. Martin's Press, 1987); and Peter D. Stachura, ed., *Unemployment and the Great Depression in Weimar Germany* (New York: St. Martin's Press, 1986).

General Interpretations of Nazism

The starting points for further study of nazism in English are the lengthy works by Karl Dietrich Bracher, *The German Dictatorship: The Origins, Structure, and Effects of National Socialism* (New York: Praeger, 1970), and Klaus P. Fischer, *Nazi Germany: A New History* (New York: Continuum, 1995). These should be supplemented with the outstanding collections of translated Nazi material in Jeremy Noakes and Geoffrey Pridham, eds., *Nazism 1919–1945: A Documentary Reader*, 4 vols. (New York: Schocken, 1983–1998).

There are also a variety of conflicting broad interpretations on the nature of nazism that could provide topics for rewarding research. These range from those explaining nazism in terms of the crisis of capitalism or nihilism and European cultural decline, to those that attempt to integrate it into the more general phenomena of fascism or totalitarianism. See Hannah Arendt, *The Origins of Totalitarianism* (New York: Meridian Books, 1964); Friedrich Meinecke, *The German Catastrophe* (Boston: Beacon Press, 1963); Franz Neumann, *Behemoth: The Structure and Practice of National Socialism, 1933–1944* (New York: Ivan Dee, 2009); Ernst Nolte, *The Three Faces of Fascism* (New York: Mentor, 1969); and Hermann Rauschning, *The Revolution of Nihilism: A Warning to the West* (New York: AMS Press, 1939).

Nazi Ideology

The most essential work for research into the ideological nature of nazism is Adolf Hitler, *Mein Kampf* (Boston: Houghton Mifflin, 1971). A good explanation of Hitler's thinking is found in Eberhard Jäckel, *Hitler's World View: A Blueprint for Power* (Cambridge, Mass.: Harvard University Press, 1981). For the origins of such ideas, see Maurice Baumont, ed., *The Third Reich* (New York: Howard Fertig, 1975); George Mosse, *The Nationalization of the Masses: Political Symbolism and Mass Movements in Germany from the Napoleonic Wars through the Third Reich* (New York: Howard Fertig, 1975) and *The Crisis of German Ideology: Intellectual Origins of the Third Reich* (New York: Schocken, 1964); Fritz Stern, *The Politics of Cultural Despair: A Study in the Rise of the Germanic Ideology* (Berkeley: University of California Press, 1961); and Peter Viereck, *Metapolitics: The Roots of the Nazi Mind* (New York: Capricorn Books, 1965).

Adolf Hitler

The most informative and balanced recent study of the Nazi leader is Ian Kershaw, *Hitler, 1889–1936: Hubris* (New York: Norton, 1998) and *Hitler, 1936–1945: Nemesis* (New York: Norton, 2000). Also still useful are Alan Bullock, *Hitler: A Study in Tyranny* (New York: Harper & Row, 1964) and *Hitler and Stalin: Parallel Lives* (New York: Knopf, 1992); and Joachim Fest, *Hitler* (New York: Vintage Books, 1975). For a contemporary study, see Konrad Heiden, *Hitler: A Biography* (New York: AMS Press, 1936). Quite illuminating and essential are the documentation of Hitler's own statements: *Hitler's Secret Book* (New York: Grove Press, 1961); *Hitler's Secret Conversations, 1941–1944* (New York: Octagon Books, 1961); and *The Speeches of Adolf Hitler, April 1922–August 1939*, ed. Norman H. Baynes (New York: Howard Fertig, 1969).

Party Development

An understanding of the organizational structure and development of the NSDAP is essential to grasping the nature and success of this movement. The basic source for this subject is Dietrich Orlow, *The History of the Nazi Party, 1919–1933* (Pittsburgh: University of Pittsburgh Press, 1969). On the SA, see Bruce Campbell, *The SA Generals and the Rise of Nazism* (Lexington: University of Kentucky Press, 1998); Conan Fischer, *Stormtroopers: A Social, Economic, and Ideological Analysis, 1929–1935* (London: Allen & Unwin, 1983); and Peter H. Merkl, *The Making of a Stormtrooper* (Princeton, N.J.:

Princeton University Press, 1980). For another aspect of the functioning of party organizations, see Donald M. McKale, *The Nazi Party Courts: Hitler's Management of Conflict in His Movement, 1921–1945* (Lawrence: University of Kansas Press, 1974).

PART TWO: THE SEIZURE AND CONSOLIDATION OF POWER, 1929–1934

Party Profile and Growth

The sociological makeup of the Nazi party remains a central area of controversy among historians. The groundbreaking study on this subject is Michael H. Kater, *The Nazi Party: A Social Profile of Members and Leaders, 1919–1945* (Cambridge, Mass.: Harvard University Press, 1983). On Nazi recruitment from various social groups, see Max H. Kele, *Nazis and Workers: National Socialist Appeal to German Labor, 1919–1933* (Chapel Hill: University of North Carolina Press, 1972); Conan Fischer, *The German Communists and the Rise of Nazism* (New York: St. Martin's Press, 1992), and Conan Fischer, ed., *The Rise of National Socialism and the Working Classes in Weimar Germany* (Providence, R.I.: Berghahn, 1996); and Timothy Tilton, *Nazism, Neo-Nazism, and the Peasantry* (Bloomington: Indiana University Press, 1975). For studies of rank-and-file Nazis, see Theodore Abel, *Why Hitler Came to Power* (Cambridge, Mass.: Harvard University Press, 1986), and Peter Merkl, *Political Violence Under the Swastika: 581 Early Nazis* (Princeton, N.J.: Princeton University Press, 1975).

Party Leadership

For general biographical studies of those prominent figures who developed and led this party, see Ronald Smelser and Rainir Zitelmann, eds., *The Nazi Elite: 22 Biographical Sketches* (New York: New York University Press, 1993), and Joachim Fest, *The Face of the Third Reich: Portraits of the Nazi Leadership* (New York: Pantheon, 1970). On specific leaders, consult Ernest K. Bramsted, *Goebbels and National Socialist Propaganda, 1925–1945* (East Lansing: Michigan State University Press, 1965); Ralf Georg Reuth, *Goebbels* (New York: Harcourt Brace, 1993); Robert Gerwarth, *Hitler's Hangman: The Life of Heydrich* (New Haven, Conn.: Yale University Press, 2011); Jochen von Lang, *The Secretary, Martin Bormann: The Man Who Manipulated Hitler* (New York: Random House, 1979); Peter Longerich, *Heinrich Himmler* (New

York: Oxford University Press, 2012); Peter R. Black, *Ernst Kaltenbrunner: Ideological Soldier of the Third Reich* (Princeton, N.J.: Princeton University Press, 1984); Peter Stachura, *Gregor Strasser and the Rise of Nazism* (London: Allen & Unwin, 1983); Ronald Smelser, *Robert Ley* (New York: Berg, 1988); Randall Bytwerk, *Julius Streicher* (New York: Dorset, 1983); Robert Cecil, *The Myth of the Master Race: Alfred Rosenberg and Nazi Ideology* (New York: Dodd Mead, 1972); and John Weitz, *Hitler's Diplomat: The Life and Times of Joachim von Ribbentrop* (New York: Ticknor & Fields, 1992). In particular, Albert Speer's Nazi career has been undergoing serious reevaluation recently. See Albert Speer, *Inside the Third Reich* (New York: Collier Books, 1970) and *Spandau: The Secret Diaries* (New York: Macmillan, 1976), and compare these to Gitta Sereny, *Albert Speer: His Battle with Truth* (New York: Knopf, 1995). On personal accounts of other prominent figures who collaborated with the Nazis, see Franz von Papen, *Memoirs* (New York: AMS Press, 1953), and Hjalmar Schacht, *Confessions of an "Old Wizard"* (Westport, Conn.: Greenwood Press, 1956).

Nazi Voters

Also contentious is the question of the Nazi electoral constituency. For two differing perspectives on which classes provided the NSDAP with its voting strength, see Thomas Childers, *The Nazi Voter: The Social Foundations of Fascism in Germany, 1919–1933* (Chapel Hill: University of North Carolina Press, 1983), and Richard Hamilton, *Who Voted for Hitler?* (Princeton, N.J.: Princeton University Press, 1983). See also Thomas Childers, ed., *The Formation of the Nazi Constituency, 1919–1933* (London: Croom Helm, 1986).

Local and Regional Studies

Several studies of national socialism in various parts of Germany have illuminated further our understanding of Nazi members and voters. They have also expanded our knowledge of how the party advanced at the local and regional levels and how such developments contrasted with events nationally. See William S. Allen, *The Nazi Seizure of Power: The Experience of a Single German Town* (New York: Franklin Watts, 1984); Rudy Koshar, *Social Life, Local Politics, and Nazism, Marburg, 1880–1935* (Chapel Hill: University of North Carolina Press, 1986); Jeremy Noakes, *The Nazi Party in Lower Saxony, 1921–1933* (New York: Oxford University Press, 1971); Geoffrey Pridham, *Hitler's Rise to Power: The Nazi Movement in Bavaria, 1923–1933* (New York: Harper & Row, 1973); Johnpeter Grill, *The Nazi Movement in Baden, 1920–*

1945 (Chapel Hill: University of North Carolina Press, 1983); and Richard Bessel, *Political Violence and the Rise of Nazism: The Storm Troopers in Eastern Germany, 1925–1934* (New Haven, Conn.: Yale University Press, 1984).

The Nazi Seizure of Power

Whether the Nazi seizure of power was inevitable and what alternatives existed is an especially intriguing subject of further inquiry and thought. For a detailed examination of the immediate circumstances leading to Hitler's appointment as chancellor, see Henry A. Turner Jr., *Hitler's Thirty Days to Power: January 1933* (Reading, Mass.: Addison-Wesley, 1996). A perceptive and essential new study is Hermann Beck, *The Fateful Alliance: German Conservatives and Nazis in 1933; The Machtergreifung in a New Light* (New York: Berghahn Books, 2008). On the various long-term factors and forces leading to this event, see Peter Stachura, ed., *The Nazi Machtergreifung* (London: Allen & Unwin, 1983). Also requiring attention is the relationship between capitalist society and the Nazi acquisition of power. The most reliable work on this subject is Henry A. Turner Jr., *German Big Business and the Rise of Hitler* (New York: Oxford University Press, 1985). And Fritz Tobias, *The Reichstag Fire* (New York: Putnam, 1964), is still quite valuable for understanding the events surrounding Hitler's establishment of a dictatorship.

PART THREE: THE NAZIFICATION OF GERMAN SOCIETY, 1934–1938

The Nazi State

The complexities and contradictions inherent in the government of the Third Reich contrast sharply with the common image of Nazi Germany as a unified, monolithic dictatorship enthusiastically supported by obedient followers. For a balanced picture of the reality of the governmental structure and practice of the Third Reich, see Martin Broszat, *The Hitler State: The Foundations and Development of the Internal Structure of the Third Reich* (New York: Longman, 1981); Ernst Fraenkel, *The Dual State: A Contribution to the Theory of Dictatorship* (New York: Oxford University Press, 1941); Jane Caplan, *Government without Administration: State and Civil Service in Weimar and Nazi Germany* (Oxford: Clarendon Press, 1989); and Edward Peterson, *The Limits of Hitler's Power* (Princeton, N.J.: Princeton University Press, 1969). A fine study of how political biology pervaded Nazi policies and practices throughout the

Third Reich is Michael Burleigh and Wolfgang Wippermann, *The Racial State: Germany, 1933–1945* (Cambridge: Cambridge University Press, 1991).

On Nazi efforts to establish dictatorial rule and nazify Germany through ritual, propaganda, and media control, see Ian Kershaw, *The "Hitler Myth": Image and Reality in the Third Reich* (New York: Oxford University Press, 1987); Hamilton Burden, *The Nuremberg Party Rallies: 1923–39* (New York: Praeger, 1967); Oron J. Hale, *The Captive Press in the Third Reich* (Princeton, N.J.: Princeton University Press, 1964); and Z. A. Zeman, *Nazi Propaganda* (New York: Oxford University Press, 1973).

Culture and Society in the Third Reich

Although not including extensive more recent research, Richard Grunberger, *The 12-Year Reich: A Social History of Nazi Germany, 1933–1945* (New York: Ballantine Books, 1972), is still the standard work on the subject. For documents in English, consult George L. Mosse, ed., *Nazi Culture: Intellectual, Cultural, and Social Life in the Third Reich* (New York: Grosset & Dunlap, 1966). To study the extent of the nazification of German society, see David Schoenbaum, *Hitler's Social Revolution: Class and Status in Nazi Germany, 1933–1939* (New York: Doubleday, 1966), and Ian Kershaw, *Popular Opinion and Political Dissent in the Third Reich* (New York: Oxford University Press, 1985). Interrelated with these questions is the issue of the anticapitalism of National Socialist ideology and the actual nature of a capitalist economy in the Third Reich. On this subject, as well as economic recovery and rearmament, see Richard Overy, *The Nazi Economic Recovery, 1932–1938* (London: Macmillan, 1982); Arthur Schweitzer, *Big Business and the Third Reich* (Bloomington: Indiana University Press, 1964); and Peter Hayes, *Industry and Ideology: IG Farben in the Nazi Era* (New York: Cambridge University Press, 1987) and *From Cooperation to Complicity: Degussa in the Third Reich* (New York: Cambridge University Press, 2004). Equally important is Gerald D. Feldman, *Allianz and the German Insurance Business, 1933–1945* (New York: Cambridge University Press, 2001).

For illuminating new research on science and medicine in the Third Reich, see Robert N. Proctor, *Racial Hygiene: Medicine under the Nazis* (Cambridge, Mass.: Harvard University Press, 1988) and *The Nazi War on Cancer* (Princeton, N.J.: Princeton University Press, 1999), and Michael H. Kater, *Doctors under Hitler* (Chapel Hill: University of North Carolina Press, 1989). On education, see Geoffrey Giles, *Students and National Socialism in Germany* (Princeton, N.J.: Princeton University Press, 1985), and Gilmer W. Blackburn, *Education in the Third Reich: A Study of Race and History in the Nazi Textbooks* (New York: SUNY Press, 1985). On other dimensions of this society, see Hans P. Bleuel, *Sex and Society in Nazi Germany* (New York: Bantam, 1973); Jonathan Petropoulos, *Art as Politics in the Third Reich* (Chapel Hill: University of North Carolina Press, 1996); David S. Hull, *Film in the Third Reich: Art and Propaganda in Nazi Germany* (New York: Simon & Schuster, 1973); Michael H. Kater, *Different Drummers: Jazz in the Culture of Nazi Germany* (New York: Oxford University Press, 1992); Barbara Lane, *Architecture and Politics in Germany, 1918–1945* (Cambridge, Mass.: Harvard University Press, 1968); and Robert R. Taylor, *The Word in Stone: The Role of Architecture in the National Socialist Ideology* (Berkeley: University of California Press, 1974).

Daily Life

The study of daily life and ordinary people under Nazi rule remains a point of contention among historians. For a truly unique eyewitness account, see Victor Klemperer, *I Shall Bear Witness: The Diaries of Victor Klemperer, 1933–41* (London: Phoenix, 1999). For other insights into this dimension of life in Nazi Germany, see Detlev Peukert, *Inside Nazi Germany: Conformity, Opposition, and Racism in Everyday Life* (New Haven, Conn.: Yale University Press, 1987); Richard Bessel, ed., *Life in the Third Reich* (New York: Oxford University Press, 1987); Bernt Engelmann, *In Hitler's Germany: Everyday Life in the Third Reich* (New York: Schocken, 1986); and Johannes Steinhoff, Peter Pechel, and Dennis Showalter, *Voices from the Third Reich: An Oral History* (Washington, D.C.: Regnery Gateway, 1989). An excellent collection of essays regarding the effects of Nazi racial policies on those classified as asocial types unacceptable within the *Volksgemeinschaft* is Robert Gellately and Nathan Stolzfus, eds., *Social Outsiders in Nazi Germany* (Princeton, N.J.: Princeton University Press, 2001). A very important contribution to our understanding of how average Germans adjusted to the Third Reich is Robert Gellately, *Backing Hitler: Consent and Coercion in Nazi Germany* (Oxford: Oxford University Press, 2001).

The Churches

For an understanding of the compromises and conflicts that characterized the complicated and vacillating relationship between religious institutions and the Nazi State, see some of the most recent scholarship: Robert P. Ericksen, *Complicity in the Holocaust: Churches and Universities in Nazi Germany* (Cambridge: Cambridge University Press, 2012); Susannah Heschel, *The Aryan Jesus: Christian Theologians and the Bible in Nazi Germany* (Princeton, N.J.:

Princeton University Press, 2010); Richard Stegmann-Gall, *The Holy Reich: Nazi Concepts of Christianity, 1919–1945* (Cambridge: Cambridge University Press, 2004); Doris Bergen, *Twisted Cross: The German Christian Movement in the Third Reich* (Chapel Hill: University of North Carolina Press, 1996); and Hans A. Schmitt, *Quakers and Nazis: Inner Light in Outer Darkness* (Columbia: University of Missouri Press, 1997). For still quite important older literature, see Robert P. Ericksen, *Theologians under Hitler* (New Haven, Conn.: Yale University Press, 1985); Ernst Christian Helmreich, *The German Churches under Hitler* (Detroit: Wayne State University Press, 1979); John S. Conway, *The Nazi Persecution of the Churches, 1933–45* (New York: Basic Books, 1968); Guenter Lewy, *The Catholic Church and Nazi Germany* (New York: McGraw-Hill, 1964); Laurence Walter, *Hitler Youth and Catholic Youth, 1933–1936: A Study in Totalitarian Conquest* (Washington, D.C.: Catholic University of America Press, 1970).

Women

Recent specialized research into the role of women and gender issues in the self-identified masculine movement of National Socialism has substantially broadened our conception of Nazi Germany, but has also raised new questions. A good starting point for further study of the relationship between women and nazism is the incisive general survey by Ute Frevert, *Women in German History: From Bourgeois Emancipation to Sexual Liberation* (New York: Berg, 1989). This should be supplemented by Jill Stephenson, *The Nazi Organization of Women* (London: Croom Helm, 1981) and *Women in Nazi Society* (London: Croom Helm, 1975); and Claudia Koonz, *Mothers in the Fatherland* (New York: St. Martin's, 1987). See also Michael Phayer, *Protestant and Catholic Church Women in Nazi Germany* (Detroit: Wayne State University Press, 1990); Gisela Bock and Susan James, eds., *Beyond Equality and Difference: Citizenship, Feminist Politics, and Female Subjectivity* (London: Routledge, 1992); and Elizabeth Harvey, *Women and the Nazi East: Agents and Witnesses of Germanization* (New Haven, Conn.: Yale University Press, 2003).

The SS

A similar broadening of our perspectives on the Third Reich has occurred through the continuing research on the SS, whose rise produced a decisive change in the nature of the dictatorship and its power structure. The information and arguments in the standard book on the subject, Heinz Höhne,

The Order of the Death's Head: The Story of Hitler's SS (New York: Ballantine Books, 1971), have been expanded in important ways by Robert L. Koehl, *The Black Corps: The Structure and Power Struggles of the Nazi SS* (Madison: University of Wisconsin Press, 1983); Herbert F. Ziegler, *Nazi Germany's New Aristocracy, the SS Leadership 1925–1939* (Princeton, N.J.: Princeton University Press, 1989); George C. Browder, *Hitler's Enforcers: The Gestapo and the SS Security Service in the Nazi Revolution* (New York: Oxford University Press, 1996) and *Foundations of the Nazi Police State, The Formation of Sipo and SD* (Lexington: University of Kentucky Press, 1990); Robert Gellately, *The Gestapo and German Society: Enforcing Racial Policy, 1933–1945* (New York: Oxford University Press, 1990); Charles Sydnor, *Soldiers of Destruction: The SS Death's Head Division, 1933–1945* (Princeton, N.J.: Princeton University Press, 1977); and Gerhard Rempel, *Hitler's Children: The Hitler Youth and the SS* (Chapel Hill: University of North Carolina Press, 1989). Old but still quite informative are Gerald Reitlinger, *The SS: Alibi of a Nation, 1922–1945* (New York: Viking Press, 1957), and George H. Stein, *The Waffen SS: Hitler's Elite Guard at War, 1939–1945* (Ithaca, N.Y.: Cornell University Press, 1966).

Nazi Anti-Semitism

For the general origin and nature of anti-Semitism, see Albert S. Lindemann, *Esau's Tears: Modern Anti-Semitism and the Rise of the Jews* (New York: Cambridge University Press, 1997). On German anti-Semitism, see Klaus Fischer, *The History of an Obsession: German Judeophobia and the Holocaust* (New York: Continuum, 1998), and Peter Pulzer, *The Rise of Political Anti-Semitism in Germany and Austria, 1867–1918* (New York: Wiley, 1964). For revealing documentation on attitudes of average Germans toward Jews and Nazi Jewish policies, see Otto dov Kulka and Eberhard Jäckel, eds., *The Jews in the Secret Nazi Reports on Popular Opinion in Germany, 1933–1945* (New Haven, Conn.: Yale University Press, 2010). Two noteworthy recent studies are Alan Steinweis, *Kristallnacht 1938* (Cambridge, Mass.: Harvard University Press, 2009), and Martin Dean, *Robbing the Jews: The Confiscation of Jewish Property in the Holocaust, 1933–1945* (Cambridge: Cambridge University Press, 2008). Differing interpretations of Nazi policies toward Jews can be found in Saul Friedlander, *Nazi Germany and the Jews: The Years of Persecution, 1933–1939* (New York: HarperCollins, 1997); Karl A. Schleunes, *The Twisted Road to Auschwitz: Nazi Policy toward German Jews, 1933–39* (Chicago: University of Illinois Press, 1990); Sara Gordon, *Hitler, Germans, and the "Jewish Question"* (Princeton, N.J.: Princeton University Press, 1984); and

Lucy S. Dawidowicz, *The War against the Jews, 1933–1945* (New York: Bantam Books, 1978). The best coverage of the Jewish experience in the Third Reich before the Holocaust is in Francis R. Nicosia and David Scrase, eds., *Jewish Life in Nazi Germany: Dilemmas and Responses* (New York: Berghahn, 2010), and Marion A. Kaplan, *Between Dignity and Despair: Jewish Life in Nazi Germany* (New York: Oxford University Press, 1998). Also insightful is Leonard Baker, *Days of Sorrow and Pain: Leo Baeck and the Berlin Jews* (New York: Macmillan, 1978).

PART FOUR: THE RISE AND FALL OF THE NAZI EMPIRE IN EUROPE, 1933–1945

Ideology and Foreign Policy

To adequately understand Nazi foreign policy and objectives during World War II, one must acquire an appreciation for Hitler's ideological motives. One of the clearest explanations of the interrelationship between Nazi ideology and the origins of the Second World War can be found in Norman Rich, *Hitler's War Aims: Ideology, the Nazi State, and the Course of Expansion* (New York: Norton, 1973). For an examination of long-term ideological currents and continuities in German foreign policy as related to Hitler's goals, see Shelley Baranowski, *Nazi Empire: German Colonialism and Imperialism from Bismarck to Hitler* (Cambridge: Cambridge University Press, 2011); Andreas Hillgruber, *Germany and the Two World Wars* (Cambridge, Mass.: Harvard University Press, 1981); and Woodruff D. Smith, *The Ideological Origins of Nazi Imperialism* (New York: Oxford University Press, 1986). The most authoritative and detailed studies are Gerhard L. Weinberg, *The Foreign Policy of Hitler's Germany: Diplomatic Revolution, 1933–36* (Chicago: University of Chicago Press, 1970) and *The Foreign Policy of Hitler's Germany: Starting World War II, 1937–1939* (Chicago: University of Chicago Press, 1980). Perceptive interpretations can also be found in Keith Eubank, *The Origins of the Second World War* (New York: Harlan Davidson, 1969); Klaus Hildebrand, *The Foreign Policy of the Third Reich* (Berkeley: University of California Press, 1970); and Donald C. Watt, *How the War Came: The Immediate Origins of the Second World War, 1938–1939* (New York: Pantheon, 1989). For Nazi perceptions of the United States, see Klaus P. Fischer, *Hitler & America* (Philadelphia: University of Pennsylvania Press, 2012).

For works on Munich and other specialized topics, see Keith Eubank, *Munich* (Norman: University of Oklahoma Press, 1962); John Wheeler-

Bennett, *Munich: Prologue to Tragedy* (New York: Viking Press, 1964); Paul Seabury, *The Wilhelmstrasse: A Study of German Diplomats under the Nazi Regime* (Berkeley: University of California Press, 1954); Jürgen Gehl, *Austria, Germany and the Anschluss, 1931–1938* (Westport, Conn.: Greenwood Press, 1979); Alton Frye, *Nazi Germany and the American Hemisphere, 1933–1941* (New Haven, Conn.: Yale University Press, 1967); Frederick W. Deakin, *The Brutal Friendship: Mussolini, Hitler and the Fall of Italian Fascism* (New York: Harper & Row, 1962); and Anthony Read and David Fisher, *The Deadly Embrace: Hitler, Stalin, and the Nazi-Soviet Pact, 1939–1941* (New York: Norton, 1988).

World War II

The debates on World War II have centered around military strategy, the nature of total war, and the brutal struggle of the German and Soviet armies on the eastern front. On the overall history of World War II, see Gerhard L. Weinberg, *A World at Arms: A Global History of World War II* (Cambridge: Cambridge University Press, 1994); Peter Calvocoressi and Guy Wint, *Total War: Causes and Courses of the Second World War* (New York: Penguin, 1979); and Gordon Wright, *The Ordeal of Total War, 1939–1945* (New York: Harper & Row, 1968). For interpretations of various aspects of the military dimensions of the war in Europe, see John Keegan, *The Second World War* (New York: Penguin, 1989), and Richard Overy, *Why the Allies Won* (New York: Norton, 1996).

For the most recent studies of the German army in the East, see Stephen G. Fritz, *Ostkrieg: Hitler's War of Extermination in the East* (Lexington: University of Kentucky Press, 2011) and *Frontsoldaten: The German Soldier in World War II* (Lexington: University of Kentucky Press, 1995). See also Omer Bartov, *The Eastern Front, 1941–1945: German Troops and the Barbarization of Warfare* (New York: St. Martin's, 1985) and *Hitler's Army: Soldiers, Nazis, and War in the Third Reich* (New York: Oxford University Press, 1992). For powerful depictions of the decisive battle on the eastern front, see William Craig, *Enemy at the Gates: The Battle for Stalingrad* (New York: Ballantine Books, 1982), and Antony Beevor, *Stalingrad: The Fateful Siege: 1942–1943* (New York: Penguin, 1998). See also Richard Overy, *Russia's War: A History of the Soviet War Effort, 1941–1945* (New York: Penguin, 1997).

Nazi Domination in Europe

A study of Nazi occupation policies should begin with Norman Rich, *Hitler's War Aims: The Establishment of the New Order* (New York: Norton, 1974).

This should be followed by more specialized works: Gerald Reitlinger, *The House Built on Sand: The Conflicts of German Policy on Russia, 1939–45* (Westport, Conn.: Greenwood Press, 1979); Alexander Dallin, *German Rule in Russia, 1941–1945* (London: Macmillan, 1957); and John F. Sweets, *Choices in Vichy France: The French under Nazi Occupation* (New York: Oxford University Press, 1986). On the ultimate Nazi plans and objectives for the Germanization of Europe, see Robert Koehl, *RKFDV: German Resettlement and Population Policy* (Cambridge, Mass.: Harvard University Press, 1957). For opposition to Nazi occupation policies and practices, see M. R. D. Foot, *Resistance: An Analysis of European Resistance to Nazism, 1940–1945* (London: Methuen, 1976).

German Home Front

Important questions still remain concerning German rearmament and the transformation of the economy of the Third Reich for total war. For the most recent interpretation, see Richard J. Overy, *War and Economy in the Third Reich, 1938–1945* (Oxford: Clarendon Press, 1994). For important earlier works, see Burton H. Klein, *Germany's Economic Preparations for War* (Cambridge, Mass.: Harvard University Press, 1959), and Alan S. Milward, *The German Economy at War* (London: Athlone Press, 1965).

Historical attention has also shifted to conditions among the German civilian population during the war. Two recommended studies on this subject are Martin Kitchen, *Germany at War* (London: Longman, 1995), and Earl R. Beck, *Under the Bombs: The German Home Front, 1942–1945* (Lexington: University of Kentucky Press, 1986). For a controversial recent interpretation, see Peter Fritzsche, *Life and Death in the Third Reich* (Cambridge, Mass.: Harvard University Press, 2008). On the bombing of German cities, see Stewart H. Ross, *Strategic Bombing by the United States in World War II: The Myths and Facts* (Jefferson, NC: McFarland & Co., 2003). The earliest effort to raise this issue is found in David Irving, *The Destruction of Dresden* (London: Holt, Rinehart and Winston, 1963). Also of importance are Edward Homze, *Foreign Labor in Nazi Germany* (Princeton, N.J.: Princeton University Press, 1967); Jay Baird, *The Mythical World of Nazi War Propaganda, 1939–1945* (Minneapolis: University of Minnesota Press, 1974); and Robert E. Herzstein, *The War That Hitler Won: Goebbels and the Nazi Media Campaign* (New York: Paragon House, 1987). The latest study of German youth, especially important for the wartime years, is Michael H. Kater, *Hitler Youth* (Cambridge, Mass.: Harvard University Press, 2004).

The Holocaust

The field of Holocaust studies is vastly and rapidly expanding. For the latest research available, consult the bibliographies published in each issue of the journal *Holocaust and Genocide Studies*. An indispensable source of the current state of the field and the latest scholarship on the Holocaust is Michael Berenbaum and Abraham J. Peck, eds., *The Holocaust and History: The Known, the Unknown, the Disputed, and the Reexamined* (Bloomington: University of Indiana Press, 1998). Quite useful in this regard also is Michael R. Marrus, *The Holocaust in History* (New York: New American Library, 1986). The pioneering study on the Holocaust, Raoul Hilberg's *The Destruction of the European Jews* (Chicago: Quadrangle, 1961), still ranks among the very best. Also recommended are Doris L. Bergen, *War & Genocide: A Concise History of the Holocaust* (Lanham, Md.: Rowman & Littlefield, 2009), and Yehuda Bauer, *A History of the Holocaust* (New York: Franklin Watts, 1982). For a new perspective on the controversial subject of the genocide of the Gypsies, see Guenter Lewy, *The Nazi Persecution of the Gypsies* (Oxford: Oxford University Press, 2000).

Essential for understanding the origin and implementation of the plans to destroy the Jews of Europe are Richard Breitman, *The Architect of Genocide: Himmler and the Final Solution* (Hanover, N.H.: Brandeis University Press, 1991); Christopher Browning, *The Origins of the Final Solution: The Evolution of Nazi Jewish Policy, September 1939–March 1942* (Lincoln: University of Nebraska Press, 2004), *Fateful Months: Essays on the Emergence of the Final Solution* (New York: Holmes & Meier, 1985), and *The Path to Genocide: Essays on Launching the Final Solution* (New York: Cambridge University Press, 1992); and Gerald Fleming, *Hitler and the Final Solution* (Berkeley: University of California Press, 1984). On the relationship between Nazi euthanasia policies and the Holocaust, see Henry Friedlander, *The Origins of Nazi Genocide: From Euthanasia to the Final Solution* (Chapel Hill: University of North Carolina Press, 1995). Also essential reading are Jeffrey Herf, *The Jewish Enemy: Nazi Propaganda during World War II and the Holocaust* (Cambridge, Mass.: Harvard University Press, 2006), and *Nazi Propaganda for the Arab World* (New Haven, Conn.: Yale University Press, 2009). Likewise indispensable is Victor Klemperer, *I Will Bear Witness, 1942–1945: A Diary of the Nazi Years*, vol. 2 (New York: Random House, 1999).

On the behavior of perpetrators, see Edward B. Westermann, *Hitler's Police Battalions: Enforcing Racial War in the East* (Lawrence: University Press of Kansas, 2005); Wendy Lower, *Nazi Empire-Building and the Holocaust in Ukraine* (Chapel Hill: University of North Carolina Press, 2005); Christopher

Browning, *Ordinary Men: Reserve Battalion 101 and the Final Solution in Poland* (New York: HarperCollins, 1992); Robert Jay Lifton, *The Nazi Doctors: Medical Killing and the Psychology of Genocide* (New York: Basic Books, 1986); and Hannah Arendt, *Eichmann in Jerusalem: A Report on the Banality of Evil* (New York: Viking Press, 1963). On the involvement of non-Nazi segments of German and European government, business, and other socioeconomic institutions, see Gerald D. Feldman and Wolfgang Seibel, eds., *Networks of Nazi Persecution: Bureaucracy, Business, and the Organization of the Holocaust* (New York: Berghahn Books, 2005).

On the response of the outside world to the Holocaust, see Joseph W. Bendersky, *The "Jewish Threat": Anti-Semitic Politics of the U.S. Army* (New York: Basic Books, 2000); Walter Laqueur, *The Terrible Secret: Suppression of the Truth about Hitler's "Final Solution"* (New York: Penguin, 1982); Martin Gilbert, *Auschwitz and the Allies* (New York: Holt, Rinehart, and Winston, 1981); Richard Breitman and Alan Kraut, *American Refugee Policy and European Jewry, 1933–1945* (Bloomington: University of Indiana Press, 1987); and David S. Wyman, *Paper Walls: America and the Refugee Crisis, 1938–1941* (Amherst: University of Massachusetts Press, 1968) and *The Abandonment of the Jews: America and the Holocaust, 1941–1945* (New York: Pantheon, 1984). Among the persistently heated debates about responses to the Holocaust, those over the actions and inactions of the papacy retain their centrality. For well-researched attempts at critical yet balanced accounts, see Michael P. Phayer, *Pius XII, the Holocaust and the Cold War* (Bloomington: Indiana University Press, 2007) and *The Catholic Church and the Holocaust, 1930–1965* (Bloomington: Indiana University Press, 2001).

Resistance and Defeat

The latest works on the problems and debate involved in the nature and legacy of the German opposition to the Third Reich are Peter Hoffmann, *Carl Goerdeler and the Jewish Question, 1933–1942* (New York: Cambridge University Press, 2011); Theodore S. Hamerow, *On the Road to the Wolf's Lair: German Resistance to Hitler* (Cambridge, Mass.: Harvard University Press, 1997); and Klemens von Klemperer, *German Resistance against Hitler: The Search for Allies Abroad, 1938–1945* (Oxford: The Clarendon Press, 1992). Equally important are older studies: Peter Hoffmann, *The History of the German Resistance, 1933–1945* (Cambridge, Mass.: Harvard University Press, 1977); Harold Deutsch, *The Conspiracy against Hitler in the Twilight War* (Minneapolis: University of Minnesota Press, 1968); Hermann Graml, Hans Mommsen, Hans-Joachim Reichhardt, and Ernst Wolf, *The German*

Resistance to Hitler (Berkeley: University of California Press, 1970); Gerhard Ritter, *The German Resistance: Carl Goerdeler's Struggle against Tyranny* (New York: Praeger, 1958); Hans Rothfels, *The German Opposition to Hitler: An Assessment* (London: Oswald Wolff, 1970); and Christopher Sykes, *Tormented Loyalty: The Story of a German Aristocrat Who Defied Hitler* (New York: Harper & Row, 1969).

On the end of Nazi Germany, see Ian Kershaw, *The End: The Defiance and Destruction of Hitler's Germany, 1944–1945* (New York: Penguin, 2011), and Stephen G. Fritz, *Endkampf: Soldiers, Civilians, and the Death of the Third Reich* (Lexington: University of Kentucky Press, 2004).

PART FIVE: THE STRUGGLE FOR JUSTICE AND HISTORICAL MEMORY

War Crimes Trials

Interest in the postwar trials of the Nazi war criminals has grown enormously in the past decade. See Nathan Stoltzfus and Henry Friedlander, eds., *Nazi Crimes and the Law* (Cambridge: Cambridge University Press, 2008); Kim C. Priemel and Alexa Stiller, *Reassessing the Nuremberg Military Tribunals: Transitional Justice, Trial Narratives, and Historiography* (New York: Berghahn Books, 2012); Hilary Earl, *The Nuremberg SS-Einsatzgruppen Trial, 1945–1958: Atrocity, Law, and History* (Cambridge: Cambridge University Press, 2009); Michael Bryant, *Confronting the "Good Death": Nazi Euthanasia on Trial, 1945–1953* (Boulder: University of Colorado Press, 2005); and Arieh J. Kochavi, *Prelude to Nuremberg: Allied War Crimes Policy and the Question of Punishment* (Chapel Hill: University of North Carolina Press, 1998). Older standard works on the subject that provide very useful general histories include Bradley F. Smith, *The Road to Nuremberg* (New York: Basic Books, 1981) and *Reaching Judgment at Nuremberg* (New York: Basic Books, 1977); and Ann Tusa and John Tusa, *The Nuremberg Trial* (New York: Atheneum, 1984). On the issue of those who escaped their proper legal and moral fate, see Donald McKale, *Nazis after Hitler: How Perpetrators of the Holocaust Cheated Justice and Truth* (Lanham, Md.: Rowman & Littlefield, 2012).

Postwar Memory and the Nazi Legacy

On the complexities of the situation in Germany in the immediate postwar years and the various early attempts to co-opt the past, see Atina Grossmann,

Jews, Germans, and Allies: Close Encounters in Occupied Germany (Princeton, N.J.: Princeton University Press, 2007). For recent studies of the continuing problems and controversies caused by the shadow of the Third Reich, see Norbert Frei, *Adenauer's Germany and the Nazi Past: The Politics of Amnesty and Integration* (New York: Columbia University Press, 2002), and Robert G. Moeller, *War Stories: The Search for a Usable Past in the Federal Republic* (Berkeley: University of California Press, 2001). For excellent broader analyses of these questions, see Jeffrey Herf, *Divided Memory: The Nazi Past in the Two Germanys* (Cambridge, Mass.: Harvard University Press, 1997); Charles S. Maier, *The Unmasterable Past: History, Holocaust, and German National Identity* (Cambridge, Mass.: Harvard University Press, 1988); Richard J. Evans, *In Hitler's Shadow: West German Historians and the Attempt to Escape the Nazi Past* (New York: Pantheon, 1989); and Peter Baldwin, ed., *Reworking the Past: Hitler, the Holocaust, and the Historians' Debate* (Boston: Beacon Press, 1990).

On the very provocative issue of German wartime victimization, see Gilad Margalit, *Guilt, Suffering, and Memory: Germany Remembers Its Dead of World War II* (Bloomington: Indiana University Press, 2010), and Helmut Schmitz, ed., *A Nation of Victims? Representations of German Wartime Suffering from 1945 to the Present* (Amsterdam: Rodopi, 2007). On the related (and equally contested) question of the bombing of German cities and civilians, the original German edition of Jörg Friedrich's *The Fire: The Bombing of Germany, 1940–1945* (New York: Columbia University Press, 2006) quickly became a bestseller and precipitated widespread public debate. See also Igor Pimoratz, *The Bombing of German Cities in World War II* (New York: Berghahn Books, 2010); A. C. Grayling, *Among the Dead Cities: The History and Moral Legacy of the WWII Bombing of Civilians in Germany and Japan* (New York: Walker & Company, 2006); and W. G. Sebald, *On the Natural History of Destruction* (New York: Random House, 2003). Two insightful literary pieces exemplifying the struggle over German memory are Gunter Grass' novel *Crabwalk* (New York: Mariner Books, 2004) and his autobiography *Peeling the Onion* (New York: Mariner Books, 2008). Both initiated far-reaching critical reevaluations of this public intellectual, who, until then, had been considered among those embodying the new moral consciousness of the Federal Republic: the former because it addressed the desperate plight of German refugees fleeing the Russians, and the latter because it revealed Grass' own hidden past as a youthful member of the SS briefly at the end of the war.

INDEX

ABOUT THE AUTHOR

Joseph W. Bendersky is professor of German history at Virginia Common-wealth University in Richmond, Virginia. His previous books are *The "Jewish Threat": Anti-Semitic Politics of the U.S. Army* and *Carl Schmitt: Theorist for the Reich*. His books have been translated into Chinese, Italian, and Japanese, and his articles have appeared in journals internationally. He is the recipient of National Endowment for the Humanities and Fulbright Fellowships, as well as distinguished lecturer and scholarship awards.